Sport in the Black Atlantic

Manchester University Press

Globalizing Sport Studies

Series editor: **John Horne, Professor of Sport and Sociology, University of Central Lancashire, UK**

Public interest in sport studies continues to grow throughout the world. This series brings together the latest work in the field and acts as a global knowledge hub for interdisciplinary work in sport studies. While promoting work across disciplines, the series focuses on social scientific and cultural studies of sport. It brings together the most innovative scholarly empirical and theoretical work, from within the UK and internationally.

Books previously published in this series by Bloomsbury Academic:

Global Media Sport: Flows, Forms and Futures
David Rowe

Japanese Women and Sport: Beyond Baseball and Sumo
Robin Kietlinski

Sport for Development and Peace: A Critical Sociology
Simon Darnell

Globalizing Cricket: Englishness, Empire and Identity
Dominic Malcolm

Global Boxing
Kath Woodward

Sport and Social Movements: From the Local to the Global
Jean Harvey, John Horne, Parissa Safai, Simon Darnell and Sebastien Courchesne-O'Neill

Football Italia: Italian Football in an Age of Globalization
Mark Doidge

Books previously published in this series by Manchester University Press:

The Greening of Golf: Sport, Globalization and the environment
Brad Millington and Brad Wilson

Sport and Technology: An Actor-Network Theory perspective
Roslyn Kerr

Sport in the Black Atlantic

Cricket, Canada and the Caribbean diaspora

Janelle Joseph

Manchester University Press

Copyright © Janelle Joseph 2017

The right of Janelle Joseph to be identified as the author of this work has been asserted by her in accordance with the Copyright, Designs and Patents Act 1988.

Published by Manchester University Press
Altrincham Street, Manchester M1 7JA
www.manchesteruniversitypress.co.uk

British Library Cataloguing-in-Publication Data
A catalogue record for this book is available from the British Library

Library of Congress Cataloging-in-Publication Data applied for

ISBN 978 1 7849 9407 5 hardback

First published 2017

An electronic version of this book is also available under a Creative Commons (CC-BY-NC) licence.

The publisher has no responsibility for the persistence or accuracy of URLs for any external or third-party internet websites referred to in this book, and does not guarantee that any content on such websites is, or will remain, accurate or appropriate.

Typeset by Out of House Publishing
Printed in Great Britain
by CPI Group (UK) Ltd, CR0 4YY

Contents

Series editor's preface		*page* vii
Acknowledgements		ix
Introduction		1
1	Community	35
2	Routes	62
3	Nostalgia	85
4	Disjunctures	108
5	Diaspora space	135
6	Nationalisms	155
Conclusion		177
Appendix		190
References		194
Index		203

Series editor's preface

There is now a considerable amount of expertise nationally and internationally in the social scientific and cultural analysis of sport in relation to the economy and society more generally. Contemporary research topics, such as sport and social justice, science/technology and sport, global social movements and sport, sports mega-events, sports participation and engagement and the role of sport in social development, suggest that sport and social relations need to be understood in non-Western developing economies, as well as European, North American and other advanced capitalist societies. The current high global visibility of sport makes this an excellent time to launch a major new book series that takes sport seriously, and makes this research accessible to a wide readership.

The series *Globalizing Sport Studies* is thus in line with a massive growth of academic expertise, research output and public interest in sport worldwide. At the same time, it seeks to use the latest developments in technology and the economics of publishing to reflect the most innovative research into sport in society currently underway in the world. The series is multidisciplinary, although primarily based on the social sciences and cultural studies approaches to sport.

The broad aims of the series are as follows: to *act* as a knowledge hub for social scientific and cultural studies research in sport, including, but not exclusively, anthropological, economic, geographic, historical, political science and sociological studies; to *contribute* to the expanding field of research on sport in society in the United Kingdom and internationally by focusing on sport at regional, national and international levels; to *create* a series for both senior and more junior researchers that will become synonymous with cutting-edge research, scholarly opportunities and academic development; to *promote* innovative discipline-based, multi-, inter- and trans-disciplinary theoretical and methodological approaches to researching sport in society; to *provide* an English language outlet for high-quality non-English writing on sport in society; to *publish* broad overviews, original empirical research studies and classic studies from non-English sources; and thus attempt to *realise* the potential for *globalising* sport studies through open content licensing with "Creative Commons."

Caribbean cricket, especially the elite, professional game, has long been recognised as a force for unifying communities throughout the entire Caribbean region. In *Sport in the Black Atlantic: Cricket, Canada and the Caribbean Diaspora*, Janelle Joseph critically examines the meanings of being black and Caribbean in Canada. She reveals how cricket operates within the ranks of the diaspora, as a force for unity but also for exclusions, hierarchies and chauvinisms and replicates social divisions in the broader society.

Joseph demonstrates the ways in which first-generation Afro-Caribbean-Canadian immigrants' culinary, musical, language, destination and, especially, sporting choices actively help the diaspora to construct homelands. She explores the ways in which playing and watching sport, and supporting or travelling with a sport club, are important to creating racialised, gendered, ethnic and/or national identities. In doing so, she extends, theoretically and empirically, the promise of intersectional analyses of race, gender and globalisation in sport.

The book's chapters explore everyday life and the construction of community, as well as the place of transnational mobility in the formation of social networks. Examining the activities of an Afro-Caribbean-Canadian cricket and social club reveals much about Caribbean and Canadian belonging, pure and hybrid racial identities, transnational social networks and performances of nation and masculinity.

Sport in the Black Atlantic also moves beyond earlier analyses to suggest that the gendering of Afro-Caribbean diasporic cultural forms leads to the occupation of different spaces and roles for men and women. In this way, it contributes to the feminist critique of black diaspora studies by showing women to be an integral part of the Black Atlantic. The book builds on foundational sport and diaspora literature to explore how borderless racial and ethnic communities are made. In doing so, Joseph provokes the need for further examinations of other black diasporas in the context of specific nationalisms, transnational networks and physical cultural forms.

John Horne,
Preston and Edinburgh

Acknowledgements

All books represent author journeys and ethnographic texts provide an especially acute representation of relationships formed along the way. I have considered where to place the origins of this text. Should it be with my doctoral supervisor at the University of Toronto, Dr Peter Donnelly, who helped me consider the possibility of switching my focus from my personal passion, capoeira, to my father's fixation, cricket? Did the journey start with my fourth-year undergraduate exchange mentor at Victoria University in Australia, Dr Chris Hallinan, who recommended that I would make a good academic, an idea I had never before contemplated. Or should I trace back even earlier? In many ways, this book began when my eighth-grade teacher at Ramer Wood Public School, Ted Cowan, told me the best athletes are "thinkers," instantly collapsing what had hitherto been two separate categories in my mind. He also taught me to think critically about the sometimes disingenuous separation of fact and fiction and the value of telling stories for both speakers and listeners.

These obvious origins were major milestones along the journey, but give exclusive credit to the educators of the academic institutions that formed me. Without their critical support, this book would not exist, but the foundations are with my first educators, my mother and father, who were born in the Caribbean, migrated to Canada in the 1970s and raised me with a love for words, a knowledge of sport and the freedom to pursue what excites me, even when it so differed from their interests. To you I give foremost thanks.

Without the cricket expertise, wise ideas, open sharing and nostalgic stories of Caribbean cricketers in the Greater Toronto Area, there would be no text. Thank you E. Bertram Joseph, Eugene Soanes, Henry Yearwood, John Verneuil, Keith Greene, Nigel Griffith, Roy Pollard and a few hundred others. I deeply appreciate the unwavering support, shrewd judgments and cogent advice from my doctoral committee and other mentors: Drs Ato Quayson Cameron McCarthy, Caroline Fusco, D. Alissa Trotz, Margaret MacNeill, Melanie Newton, Patricia Landolt, Peter Donnelly, Rinaldo Walcott and Russell Field. I am truly grateful for the critical insights, careful editing, creative input and patient reading the following people have offered me since I stepped into fieldwork in 2008: Chris Nock, Dian Bridge, Eileen Joseph, Kyoung-Yim Kim, Parissa Safai and Yuka Nakamura. And certainly, each member of the publication teams and manuscript reviewers for Bloomsbury and Manchester University Press deserve accolades, especially for your patience.

The financial, intellectual and emotional support I have received over the past decade was essential for me to persevere and remain healthy. I am thankful for a doctoral award from the Social Sciences and Humanities Research Council and my colleagues at the University of Toronto including Bruce Kidd, Sandy Wells, Simon Darnell, and Tanya Lewis. Two postdoctoral awards, one from the School of Physical Education at the University of Otago and the other, a Social Sciences and Humanities Research Council Banting Fellowship hosted by the Faculty of Education at the University of Ontario Institute of Technology, sustained me. I give a sincere thanks to the School and the Faculty for supporting my research. At those institutions, Drs Doug Booth, Josh Newman, Marc Falcous, Steve Jackson and Wesley Crichlow taught me immeasurably about the art, science and politics of ethnography and academia.

The energies of my closest friends and family members continue to nourish me every day, and the tenacity with which they tackle a wide range of professional, intellectual, familial, and emotional projects gives me the resolve to continue my own. Thank you, Alex Karolyi, Chris Nock, Claudia DeSimone, Crystal Burke, Jamaal Joseph, Jane Lee, Jeffrey Rawlins, Jill Russell, Josephine Mullally, Laura Molinari, Nataleah Hunter Young, Tafiya Joseph Nock, and Tiombe Joseph Nock. Thanks to all of you for keeping me whole and happy, encouraging me to set my goals ever higher, and helping me to complete this difficult journey.

Introduction

First Caribbean Days in Canada

I play cricket for de telephone company in Barbados. It was June of 1975. I went to dis one game up in St. Andrews village and everyt'ing set for me to leave for Canada de following day. And I remember, like it yesterday, as I walkin' off de fiel' one of de guys on my team come runnin' and literally dive at my feet. I had a pair of Gary Sobers boots dat my father brought me from Englan', see? Dey had de autograph on de side, you know? Dey were pretty new and it hadn't really occurred to me what I would do wit' dem when I was leaving, but dis fella, boy, he knew! He dive at me and tek me off me feet. He strip dose boots off me quick fas' and say "You're not going to need these where you're going!" and run away. Well, dat's what I thought too. I thought, well you know, it's not likely I play cricket in Canada and I'm not going for life, anyway. I plan to come here for five years and further my education, make some money and den head back. I thought, I'll get dose boots back soon enough. So I walk de rest of de way home in my bare feet.

Den, t'ree weeks later I in my sister's front room. De doorbell ring an' I look out de window an' see dis man dress all in white. I thought, wow, in Canada de bakers deliver de bread! Den I see he don't have no bread. When my sister get de door dat man come in like he familiar wit' de place. "Hello an' good afternoon," he said. I recognise his Jamaican accent straight away. We lived next to a Jamaican woman growing up an' she always say dat. "Hello an' good afternoon." It end up dat he was my brother-in-law Trevor's buddy, and it wasn't a baker's uniform but cricket clothes he wearing. I couldn't believe my eyes. I say "You play cricket?", stunned. I thought he'd say, "You know, just a few West Indians get together every once in a while," but he tell me he play in de Toronto and District League every weekend and I should come. A league! Well, I went wit' him and Trevor, and I joined de team dat Sunday afternoon. Dat was a very bright spot in my first days in this country because dere was a hope of continuing playing cricket.

We get to de groun' and I see dey rolling out dis t'ing looks like carpet. I hear dem calling, "Where's the spikes? Where's the hammer?" And dey nail it down right on de grass. Dat shock me. I ask, "What's dat?" and Trevor explain to me dat in Canada we play on dis stuff called matting 'cause de pitch don't have turf. I was used to playing on turf so dat was strange, but other than dat, it was basically like walking onto e fiel' at home. There was women selling all sweet bread, and fish cakes, and black pudding, and what you call souse. And de people dem sell beer, and pop, and stuff from their cars. But Trevor tell me not to drink beer straight from de bottle in case de cops come around, since it illegal here. Luckily, everyone have dem plastic cups ready! You would see de whole fiel' pack wit' people and their kids. On a Saturday or Sunday everybody come out to watch de game. I ran into guys here at de cricket grounds who were cousins or brothers of my friends from back home. Before I got here I never expec' fe see so many black people.

De next week at cricket a guy tell me dey hiring at de phone company in Scarborough. So I go to dis job fair, get hired on de spot by Bell Canada, and end up doing an easier job than I did home. Even though lots of West Indians worked dere, you know, I don't know if I could have survived without cricket. Some of us guys been playing together at dese grounds over t'irty years. You know, we had some good times just being outside on a nice sunny day. Seeing de blue sky, green pastures, white cricket clothes, a bright red ball. Being able to score some runs and have my friends give me de accolades I deserve. You know, dat's something I would give almost anything for. During de summer I give up picnics, parties, whatever, just to be in a cricket game. My wife is of de opinion dat cricket is my mistress. I say, "Well, of course!"

The above narrative, "First Caribbean Days in Canada," weaves together the experiences that four Afro-Caribbean-Canadian men shared with me to depict the common story of hundreds of migrants to Canada.[1] In the 1960s and 1970s, Canada was the location of choice for thousands of Caribbean men and women. The majority ended up in the "Golden Horseshoe" area of southern Ontario, predominantly in the Greater Toronto Area (hereafter, Toronto).[2] My father, a black man native to the island of Antigua, who migrated to Canada in 1975, played cricket when he arrived. For him, this was an expression of his race and masculinity, a source of friendship, fitness and, ultimately, bodily disrepair. Many Caribbean men's stories about their migration experiences, settling in Toronto's urban and suburban neighbourhoods, finding jobs, returning home for visits and travelling to other diasporic locations, involved some contact with a cricket and social club. These clubs provided family, social and professional networks that were essential for black men's survival in a city rife with interpersonal and systemic racism. Talking with men of my fathers' generation made me appreciate C. L. R. James' sage comments made in the introduction to a collection of his writings: cricket is not "some specific unit that one adds to what really constitutes the history of a period. Cricket is as much part of the history as books written are part of the history" (1986, p. xi). Given that, according to James (1963) cricket is not only the central, but also the most ideologically loaded Caribbean cultural practice, any documentation of the history and culture of the Afro-Caribbean diaspora must include an examination of cricket.

At the same time, cricket is an integral part of Canadian history. Canada comprises many diasporas and its history is composed of migrants' experiences. Cricket in Canada, once the exclusive pastime of dominant English migrants, has been a popular culture of minority ethnic groups since the middle of the twentieth century. As is the case for African-American blues music, which "was once unrecognized by America's Anglophone establishment ... [and] characterized by its informality, its nontraditional grammatical structures, its discursive hybridity and its proclivity for drawing on and incorporating other cultural formations, even other languages" (Farred, 2003, p. 18), cricket is often dismissed from the canon of Canadiana. The fact that many cricket players in Canada have dark skin and incorporate cultures and languages other than English as they play has resulted in their experiences being obfuscated from Canadian sport history. Though the nation is no main player on the international cricket stage, there are thousands of Canadians playing the game recreationally, including a group of Afro-Caribbean-Canadian men that are referred to here as the Mavericks Cricket and Social Club (MCSC).

When the Mavericks left their nations of origin, most believed it would be temporary. Most played at a high level, but gave up hopes of playing professional cricket, finding competitive recreational leagues instead. Through the leagues they found a sporting outlet as well as the social capital necessary for employment, many in government-sponsored fields such as education, policing and postal services. Many developed middle-class status, friendships and a permanent life in Canada. At the cricket ground, they were immediately introduced to a uniquely Canadian environment. For example, they needed to use matting (a canvas carpet) on the pitch because the soil was too hard, but they found it easy to carve out a space in which to celebrate their heritage in a multicultural milieu, and therefore to *be Canadian men*.[3] Through playing and watching cricket, they enacted many characteristics of Canadian masculine identity, including athletic prowess and diasporic pride. One of the defining characteristics of diasporas, according to Cohen (1995) and Safran (1991; 1999) is a desire to "return to origins." For the Mavericks, this required neither a trip to Africa nor a flight to the Caribbean. They only needed to travel across the Peace Bridge for a 10-hour drive to New York City, or merely to Ross Lord Park, 30 minutes north of the City of Toronto, in order to forge close bonds with other black people, enjoy Caribbean sport, food, drink and music, and share nostalgic stories in their native languages. Afro-Caribbean migrants used sport and travel within the Black Atlantic as vehicles to recreate their homeland cultures, resist and promote integration in Canada, overcome racism and therefore to *be black and Caribbean and Canadian men*. The use of sport to create their gender and tripartite racial, ethnic and national identities is the focus of this text.

This is not a book about the sport of cricket per se. Rather, it is a narrative of what I call black plurilocal homespaces, created in Canada and the Caribbean diaspora through cricket, cricket-related travel and imaginative rediscoveries of communities. Of the diaspora experience, Salman Rushdie (1991, p. 9) writes that we "are haunted by some sense of loss … our physical alienation from [the homeland] almost inevitably means that we will not be capable of reclaiming precisely the thing that was lost; that we will, in short, create fictions, not actual cities or villages, but invisible ones, imaginary homelands." Homelands come alive through our activities and the stories we tell about them. These are what Stuart Hall (2003, p. 235) calls "imaginative rediscoveries" that help to define diasporic identities and make sense of the discontinuous and seamless connections to families, ancestors, others in the diaspora, others in the racial group and other Canadians.

Journalists, scholars and fans alike have noted that Caribbean cricket is a force for unifying communities throughout the entire Caribbean region and the diaspora, though they typically focus on the accomplishments in the elite ranks. It has been equally observed that cricket is a force for exclusions, hierarchies and chauvinisms and replicates social divisions in the broader society. This study examines both sides of what cricket offers to a sense of home for Afro-Caribbean migrants by exploring the processes of making and crossing boundaries.

Within the sport of cricket, making boundaries is one of the primary goals of the cricket players. That is, in cricket parlance, players attempt to score four or six runs by hitting the ball across the boundary rope that encircles the field of play. Making boundaries is a highly masculinised achievement that brings accolades to the individual, team, city of Toronto, province of Ontario, Canada, Barbados, Guyana or the entire West Indies, depending on the location of the game and the composition of the opposing teams. In a sociological sense, MCSC members also use sport to make boundaries around their community, defining who is inside and who is out through language, food and performances of ethnicity and gender.

Scholars and novelists within sociological and anthropological disciplines have long emphasised the importance of studying boundaries, the processes of boundary maintenance and the ways in which boundaries are crossed to understand the fluidity of ethnic and diaspora identity formations and expressions

(Cohen, 2007; James, 1963; Lamming, 1953; Marshall, 1983; Mintz, 1996). The sense of difference that boundaries distinguish is created through human action, that is, ethnic or racial difference is a cognitive–social–cultural–historical phenomenon created and maintained by both inside and outside actors. Arguing that ethnic identity becomes meaningful only at its boundaries, Fredrik Barth notes that "it is clear that boundaries persist despite a flow of personnel across them" (1998, p. 9) and our attention should be drawn to the boundary, how it is maintained and who or what is allowed to pass through, rather than solely "the cultural stuff that it encloses" (1998, p. 15). Barth suggests it is the processes of exclusion and selective incorporation within a context of acculturation and inter-ethnic interdependence that allow immigrants to maintain their cultures. It is through the (near) crossing of boundaries drawn around Barbadians, men, Canadians, or other categories, that we come to understand where the limits of the community lie. For example, it was not until one team member suggested that the team save money and time by ordering and serving pizza for the game after-party that the boundaries of the community were clarified. That individual met a resounded "Noh man, we mus' have curry goat an' t'ing! Dat what dey serve us last game!" Although pizza is consumed throughout nearly every region of the Caribbean, and by some of the MCSC members in Canada, many club members felt that the opposing teams' hospitality must be repaid only with traditional Caribbean dishes such as "curry goat" at game after-parties, thereby marking cricket spaces as Caribbean homespaces. At the same time, when they compete against their US "brothers," there is a discussion of the journey across the border as travelling the Underground Railroad, marking the cricket field as a safe black space.

Whether they are framed as black or Caribbean, after attending just a few of the sport and social activities of the MCSC, I was immediately able to appreciate the ways in which unity was promoted in the production of their homespaces. There was a convivial atmosphere among a group of men that appeared to be relatively homogeneous. They used native, colloquial languages, and shared a joyful sense of connectedness with each other in a fun, celebratory, music-, food- and drink-filled environment. They turned to cricket spaces to celebrate, relax, travel and be with (fictive) kin; however, these celebratory events were also sometimes sad and nostalgic, especially for the eldest participants. They sometimes used the cricket grounds as spaces in which to come together to commemorate their loved ones. They marked the surgeries, retirements, and sadly, deaths of their friends and family members. The cricket ground brings black Canadians together as a unified community, not only to celebrate their homeland cultures or assuage the pain of what Gilroy calls the "racial terror" that unifies the Black Atlantic, but also to allay the pain of ageing in the diaspora. The ongoing efforts they put into their boundary-making mechanisms – that is, to mark their spaces as masculine, Caribbean, black, Canadian, or exclusively for cricket or socialising, depending on the setting – reveal that they share an understanding of common traditional values.

Diasporas, nations and sporting cultures that appear to be unified can, nevertheless, "act as repressive or normalising structures that, by virtue of an inability to tolerate discord, constantly attempt to produce conformity and sameness, and disavow difference and inequality" (Abdel-Shehid, 2005, p. 3). As they erect boundaries, for example, around cricket as a men's sport, they promote unity among cis-gender men and exclusion for their Afro-Caribbean sisters. When they promote broader cricket spaces as family oriented, a closer examination of women's peripheral roles, as scorekeeper, cook, or fundraiser, raises the question of who should participate in the regeneration of the Black Atlantic and in what way. The making of boundaries can result in the reinforcement of gender, class, nation and ethnic hierarchies. In the only other book-length examination of the black sporting diaspora in Canada, Abdel-Shehid (2005, p. 8) describes black masculinities in sporting contexts as "heterosexual at minimum, and misogynist and hypermacho at maximum." Among the Mavericks, gay men were occasionally disparaged and positioned as inauthentic, improper, or unwelcome as players or spectators. Cricket was used by some men as a space for their mistresses and not their wives. Players attempted to maintain Afro-Caribbean communities and cultures to the exclusion of their cricket-playing Indo-Caribbean and South Asian peers, and spent hours discussing which nation's cricketers, politics, foods, or carnivals were "the best." This cricket and social club demonstrates the disunities that manifest within diasporas.

An examination of the making of boundaries, whether to include or exclude, must also be paired with an analysis of the crossing of boundaries. In the 1970s, when the field of anthropology turned its attention away from "traditional" sites and towards the relationships between core and periphery, the binary dissolved between the modern, metropolitan worker and the traditional, rural peasant. By following the realities of subjects who regularly (if not easily) flow back and forth across borders, the fieldwork of scholars such as Kearney (1996), who examined changing life in rural Oaxaca, southern Mexico, revealed that subjects end up inhabiting many diverse niches, or plurilocal homelands, simultaneously. The crossing of geopolitical boundaries, by car, bus, plane, or imagination is an essential component of diasporas. Club members' initial migration created a home–away dyad that had to be negotiated. MCSC's repeated cricket-related trips are, as Trotz (2011, p. 60, emphasis in original) describes of bus trips from Toronto to New York, "gendered and routinized modes of travel across sites that displace the home–away dyad … [V]isits to Caribbean people in places other than the Caribbean and to Caribbean places in North America" and the UK have much to "offer to discussions of Caribbean culture and identity". Regular visits, compounded by their storytelling about those trips and sharing memories of their nations of origin, mean that cricket club members are multiply placed in plurilocal homelands at any one time.

Sociology, once primarily concerned with nations as societies, has recently been reshaped around notions of the border zone, global society, and postnational, international and transnational formations that cross, but certainly do not erase, boundaries. As Gilroy (1993) has pointed out through his conception of the Black Atlantic, the travelling black man is an iconic figure for understanding how embodied, personal understandings of new geographies, racial formations and cultural identities develop as boundaries are crossed. The Black Atlantic is what Nederveen Pieterse (2009) refers to as a hybridised community that comes into existence through the continued flux and reorganisation of culture that occurs when migrants have been living in a "new" land for longer than they lived in the "old" one. At the same time, Canadians (and Torontonians in particular) are embedded in a mixture of cultures that welcome and reject them, and although they may celebrate hybridity, they may also cling vigilantly to their boundary-making process and purity discourses.[4] Rather than investigating whether migrants are either hybrid or pure, my attention is drawn to the ways and contexts in which they imagine themselves as both and I seek to deepen our understanding of diasporas by writing a history of boundary and border making and crossing. Examining the activities of an Afro-Caribbean-Canadian cricket and social club helps us learn about Caribbean and Canadian belonging, pure and hybrid racial identities, transnational social networks and performances of nation and masculinity, to name but a few themes covered in this text.

The Caribbean diaspora is a diverse, deterritorialised community. Not only in terms of their present locations (e.g., Ohio and Georgia in the United States, London and Birmingham in England, Toronto and Montreal in Canada), but also in terms of the diversity in languages, political perspectives, nations of origin and ethnic groups (see Harney, 1996). This study does not attempt to capture all the makings of the Caribbean diaspora. Rather, it focuses on a select group of men and women, primarily from the Anglo-Caribbean and predominantly of African descent. They are referred to here collectively as the Afro-diaspora, Afro-Caribbean-Canadians and the black diaspora. Other than occasional team newsletters and brochures arranged for 25- and 30-year club anniversaries, there is little documentation of what these first-generation immigrants do with their recreational time. There is no in-depth analysis of the sporting practices and important associated social activities such as team banquets, fundraising dances and picnics of the Caribbean men and women who were among the first to arrive in Canada from that region. The stories of the Mavericks, black men born in the Caribbean in the 1950s and 1960s, who migrated to Canada in the 1970s and 1980s, and now continue to play friendly cricket, have much to tell us about the history of the Afro-Caribbean diaspora. Their friends and female partners' storied and performative productions of the spaces they visit, including national locations (St. Lucia or England), local sites (stadia or community parks) or specific sporting or social environments (award ceremonies or "Memorial Matches"), tell a history of racialised, gendered and diasporic identities.

This book demonstrates the ways in which first-generation Afro-Caribbean-Canadian immigrants' culinary, musical, sporting, language and destination choices actively create plurilocal homelands throughout the diaspora. The aim is to broaden the understandings of intersectional analyses for those who study race, gender and/or globalisation in sport and it is therefore written from a discursive space where physical cultural studies, black diaspora studies and Caribbean studies overlap. A thorough understanding of the concept of diaspora is necessary in order to comprehend how these disciplinary boundaries are crossed.

Diaspora unpacked

Diaspora is conceptualised in a variety of ways depending on the region, case study and actors involved. Its overuse and increasingly imprecise application makes it difficult to use as a heuristic device (Edwards, 2001). The word "diaspora" comes from the Greek verb *speiro*, meaning "to sow" and the preposition *dia*, meaning "over" (Cohen, 1995), and is most often used to refer to real or imagined communities scattered from a homeland over multiple sites. In this study, diaspora is theorised broadly, using a cultural studies approach that draws from black and Caribbean diaspora as well as transnationality literatures, to study the racial, ethnic, local and national (imagined) communities and cultures that span borders as a result of historic and contemporary migrations.

The notion of diaspora depends on an understanding of flows, boundaries and hybrids, outlined as key terms of transnational anthropology by Hannerz (1997). He writes, "One fundamental fact about flows must be that they have directions. In the case of cultural flows, it is true, what is gained in one place need not be lost at the source. But there is a reorganization of culture in space" (p. 5). Just as cultures become reorganised in unpredictable ways, as migrants transplant from one place to another, their movements need be neither unidirectional, nor permanent, especially when technological, material and nostalgic connections to the homeland are considered. Flows suggest continuity and freedom and are typically contrasted with boundaries, which prevent passage and restrain. However, as Hannerz (1997) notes, drawing from Barth's (1969) *Ethnic Groups and Boundaries,* "'boundaries' have to do with discontinuity and obstacles ... sharp line[s] of demarcation ... *across* which contacts and interactions take place; they may have an impact on the form and extent of these contacts, but they do not *contain* natural isolates." (p. 7, emphasis in original). When cultural and migrant flows cross boundaries, they create spaces that are neither culturally homogenous nor ethnically pure. The black diaspora, while it may hold onto certain heritage practices, is also a deeply creolised community. It features the histories of complex cultures that subverted and destabilised colonial authority, as well as the adoption of local traits based on the dominant customs and structures of the nations in which migrants have ended up. This text aims to show the human face of the flows, boundaries and hybridity of the Black Atlantic and specifically the Afro-Caribbean-Canadian community.

Blackness as a concept is not an African phenomenon, according to Manthia Diawara (1990); rather, blackness emerged in the Americas "by the performative acts of liberation by black people through Western arts, religion, literature, science, and revolution ... [B]lackness is therefore a way of being human in the West or in areas under Western domination" (Diawara, 1990, p. 831). In studies of blackness, sometimes referred to as African diaspora studies or black diaspora studies, there is a long history of research on the maintenance of culture across the middle passage; the syncretism that results from the fusion of African and Western cultural forms; and the desire for origins that results from the present complex experiences of racism, hybridity and in-betweenness of postcolonial peoples. Anthropologist Melville Herskovits made it his life's work to recount many of the repossessions of black heritage occurring in the Americas. His studies of the simultaneous survival and rupture of African cultural forms in the Americas remains foundational to black diaspora studies. Influenced by the respective Afro-Cuban and Afro-Brazilian scholarship of Fernando Ortiz and

Arthur Ramos, and also by Jean Price-Mars (1928), who traced the rich cultures of early African kingdoms in western Sudan, Ghana, Mali and Songhai to the rural voodoo cults of Haitian peasants, Herskovitz helped to elevate the rank of African heritage hitherto despised as semi-heathen. Sidney Mintz, known for his anthropological research with Richard Price on the cultural heterogeneity of enslaved Africans in the New World and the significant impact of their mixed cultures on the diversity of beliefs and practices of the Americas, notes that no single culture can be studied in isolation, because "the peoples we study are forever subject to influences from elsewhere" (1996, p. 292). I raise this history to show that Caribbean sites have been foundational to the study of the black diaspora since its founding as an academic discipline.

Building on this legacy, black diaspora scholars demonstrate the prevalence and transformations of Igbo, Kongo, Yoruba and other African art (Thompson, 1984), religion (Routon, 2006) and food (Houston, 2005) traditions in the Americas. For example, Afro-Caribbean cooking styles and cuisine also owe a debt to enslaved Africans and colonisers who brought their culinary habits to the region. Cornmeal, okra and root-crop dishes; use of hot peppers, salt, tripe and tail; one-pot stews; and the preference for cooking outside derive from African traditions (Houston, 2005), but these are also mixed with Indian and Chinese spices, foods and customs to create the cuisine that Afro-Caribbeans call their own today. These sophisticated analyses recognise the ongoing dialogue between Africa, Europe, Asia and the Americas, and describe cultural forms as drawing on African roots, yet constantly evolving. While this work continues, the year 1993 signalled a significant shift in black diaspora studies with the publication of Paul Gilroy's *The Black Atlantic: Modernity and Double Consciousness* (1993).

Gilroy's concept of the Black Atlantic was revolutionary in its subordination of the study of emotional and cultural links to continental Africa, enslaved Africans and transplanted elements of African cultures, which he suggests essentialise blackness. Rather, he is in favour of research on contemporary individual and community travel and cultural productions that cross borders and allow black groups to form distinctive cultural and political identities by borrowing from elsewhere. Specifically, Gilroy (1993) outlines a complex genealogy of Afro-Caribbean/Afro-British/Afro-American cultural and political formations. He calls this triad the "Black Atlantic" and argues that it is the cultural flows through these three nodes, abiding racism and racialised conditions, political (dis)empowerment and resistance practices that form what he refers to as the "changing same" that keeps black people unified, striving "continually towards a state of self-realization that continually retreats beyond its grasp" (Gilroy, 1993, p. 122). An examination of the cultural interdependencies between peoples in the Caribbean, Britain, the United States (and Canada) helps in understanding how a borderless or deterritorialised identity forms for black people.

The notion of "movement" or "routes" has long been recognised as central to black diasporic consciousness. From the ships that began the journey of millions of enslaved Africans, to the sea and train porters who comprised a majority of North and South American and European black proletariat, to the contemporary refugees, fugitives and migrants that leave their homelands daily, the routes of black people have created a dispersed community on the move as an alternative to national allegiances. As Gilroy (1993, p. 16) writes:

> The history of the Black Atlantic since 1942, continually crisscrossed by the movements of black people – not only as commodities but engaged in various struggles towards emancipation, autonomy, and citizenship – provides a means to reexamine the problems of nationality, location, identity and historical memory.

To examine Canada from the perspective of the Black Atlantic is to raise unique questions about the project of nation building. However, to speak of *the* Black Atlantic, with common cultures and ongoing desires for elsewhere, obscures the heterogeneity of the black diaspora.

More recently, several scholars have made important incursions into Gilroy's Black Atlantic framework. Jacqueline Nassy Brown's (1998) research on black seafarers and Brent Hayes Edwards (2003) study of literary and political figures in France and the United States in the early twentieth century reveal that power asymmetries within black communities make it difficult to locate common ground within these transnational communities; therefore, they highlight the importance of historical, local and gender specificity. These authors argue that Gilroy's influential theory elides the specificity of nation-states and suggest that the assumption that black cultures and outer-national identifications arise solely as antidotes to racism is limited.

Gilroy, in *Ain't No Black in the Union Jack*, argues that the culture and politics of black America and the Caribbean have become the "raw materials for creative processes which redefine what it means to be black" in Britain (1987, p. 154). Nassy Brown builds upon Gilroy's notion of "raw materials" and uses the term "diasporic resources" to describe the tools, images, events, organisations, artefacts and expressive cultures that operate beyond the anti-racism paradigm and allow membership in the black diasporic community. Her description of diasporic resources is worth quoting at length. Diasporic resources:

> include not just cultural productions such as music, but also people and places, as well as iconography, ideas and ideologies associated with them. 'Place' is an especially important resource, for the practice and politics of travel serve to map diasporic space, helping to define its margins and centers, while also crucially determining who is empowered to go where, when, under what conditions and for what purposes ... [resources are appropriated] to meet particular needs – but do so within limits, within and against power asymmetries, and with political consequences. (1998, p. 298)

Nassy Brown describes the Black Atlantic as both bound to and free from "place," captured in a "racialized geography of the imagination" (1998, p. 291); though their ethnic roots, territories and customs are varied, black people's imagined connections remain strong because they are able to access similar resources that link them to particular places. Cultural practices such as wearing kentia fabric or natural hairstyles, or listening to and creating hip hop music may all signify dissatisfaction with, and resistance to, dominant discourses and mainstream cultures. Notably, these diasporic resources are gendered and attention to making of masculinities and femininities via diasporic resources deepens our understanding of the Black Atlantic. Cultural expressions such as the philosophies of Muhammad Ali or the batting of Vivian Richards, to use two gendered sport examples, are anti-hegemonic cultural practices that permit the mapping of the black diaspora onto particular locales (such as the United States and Antigua) and broad regions (such as the Black Atlantic and the Caribbean) at the same time.

Another important challenge to Gilroy's framework includes the general occlusion of Canada from black diaspora studies. Expanding the Black Atlantic to include Canada allows for greater understanding of the supra-national, transnational and multinational contexts and cross-border flows that create black diasporic cultures. Burman (2010), Campbell (2012), Joseph (2012), Trotz (2006), Walcott (2001; 2003) and others have shown black popular culture in Canada to be dependent on transnational relationships and movements to and from the Caribbean, North and South America and England. Abdel-Shehid, in his assessment of sporting black masculinities in Canada argues "that we need to eschew the nation as an interpretive framework for thinking through sport and nationalism" (2005, p. 6), particularly due to "the inability of Canadian state narratives to produce local versions of black masculinity" (p. 112). The Black Atlantic provides an appropriate alternative interpretive framework.

In Canada, black aspirations for belonging are activated by specific local debates about the exclusivity of Canadian national white belonging, and also by desires for membership in an inclusive community that happens to be dispersed across borders. Thus, expanding the Black Atlantic to include Canada and drawing from a mode of cultural production such as sport exposes how the Canadian nation-state intersects with local dynamics of the countries from which black Canadians have come and the nations to which their kin and kith have dispersed. Below is detailed the history of Canada's black diaspora, focusing specifically on peoples and cultures from the Caribbean and research trends in (Afro-)Caribbean diasporas.

The Caribbean, arguably more than any other region, has felt the impact of international movements of people throughout its history. Transnational social and family networks, emotional connections to a homeland, and cultural formations that transcend borders can be regarded as fundamental aspects of Caribbeanness (Foner, 2001; Gmelch, 1992; Mintz, 1998; Nurse, 2004; Richardson, 1992). The Caribbean diaspora's story begins with the story of slavery. As a result of the need for staples (such as sugar, molasses, rum, tobacco, cotton, indigo and coffee) for rapidly expanding metropolitan markets, European colonisers began the import of slaves from various African nations as early as the mid-sixteenth century; from the early 1500s to late 1800s, the Caribbean "received perhaps one-third of all enslaved Africans who reached the New World alive" (Mintz, 1996, p. 294). When the legal systems of slavery were reluctantly dismantled in 1838, the British colonies expressed a need for replacement labour and a need to depress wages where former slaves had begun to agitate for more income. Eventually a system was devised for recruiting labourers, from Portugal, China and especially the Indian subcontinent (Niranjana, 2001; Peake and Trotz, 1999; Williams, 1991). "The end of slavery did not put a halt to slavery's habitual social and economic accompaniments," Mintz (1996, p. 298) argues. Workers continued to be abused and exploited. For example, Munasinghe (2001) notes that working conditions on plantations were so poor that thousands of Africans and Indians after them were ill, punished for constant ill health and worked to death, and little was done to improve their circumstances or integrate them into society by way of education. Enslaved, indentured and free Africans and Indian labourers engaged in numerous forms of rebellious activity, ranging from feigning sickness, stealing and burning crops, to "maroonage" (running away and forming free communities) and ultimately migration.

Gmelch (1992) points out that for Caribbean peoples migration is not only a result of global economic push–pull factors. Migration is embedded in the social, cultural and mental fabric of Caribbean people and a predominant feature among men and women, including not only working class, but also skilled and highly educated groups, as the main means of upward social mobility and family reunification. For many Caribbean countries, more members of the population live in other areas of the Caribbean, North America and Europe than in their homelands: "In the eastern Caribbean, particularly where small, resource-poor islands predominate, migration is a way of life, a common household strategy for dealing with economic scarcity … On many islands migration is so pervasive that nearly every household has a relative living in Britain or North America" (Gmelch, 1992, p. 3). The first emigrants, beginning shortly after the formal end of slavery in the late 1830s until the 1880s, moved away from plantations to small landholdings on other islands with expanding sugarcane cultivation and high demands for labour. Afro-Caribbeans migrated within the region, going to Spanish and other non-British territories to work on sugar estates or banana plantations and for jobs such as the building of the Panama Canal (Gmelch, 1992). They also went to the Netherlands, the United Kingdom and the United States after the Second World War to help with unskilled and semiskilled labour shortages in the 1940s and 1950s (Nurse, 2004; Thomas-Hope, n.d.).

Immigration to Britain was mainly from Commonwealth Caribbean regions, especially Jamaica, in the 1948–62 period, in part thanks to the 1948 British Nationality Act, which created shared rights (including the right to live and work in the United Kingdom) to all citizens of the Commonwealth. Nurses and students were the two biggest groups of those who gained entry from the Caribbean during this time. As Britain began to impose more stringent immigration requirements on Commonwealth Caribbean migrants, the systems of the United States and Canada became more liberal, and immigration shifted primarily to these countries in the early 1960s. Significantly, since the 1960s, more Caribbean migrants have left Britain than entered, with Canada, the United States and also their nations of origin as destinations. The ageing population combined with low immigration rates means that although the British-born, Caribbean ethnic population will remain, the stock of Afro-Caribbean immigrants in Britain will soon be diminutive, while the population in Canada continues to grow.

Ropero (2004, p. 156) explains that new regulations in Canada that de-emphasised nationality (and, indirectly, race) as a criterion for selection, and instead prioritised educational and occupational qualifications, led to a boom in migration from the Caribbean:

> [A] points system was introduced in 1967, whereby immigrants were assessed in terms of their skills and employability, regardless of race or nationality ... Thanks to the points system, Caribbean immigrants gained access to Canada, coming in large numbers during the late 1960s and 1970s. Canadian immigration offices were opened in Jamaica, Trinidad, Barbados and other islands in order to recruit skilled immigrants. Thus, the Caribbean jumped from fourteenth place to third as a source of Canadian migration during these years.

During the period 1960–81, Canada received migrants mainly from the Anglophone Caribbean. Over one-tenth of these were female domestic workers and nurses who started on 1-year visas as a result of government-supported work schemes. The majority were able to become long-term migrants during the period between 1968 and 1973, when migration reached its peak and persons who had been admitted as visitors could apply for landed status. Females from the Caribbean have always outnumbered male migrants to Canada owing to the opportunities for work in the service, clerical, domestic help and nursing fields. The majority were from Jamaica, Trinidad and Tobago and Haiti, although all Caribbean regions have supplied migrants to Canada. The population was generally younger than migrants to the United Kingdom and the United States, with a concentration in the 25–29-year-old age group, and a higher proportion of migrants to Canada entered as students (Thomas-Hope, n.d.).

With regard to geographic distribution, Henry (1999) notes that 84 per cent of Caribbean immigrants to Canada are from the former British colonies: Anguilla, Antigua, Bahamas, Barbados, Cayman Islands, Grenada, Guyana, Jamaica, Montserrat, St. Christopher and Nevis, St. Lucia, St. Vincent and the Grenadines, Trinindad and Tobago, Turks and Caicos Islands, and British Virgin Islands. However, only four of these countries – Jamaica, Guyana, Trinidad and Tobago and Barbados – account for 93 per cent of the immigrants. Notably, Afro-Caribbeans responding to racism and declining work opportunities in Britain are listed as British in the Canadian census, but it is estimated that as many as 15,000 Afro-Caribbeans have migrated twice, first to Britain and then to Canada. In 2001, there were over 500,000 Caribbean peoples in Canada, representing 2 per cent of the total Canadian population, and this population continues to grow. The majority live in Quebec (22 per cent) and Ontario (69 per cent), primarily concentrated in Toronto (Lindsay, 2007a). Vibrant Afro-Caribbean communities were created in various neighbourhoods such as Eglinton-Oakwood and Jane-Finch. In the intervening decades, many middle-class Afro-Caribbean immigrants have dispersed into suburban areas including Scarborough, Markham, Pickering, Brampton and

Mississauga, creating an Afro-Caribbean community that spans Toronto's urban and suburban zones.

Despite Toronto's celebrations of multiculturalism and a three-week-long summer festival dedicated to Caribbean culture, institutionalised racism remains part of the foundational moral and social climate of the city and nation. Canada's ethnic minorities, Afro-Caribbeans in particular, are in a disadvantaged position with respect to the distribution of power, prestige and resources. For decades Afro-Caribbean-Canadians have waged a number of legal battles around improved working conditions, enhanced access to jobs and non-discriminatory education.

The crossing of borders and meeting of other Afro-Caribbeans in Canada, drawing from African-American and black British cultures, and being lumped together as one based on racial difference from the dominant white group, led to a pan-Caribbean, transnational, deterritorialised sense of black consciousness for many migrants in Canada. This diasporic identity, as Gilroy (2010) writes, seems "to have cultivated its own forms of blackness, which were not African, or more accurately, not *just* African" (p. 115, emphasis in original). A migrant from Barbados living in Toronto may have family in the United States, England, Jamaica and Barbados, and a reunion may take place in New York City, which is considered the "homeland" for many members (Foner, 2001; Sutton, 2008). Therefore the Afro-Caribbean diaspora is a deterritorialised community, connected to multiple geographies at once.

In his analysis of black diaspora "routes," Edward (2001, p. 63) observes, Gilroy is "more concerned with individual stories of travel ... and abstract notions of transnational circuits of culture than with specific ground-level histories." This study draws from Gilroy's (1993) theoretical framework of the Black Atlantic, but expands his geographical and theoretical purview in five important ways: (1) rather than exploring meanings created by individual sojourners such as W. E. B. Du Bois and Richard Wright, I specifically examine ground-level experiences of a group of Afro-Caribbeans; (2) I raise the importance of Canada to the Black Atlantic, instead of focusing on relations among the Caribbean, England and the United States; (3) rather than examining cultural forms such as music and literature, I investigate the activities associated with sport to illuminate the cultural ingenuity, resilience, heritage and creolisation of the black diaspora; (4) I highlight gender performances and relations and show how spaces come to be not only raced but also gendered, especially through women's absences; and (5) I shift attention away from racial terror and exile as factors driving black consciousness to consider how the terror associated with ageing can bring older black men together.

Much of the writing about black Caribbean men in anthropology, cultural studies and sociology of the Caribbean draws from the gender analysis of Peter J. Wilson's (1973) text, *Crab Antics*. In his study of the island of Providencia, the two separate value systems Wilson explicated, "respectability" and "reputation," have been found to be characteristic of Afro-Caribbean cultures throughout the islands, territories and diaspora. The "respectability" value system is derived from the cultures of the upper classes (originally the British colonisers) and is adopted by black and creole middle-classes, the Church and women, primarily. These groups value the home, self-restraint, work, education, family and hierarchies. The opposite locations and characteristics (the street and rum shop, playful self-expression, idle pleasures, infidelity and egalitarianism) are the domain of men, especially the working classes.

Further elaborating on Wilson's reputation thesis, Roger D. Abrahams made a crucial contribution to Caribbean studies in his studies comprising *The Man-of-Words in the West Indies*. He clarifies the acts of playful self-expression that are central to building reputation by distinguishing between *broad talkers* and *sweet talkers*. *Broad talkers* are predominantly working-class men who rely on wit, repetition and a local dialect. Working- and middle-class *sweet talkers*, in contrast, use elevated diction, elaborate syntax and received pronunciation to enhance their reputations. Both of these groups use a stylised performance of speech and verbal agility to perform masculinity in outdoor spaces. Abrahams' (1983) analysis was not only limited to men. He highlights the verbal acuity of working-class women as part of their reputation building as well. Caribbean people appear to be talking all at the same time, with call and response, interruption, gestures (e.g., cut-eye) and noise (e.g., kiss-teeth) being more important at times than the content of the words used.[5] Although reputation and respectability are not complete binaries divided along space and class lines, their value for understanding black diaspora cultures and gender, with the Caribbean case in particular, remains undeniable. Wilson (1973) espoused reputation as the autochthonous value system of Afro-Caribbeans. While I do not agree that the predominantly masculine activities of talking, drinking, storytelling and gaining respite from the workplace and homespace are any more "purely Caribbean" than the work, decorum, discipline and polite exchanges of some women's spaces or workspaces, the case study presented below helps to illuminate the ways in which Afro-Caribbean men and women in the diaspora draw from both value systems to mark their home culture. Afro-Caribbean men and women generally inhabit distinct cultural spheres, and the cricket grounds and the club's associated parties and picnics are primarily spaces of "reputation"; however, club members cannot escape some of their religious and middle-class principles that result in "respectable" behaviour. Club members are embedded in both reputation and respectability value systems, more or less, at different times, and both will be used as a hermeneutic thread in the pages that follow to show how gender, class and racialised performances reflect their (aspirations for) belonging to different communities.

Within Canada, there is a corpus of theatrical, literary, poetic and artistic works that examines the multiply-identified members of the Afro-Caribbean diaspora. It would be remiss of me if I did not preface this study of race and gender in Toronto cricket communities, and if I did not specifically pay homage to Trey Anthony's *Da Kink in My Hair* (2005), set in a Toronto hair salon. The play, which inspired a television series, highlights the emotional, financial and family-related struggles of Caribbean women and men in Canada. Member of the Order of Canada, novelist Austin Clarke, as well as poets, playwrights and novelists Althea Prince, Claire Harris, Dany Laferrière, Dionne Brand, Everard Palmer, Makeda Silvera and M. Nourbese Philip rewrite Canadian history from the perspectives of disarticulated Afro-Caribbean people who remain confronted with conflicts of idyllic multiculturalism embedded in a racist society. They demonstrate that differently positioned Afro-Caribbeans have real and imagined journeys and communities that are important to narratives of nation, (dis)location, loss, safety, horror, hope, (return to) home and belonging. These contributions highlight the ongoing importance of storytelling and demands for social justice among Afro-Caribbean-Canadians.

From a social science perspective, Katherine McKittrick's (2002) study highlighted a creative tension between Canadian black diaspora "communities that are elsewhere (remembering, imagining, travelling) and here at the same time" (p. 33). Important in this dimension of diaspora is the critical role of the spatial production of race; of dwelling, settling and nostalgic memory in the diasporic experience; or as McKittrick puts it, "a politics of location – geographical, linguistic and imaginary – is importantly rooted in a politics of (un)belonging" (2002, p. 33). Diasporas do not necessarily travel regularly to feel connected to "home." Turning attention to the national discourses, recollections and cultural resources of those who left their homes and *then* chose to make their new homes in Canada, broadens our understandings of Afro-Caribbean diasporas and the Black Atlantic. Alissa Trotz (2006; 2011) also provides a formidable analysis of space, race and transnational networks within the Guyanese diaspora in Toronto, Canada, that hosts school reunions and travels to New York on shopping trips. Ostensibly, the Guyanese community is brought together and the porosity of nation is demonstrated through links made between Canada, the United States, England and Guyana; however, class hierarchies and specifically gendered roles of the homeland are also reinforced revealing that diasporic communities are not homogenous. Although national borders are regularly crossed – and for some, essentially dissolved – the political and cultural salience of nation-states remain.

Hundreds of thousands of Afro-Caribbeans insist on making Canada their residence. They establish networks, raise children and embed themselves in local communities; yet, they remain out of place, as others assume that they are new, and they choose or are forced to refer to other locations as home. Afro-Caribbeans are aware of the limits of belonging and thus prefer not to place all their hopes and dreams in this nation. Rather, they turn to the black and/or Caribbean diaspora for a sense of belonging. Organised physical activity at a recreational level is largely overlooked as a diasporic resource that Afro-Caribbean people deploy (Walter et al., 1991 is one exception). Cultural or ethnic organisations and associations and their sporting clubs are important spaces for the formation of an Afro-Caribbean diaspora consciousness through what Clifford (1994) refers to as "roots" and "routes." That is, diasporas develop (1) relationships with their "roots," their ideas of ancestry and home that shift with changes across the lifespan, varying political (un)certainties in the states of origin/dwelling, and transformations in degrees of economic and social power, and (2) access to "routes"; that is, flows of kin and cultural resources and the ability to forge real and imagined transnational networks.

A recreational cricket field in Toronto operates as, in Gilroy's (1993, p. 95) words, "an important junction point or crossroads on the webbed pathways of Black Atlantic political culture." This text examines the many ways that cricket is a useful diasporic resource for Afro-Caribbean-Canadians. Cricket has many associated elements including travel, food, drink, socialising and fundraising, to name a few, which help Afro-Caribbean-Canadians to develop a sense of connection to a broader Afro-Caribbean and black community, restore their homelands, reproduce gendered cultures and class hierarchies, and create an anti-hegemonic space in their local neighbourhoods. At the same time, the black cricket club members demonstrate their status as Canadians and show ways in which they are locally embedded in and intertwined with the dominant culture. A closer analysis of what has been written about the sporting experiences of different diasporas helps to situate the research on the Mavericks Cricket and Social Club (MCSC).

Sport and diaspora

It is only in the past two decades that a few illuminating studies emerged to examine the intersections and experiences of diasporas in sport. Within multicultural societies, diasporic communities, consciousness and cultures come to life in professional sport stadia and on recreational fields. It should come as no surprise that much of this research is on cricket, given the importance of the sport in nearly every British colony and the high rates of postcolonial migration from those same sites.[6] In England, national belonging was "tested" via sport in 1990, when conservative British politician Norman (now Lord) Tebbit's infamous "cricket test" called on diasporic ethnic minorities to prove their loyalty and desire to integrate into Britain by showing support for the English cricket team (Werbner, 2005, p. 756). South Asian diasporic groups often show allegiance to Britain and investment in British teams and leagues, but they also gather to celebrate their homeland cricket team – Bangladesh, India, Pakistan, or Sri Lanka – in international competitions to connect with other local and distant compatriots, thus forming an imagined community and symbolic link with the subcontinent. Their support is also an anti-colonial and anti-local act of resistance, a symbolic rejection of "Englishness" (Burdsey, 2006, p. 17). South Asian cricket fans now living in the diaspora subvert national identities through their sporting allegiances as they express their homeland cultures, including sometimes re-enacting political conflicts such as between India and Pakistan (Davis and Upson, 2004).

International Test cricket spectatorship offered the same openings for black Britons. In 1984, when the black West Indies (Windies) team executed a historic massacre of a white English team in England (5–0 in five matches), with the result being repeated at home in the Caribbean four years later, celebrations abounded in black inner-city areas from Bristol to Leeds. The wins were labelled by these supporters as a "blackwash" (as opposed to a whitewash): "[I]t was very clear that they were celebrating not just a cricket victory but a far wider one in the wake of the Notting Hill and Brixton riots, inquiries into which revealed the full social and political plight of West Indian communities in Britain" (Stoddart, 2006, p. 804).

Anecdotal evidence suggests that the reactions to the wins were similar in New York and Toronto. Afro-Caribbean immigrants were glued to their radios and televisions for the duration of the matches and they gathered at parks to celebrate, play their own cricket and rehash the victories of "their team." In addition to watching professional cricket, playing recreational cricket offers an opportunity to cathect an explicit anti-racism platform, eschew exclusion from elite leagues, symbolically overturn hierarchies of dominance, subvert police harassment and destabilise class subordination in the diaspora (Carrington 1998; 1999; Williams, 2001). It is at their own games that Afro-Caribbean migrants related Windies victories and their own successes to vanquishing the colonisers, and played the calypsos "Cricket Lovely Cricket" by Lord Beginner and "Sir Garfield Sobers" by The Mighty Sparrow as soundtracks for their local celebrations. Although these types of celebrations do little to interrupt local and historical racial antagonisms, and mask internal divisions, it is clear that they are a necessary part of survival in the diaspora for some men. Athletes of Afro-Caribbean descent connect to their homeland, native language, ethnic pride, racial group, dispersed populations and local communities through sport.

The ethnographic research conducted by Ben Carrington in the mid-1990s with a black cricket team, "the Caribbean Cricket Club (CCC) one of the oldest black sporting institutions in Britain" (2008, p. 431), is instructive for the analysis being conducted here. The CCC plays in a league, "representing" an area of Leeds racialised as black, in a sport invested with the English habitus, in a county renowned for its chauvinism and racially exclusive form of identity (Carrington 2008, p. 431; see also Carrington 1998; 1999). He demonstrated that participation in the CCC and playing the sport of cricket itself could be read as a form of cultural resistance to white racism in this context. Though he acknowledges the diasporic dimension of racial formation, and even highlights regional differences in black Britishness (Carrington, 2008, p. 435), he pays less attention to the transnational connections of the CCC members. The "friendly" (non-league) games that the Mavericks played in England against teams like the CCC tell us something else about the *"complex, relational, and dialogic* nature of racial formation" (Carrington, 2008, p. 430). By situating their play in the context of the Black Atlantic, with itinerant, older, Canadian cricketers, I build on the cogent understanding of race provided through Carrington's local study from two decades ago.

Gilroy's concept of the Black Atlantic has been used in sport studies to understand the bonds across borders shared by racialised athletes with and without African origins. For example, black athletes in Norway have been shown to be bonded through their imagined connections to black people in other countries, and their exclusion from white privilege and power, rather than a link to a common, mythical African homeland (Andersson, 2007). Andersson's examination of Norwegian football, basketball and track and field reveals that black athletes do not always feel included in Norwegian society. The local history of the sport, national origins of the athlete and individual desire to risk being seen as "too sensitive' by openly resisting racist labels such as "negro" all influence black Norwegian athletes' experiences of what Gilroy, drawing from W. E. B. DuBoiss calls a "double consciousness." In his examination of the othering of Samoans (even those representing New Zealand's preeminent national rugby side, the All Blacks), Grainger (2006) demonstrates the complicated questions of ethnicity and national belonging, cultural networks, deterritorialised identities and anti-colonial resistances that form within what he calls the "Black Pacific" – akin to Gilroy's (1993) conception of the Black Atlantic. Samoan professional and recreational athletes' emotional, economic and political relations to the "homeland" in conjunction with racist exclusions in the "hostland" often prevent them from aligning themselves as national subjects; Samoan rugby players "negotiate an identity simultaneously informed by colonial legacy, notions of 'homeland,' and the economic demands of global capitalism – they occupy, and identify with, more than one national space" (Grainger, 2006, p. 46). Samoan players' blackness allows them to mobilise both national and diasporic consciousness, which may or may not be associated with the cultures, resistance efforts, sport figures or political icons of the Afro-diaspora.

The broad social significance of sport in the Black Atlantic has been clearly shown by Grant Farred (2003), who argues that sport figures may act as symbols for a borderless black community. His detailed treatise of Muhammad Ali describes the diasporic and political nature of this icon when he states: "It is no accident that Ali, more than [Bob] Marley was (at first) more readily accepted by the Third World and the black diaspora than he was by mainstream America" (p. 25). Farred continues:

> The impact of his victories and his (rare) defeats resonated well beyond the United States, particularly (and surprisingly, in those pre-TV and -satellite days) in those places where previously – or still-colonised – people saw Ali as championing the same struggles in which they were engaged. (2003, p. 41)

Ali was sometimes commodified, unlearned in some aspects of postcolonial politics and a patriot (e.g., when he competed for America at the 1960 Olympics). Yet, when the boxer demanded to be recognised not as "Cassius Clay" (which he referred to as his "slave name"), but instead as "Muhammad Ali," (which represented his conversion to the Nation of Islam and commitment to the liberation of black people), he registered political dissent in a public sport forum. As "the poet laureate of black global expression" (Farred, 2003, p. 54), Ali brought into public view the effects of slavery and colonialism and the struggle for anti-hegemonic and non-pejorative black identity in the United States and the postcolonial world.

There are only two book-length texts that purport to describe the intersections of sport and the black diaspora. *Race and the Sporting Black Diaspora* (Carrington, 2010) describes the roles of pugilists Jack Johnson, Mike Tyson, Frank Bruno and Joe Louis as transcending the sporting realm and becoming meaningful icons for black people in and outside the United States. Like Ali, these black athletes were commodified by a racist media as they used sport as an arena for public resistance to white racism. Carrington (2010) shows the uniqueness of sport in providing an international stage for black voices and the centrality of the athlete to crafting a specifically black and masculine global imaginary within the context of the twentieth century. However, Carrington reproduces Gilroy's elision of ground-level group activities and the Canadian nation-state within the Black Atlantic. In Abdel-Shehid's (2005) text, *Who Da Man?*, Gilroy's seminal notion of the Black Atlantic "and its emphasis on black performance, movement and permanence both inside and outside national frameworks, helps us understand sport in Canada much more thoroughly" (p. 6) and "allow[s] us to hear the complexity of black voices here in Canada and their engagements with other parts of the world" (p. 7). Abdel-Shehid uses case studies of Afro-Caribbean track athlete, Ben Johnson and African-Americans in the Canadian Football League to show that crossing national borders is central to black sporting presences in Canada and that a Manichean response to colonialism still exists within dominant Canadian culture.

Yet, Carrington's (2010) and Abdel-Shehid's (2005) texts do not go far enough. They opine that much of the literature on sport and race leaves out the complexities of the diasporic condition, when much of their own texts focus on a capacious black category and theories of "invisibility," "erasure" and "marginalisation." One is left wondering, other than (overcoming) racism, what are the complexities of the diasporic condition? How do black groups interact with other diasporas? What are the black women doing while the black men are playing sport and how is gender produced relationally? How do the historical and contemporary manifestations of culture and politics in the nation of origin and the new home influence the production of racial categories? How do the heterogeneities of Caribbean diasporas manifest in specific national contexts outside the Caribbean and how do these influence Afro-Caribbean identity? If the Black Atlantic is produced through collective cultures and memories, how do these concepts come into play on and around sport playing fields?

This book owes a debt to the foundational sport and diaspora literature, building on it in order to decipher how borderless racial and ethnic communities are made. This research forces us to examine black diasporas in the context of specific nationalisms, transnational networks and physical cultural forms. Whereas Carrington (2010) and Abdel-Shehid (2005) concentrate on professional, celebrity, black male athletes as icons who represent power, strength and overcoming oppressions in mainstream sport, this text is interested in how itinerant, recreational athletes use a relatively marginal (in Canada) embodied activity to generate a black racial consciousness and ethnic community, for themselves and their families. This book also moves beyond their analyses to suggest that the gendering of Afro-Caribbean diasporic cultural forms leads to the occupation of different spaces and roles for men and women. I contribute to the feminist critique of black diaspora studies by showing women to be an integral part of the Black Atlantic. Women contribute to men's gender performances in sport communities, even if they are relegated to the area outside the playing field. Also, a particular subset of the Black Atlantic, Afro-Caribbean-Canadians, is examined using a particular sport, namely cricket. This popular culture is as germane to the Caribbean region and a supra-national consciousness as reggae music and carnival parades.

The unification of the Caribbean territories via the Windies cricket team (there is no equivalent in other sports in the Caribbean) anticipates the diasporic condition of racialised unification of black Caribbean people from a range of nations of origins; therefore, an examination of Afro-Caribbean diasporas and cricket go hand in hand. Given that sport is an embodiment of culture in Canada and, moreover, associated with so many other cultural manifestations such as music, dancing and socialising, sport is a powerful mode of cultural production for thinking through the Afro-Caribbean diasporic subjectivities that are forged in Canada.

Researching the Mavericks Cricket and Social Club

The majority of the cricketers involved in this study played the sport as boys informally in the roads and fields, on the beaches and in an organised fashion in school, parish and national leagues in their respective Caribbean homelands. When they decided to immigrate, they knew they were not going to arrive in a country featuring clay pitches and regular test matches;[7] in fact, many did not believe cricket was played in Canada at all, but they began playing in recreational cricket leagues when they arrived in the late 1960s and 1970s. They dominated the Hamilton and District, Montreal and District,

Toronto and District and Commonwealth Cricket Leagues as well as the appropriately named SOCA (Southern Ontario Cricket Association) for over 20 years. Some even enjoyed elite cricket at the provincial and national levels in Canada; however, as they aged they were unable (or unwilling) to run or bowl as fast, sacrifice their bodies as much or see the ball as well. Many stopped playing as a result of acute muscular and joint injuries or illnesses such as stroke or heart attack, and they never returned to the action. The increasing drop-out rates, in addition to the changing cultural demographics of league cricket in Toronto, caused the majority to opt to end their competitive careers, amalgamate some of their teams, and as they crossed the threshold of 50 years of age, focus on the pleasures associated with watching or playing what they call "friendly master's cricket" instead. Because they play with and against each other, and members of a few different teams join together to travel, I have aggregated several first-generation immigrant-friendly cricket clubs into one group, which is referred to as the Mavericks Cricket and Social Club (MCSC).

Approximately 200 Afro-Caribbean-Canadians, mainly living in Toronto, make up the MCSC. In particular, I focus on a group of approximately 50 male players (the Mavericks), with 100 male and 50 female supporters. This latter group comprises the daughters, sisters, friends, girlfriends, mistresses and wives of the cricketers. They do not play cricket, but a few remain embedded in the club culture nonetheless. A rare few come to every game and may cook meals for the after-parties, score keep, or enjoy the black/Caribbean cricket culture alongside male supporters. Other women are linked to the club only through their absence from games, attendance at dances and other social activities, or through their chauffeur and laundry services.

In order to study populations that are scattered across multiple locations, maintain networks across borders and live their lives embedded in multiple communities, researchers are required to live among and travel along with their participants, observing and engaging in cultural patterns and intimate social interactions in many different locations. I performed a multi-sited ethnography, observing and participating in MCSC cricket practices, games and trips for 21 months in 2008 and 2009.[8] I did not play cricket but engaged as much as possible with the associated practices of the sport, including the (grand)child minding, score keeping and sideline cheering undertaken by female MCSC members, and the dancing, socialising and drinking of the males. I also attended team meetings, award ceremonies, house parties, street fêtes, picnics, dances and banquets.

Cricket-related travel is a highlight of the year for many of the members. The MCSC relies on members' diasporic social networks to arrange weekend bus trips to Canadian cities in southern Ontario, Quebec and US states including Connecticut, Massachusetts, New Jersey, New York, Ohio and Pennsylvania. They also travel for two-week-long cricket tours and tournaments in England and numerous Caribbean islands, including Antigua, Barbados, Grenada, St. Lucia and Trinidad. I formally interviewed (digitally recorded and transcribed verbatim) 29 players, and held dozens of informal interviews with former players, supporters, team managers, tournament administrators and MCSC members, including members of the teams that came to play against the Mavericks from abroad and players' wives and girlfriends. Every participant was given a pseudonym. I deliberately chose names common to the Caribbean: some are Christian (e.g., Michael) and others Afro-Caribbean (e.g., Kundell) or Indo-Caribbean (e.g., Hussein) in keeping with the diversity of the real names of the Mavericks. Over 21 months, I spoke with hundreds of community members at games, practices, parties, picnics, dances, meetings and cricket-related trips. It would be impossible to collect demographic information from everyone, but the major characteristics of participants formally or informally interviewed and observed, whose words and actions compose the majority of the data analysed below, are displayed in Table A1 (in the Appendix).

In as few as 10 years, a study of the MCSC will not be possible. The majority of the members' children do not play cricket, and the ratio of cricket players to cricket spectators in the club is rapidly shifting to favour the latter. The Mavericks' average age was 61 years and many will soon cease play as a result of their physical degeneration; this community of Afro-Caribbean-Canadian cricketers is literally dying out and not being replaced. The members of the MCSC are uniquely positioned to offer insights into questions of diaspora, community, culture and (trans)nationalisms, particularly because a sense of "alienation may be relatively more pronounced among the earlier cohort of migrants" (Roberts, 2004, p. 650) and older, middle-class migrants may have more sufficient resources to travel and perform elaborate rituals that connect them to home (Werbner, 2005). Canadian census data show that immigration from the Caribbean reached a peak in the mid-1970s and migrants from the Caribbean represented more than 10 per cent of all landed immigrants admitted to Canada between 1973 and 1978, with the majority residing in Ontario and Quebec (Richmond, 1989, pp. 3–5). The Mavericks reflect these demographics, having an average year of migration to Canada of 1976 and having played the vast majority of their cricket in Ontario and Quebec.

Members of the MCSC were mainly middle- and working-class (discerned from their reports of their careers: e.g., autoworker, engineer, home renovator, police officer, postal worker, plumber, teacher). In 2007, a Statistics Canada report indicated that people of Caribbean origin aged 45–64 years and aged 65 and over had an average income of $32,502 and $20,944 respectively (Lindsay, 2007a, p. 15). Based on their reports of their careers, MCSC members probably make between $40,000 and $140,000, putting them in a higher socio-economic bracket than many of their Afro-Caribbean-Canadian peers. The majority of club members were Afro-Caribbean. They originally migrated from Antigua, Grenada, Guyana, St. Lucia, Trinidad and Jamaica. Also, approximately half were from Barbados. Most spent over half their lives in Canada, yet they remain connected to the Caribbean through their real, imagined and "corporeal travel" (Joseph, 2008) to Caribbean spaces.

A discussion of my positionality is necessary, given that questions of the participants' and the researcher's race, nationality and gender "have to be accounted for and *theorized*" in all sociology research, not to mention research on race issues (Carrington, 2007, p. 58, emphasis in original). My status as a 30-year-old black Caribbean-Canadian woman, who understands Anglo-Caribbean dialects, enjoys Caribbean music and food and easily socialises, is likely to have helped me to gain rapport and entry into many spaces with the club members. As I wrote previously, "my relative youth, female and researcher status *required* that I befriend some female club members, who were constantly on guard against any (especially younger) woman, talking with their husbands or boyfriends due to the potential of sparking romantic interest" (Joseph, 2015, p. 171, emphasis in original). The friendships I made with female club members proved invaluable for finding people to interview, discussing what I had observed and editing my writing.

My relationships with many of the male club members were also friendly. Sometimes *too friendly*, but even those uncomfortable moments, when I was being pursued as a love interest or object for sexual harassment, were rich research moments, revealing much about gender politics in the Black Atlantic (see Joseph, 2013). In this text, I avoid "the worst type of identity politics … a static standpoint epistemology" (Carrington, 2007, p. 58) by describing the ways my various relationships, embodied experiences, age and gender performances influenced the observations I was able to make and interviews I engaged in (or not). Although this book is by no means an auto-ethnography, I recognise the following:

> To write about the sexual politics and gender performances of the Mavericks' cricket tours in Canada, England, and the Caribbean, or to describe what the players and spectators wore and the ways they wined (a sensual dance) at fêtes

> (parties) and other social events, and leave my own embodied, erotic experiences out of the account is tantamount to disregarding the very social phenomena and cultural boundaries I set out to study in the first place. (Joseph, 2013, p. 7)

Therefore, I draw inspiration from Rinaldo Walcott (2001), who taught me to intertwine the popular, personal and academic, to write myself into this community – as the Mavericks' adopted (grand)daughter, friend, romantic date and researcher. I also embrace the directive from Ben Carrington (2008), whose obdurate calls for reflexivity in writing about race and sport have helped create a reflexive cultural studies/critical sociology of sport methodology that is sensitive to embodied performances of racialised identity by both the participants and the ethnographer. Owing, in part, to his status as a black male and his working-class background, in combination with his ability to play cricket to a relatively high level, Carrington was accepted as a player by the Caribbean Cricket Club he studied. He does not revel in this "insider" status, however. He explains, "[a]ll our ascribed, learnt, and behavioral characteristics – as well as simply the degree of rapport that has been built up before and while in the field – will shape, though not determine, how successful the research process is" (Carrington, 2008, p. 430). Every researcher should reflect on how their various social identities help or hinder them in the field and influence their understandings of their observations, and these reflections should be included in the research narrative. Although I was unable to play alongside the Mavericks on the field, and was excluded from or chose to avoid some parties, locker rooms and late-night hotel activities, I gained a unique perspective on the use of a Caribbean sport to create a sense of a transnational black identity through the "play" I engaged in with club members around the boundary, and at parties, picnics and meetings, as well as through my entrée into women's club activities.

Book overview

In the remaining chapters, out of acknowledgement of the inseparability of the poetic and political, and the rhetorical construction (not merely reporting) of cultural accounts – or as Clifford (1986, p. 10) puts it – because cultures "do not hold still for their portraits" – I have recreated the MCSC members' storied means of communication as well as my own accounts of personal and research experiences using a variety of strategies. Often, participants would rise from their seats, not merely to tell a story but to perform a re-enactment, exaggerate a characteristic, or emphasise a memory. They sometimes spoke in clichés, rhymes and lyrics, answered questions in a confusing or poetic manner, and on occasion engaged in lewd, offensive or illegal behaviour. To render what was fragmentary coherent and meaningful, to protect anonymity without stripping away the rawness of real events and to capture the Caribbean bent for performing oral histories, a narrative inquiry approach is useful.

Narrative inquiry involves collecting and then mining the stories people tell about their experiences in the world for data to analyse. Research findings are then presented as narratives of experience. The fictionalised narratives presented in each chapter are the result of "restorying," which Connelly and Clandinin (1990, p. 4), based on their educational research, describe as the process of a "reserarcher listen[ing] first to the practitioner's story … so that it too gains the authority and validity the research story has long had." Participants are encouraged to engage in storytelling in formal and informal interviews and stories are recorded digitally and in field notes. Then researchers and participants become involved in "a process of collaboration involving mutual storytelling and restorying as the research proceeds … the researcher needs to be aware of constructing a relationship in which both voices are heard" Connelly and Clandinin (1990, p. 4).⁹

In 2000, Clandinin and Connelly highlighted that the process of reporting on ethnographic research does not begin only after data collection has ended. In fact, as the researcher enters the field, scenes, characters and plot become evident and the writing process has begun. Some ethnographers within sport studies (e.g., Sparkes, 2002) make the case for poesis in qualitative research representations, which stimulates different kinds of analyses, enables readers to feel the world in new dimensions, and "reduces the distance between the 'I' and the 'Other', and between the 'writing-I' and 'experiencing-I' of the writer" (Sparkes et al., 2003, p. 154). Stories require general descriptions of context and particular details of experience to allow the reader to understand the actual life of a community. They must be plausible, authentic and create further meaning based on the polyvocal contributions. As such, in combination with traditional ethnographic reporting, I have tried to recapture the black diaspora penchant for performing oral histories in this text with some fictionalised narratives. I follow George Lamming's (1953) coming-of-age narrative, *In the Castle of My Skin*, which provides a behind-the-scenes look at Caribbean life, communities and hierarchies, in a globalised world; I present participants' voices as they were spoken, in a mix of Caribbean patois and Canadian English to affirm participants' multiple attachments.

In addition to fictionalised narratives, I have included segments of interview transcripts and field notes in an attempt to capture the richness of the sporting Black Atlantic and Caribbean diaspora. Marcus (1998, p. 189) and other proponents of performing and inscribing reflexivity and polyvocality in qualitative research have argued for more open-ended, polyvocal and ultimately "messy" forms of dialogic writing that do not hide behind authorial authority. This self-consciously polyvocal text honours the Mavericks' and my own myriad voices, performances, politics and means of communication.

I have separated the following chapters into six themes primarily drawn from (critiques of) Gilroy's (1993) *Black Atlantic: Modernity and Double Conscious*: community, routes, nostalgia, disjunctures, diaspora space and nationalisms.[10] I begin by paying attention to the quotidian practices used to maintain unity among MCSC members in Chapter 2, "Community." Their *liming*, a patois term used to describe (especially outdoor) socialising with food, drink, chat, banter and music, is central to their recreation of a sense of home and the forging of connections with real and fictive kin. I begin in this way to highlight the performative and life-sustaining qualities of Afro-diasporic culture in Canada, and because *liming* as community regeneration is key to all of the subsequent chapters. In Chapter 3, "Routes," I show the ways the concept of transnational mobility is central to creating a deterritorialised Black Atlantic community. I provide examples of the cross-border paths Afro-Caribbean-Canadians take, and the family and friend reunions they create, to demonstrate how transnational social networks form. The chapter describes MCSC travel to their nations of origin, other Caribbean diaspora locations and hosting visiting teams in Toronto. These practices are integral to their ability to make meaningful financial/material investments that regenerate community in multiple Caribbean locations. Through cricket and other social events they create homespaces outside of the Caribbean and outside of Canada, an often overlooked aspect of the Afro-Caribbean-Canadian diaspora experience.

Chapter 4, "Nostalgia," highlights memory sharing and making as critical processes of connecting to the past, to regional imagined communities and to the dispersed people of the diaspora. Gilroy (1993, p. 212) asks "How do black expressive cultures practice remembrance? How is their remembering socially organised ... and marked out publicly?" A view of sport settings offers some answers. Within black cultural studies, nostalgia has been analysed and critiqued for its positive and negative constructivist aspects. James Lorand Matory (2008) has shown that remaking the past through myths, legends and stories, which are based on "facts," but not necessarily "true," are central to black identity. The

Mavericks stories of their pasts, including details of their childhoods, Windies cricket histories and memories of their travels are fundamental not only to their creation of community in the present, but also to easing the pain of ageing in the diaspora.

The disjunctures of diaspora is the subject matter for Chapter 5. While a diaspora is described as a deterritorialised community, a local group of people who share an identity with people dispersed to other nations, they are also a group divided. Women are often left out of the story of the black diaspora, portrayed as non-agents, erased from the history of diaspora movements and travel. However, an examination of the female club members' experiences – in addition to my own – reveals gender performances, power struggles and hierarchies within diasporas. Female club members gossip about people from different nations within the Caribbean ecumene, marking themselves as national citizens and respectable women, and making the values of the community known. Furthermore, I show that Afro-Caribbean-Canadian men's performances of race are gendered and that their masculinities are classed, sexualised and performed *relationally* with women who are present at the ground as lovers and supporters, and even with women who are absent.

In Chapter 6, "Diaspora Space," I attend to the lateral connections among diasporas, that is, how Afro-Caribbean-Canadians define themselves in contradistinction to Indo-Caribbean- and South Asian-Canadians. Much of the literature in Caribbean studies has been accused on ignoring, erasing and subordinating the Indo-Caribbean experience in favour of Afro-Caribbean domination. Although the majority of participants identified as black and Afro-Caribbean culture was dominant, I do not take those as uncontested facts. Rather, I investigate the cricket field as a site of ethnic conflict, which is loaded with the history of slavery, indentured service and nation building projects in the Caribbean and in Canada. The efforts to make a boundary around a cultural group and represent "authentic" Afro-Caribbeanness reveal the power struggles and impurities in seemingly homogenous diaspora cultures.

The nuances of Afro-diasporic life in Canada are highlighted in my descriptions of how both movement and stasis are equally relevant to black popular culture in Chapter 7, "Nationalisms." Although we know identities shift and change over time, drawing from fixed, essentialist ideas of nationhood creates a rootedness that is essential to a black sense of self. Stuart Hall's ideas of *roots* is critical to Chapter 7, which stresses the ways static Canadian and Caribbean nation of origin identities are performed in cricket spaces. Although diasporas are deterritorialised communities, Canadian nation-state discourses, histories of participants' nations of origins and their assumed allegiances remain salient. The fact that many participants have lived in Canada longer than they were in their nations of origin requires us to address their hybridity and notions of themselves as (assimilated or resistant) Canadians. In the "Conclusion," Chapter 8, I link together various threads within the book to deal with the questions of black belonging, dispersed and local Caribbean communities and the globalisation of cricket. I show how the activities of the members of a cricket and social club allow us to see both unities and hierarchies within a group, and the efforts made to create racial and ethnic boundaries which are inevitably crossed. I interrogate what we might gain from thinking about those who were largely missing (e.g., women, Indo-Caribbean-Canadians and second-generation Afro-Caribbean-Canadians) from MCSC games and events.

As I watched cricket players and supporters at games and social events, listened to them speak about the pleasures and frustrations of their lives in Canada and in their nations of origin, and followed them to near and far diaspora locations, they introduced me to their complex senses of community, culture and consciousness. They are locally embedded and globally attached. Their sense of themselves as authentically Caribbean is linked to their knowledge of and experiences within cricket settings. Yet there is no denying that they have a permanent presence in Canada and an indelible connection to black people across the Atlantic. The following chapters articulate some of the meanings of being black and Caribbean in Canada. Playing and watching sport, or supporting or travelling with a sport club, are important to creating racialised, gendered, ethnic and/or national identities. I begin with an analysis of the bounded communities club members create at and around the cricket grounds.

Notes

1 In scholarship on migration from the Caribbean, specifically from the English-speaking Caribbean, there persists an insistence upon using "West Indian" as opposed to "Caribbean." The persistence of the term "West Indian" is owing, in part, to the lexicon of the people themselves and the popularity of the internationally competitive West Indies cricket team, so named because of its origins in the colonial era, and Columbus' mistaken belief that he had landed in the "Indies." I employ the label "Caribbean" to refer to the region that includes Guyana as well as the string of islands between North and South America, and even spaces within Canada, following Gadsby's (2006, p. 10) suggestion that we use "Caribbean in an effort to move beyond the legacies of colonial designations" and that "Caribbeanness as a concept cannot be narrowed down to a particular space."

2 The Golden Horseshoe Area spans a region from Niagara Falls in the south-west, around the western end of Lake Ontario and ends at Oshawa in the east. The region includes the City of Toronto as its major metropolitan centre. The cities where the majority of the research participants lived and played include Ajax, Brampton, Brantford, Cambridge, Hamilton, Kitchener, Mississauga, Pickering, Richmond Hill, Scarborough, Toronto, Vaughan and Woodstock. Though each city has a different history of black and Caribbean migration, socio-economic demographics, and mixture of ethnic groups, I have amalgamated them under "Toronto" because most participants were closest to this city, Torontonians is usually how they described themselves when interacting with others across the Black Atlantic, and also for ease of communication in this text. I use the names of particular cities where relevant.
3 Although matting is used in some Caribbean nations – James (1963, pp. 61–63 and 83–85) describes the use of matting wickets – many MCSC members described their surprise when they encountered matting for the first time in Canada.
4 When they refer to themselves as "pure" blacks or "truly Jamaican," migrants refuse hybridities and border crossings, which "may have less to do with a modernist nostalgia for secure origins than with a will to physical survival and a struggle for political self-determination" (Puri, 1999, p. 15) in an unwelcoming society.
5 "Cut-eye" is a visual gesture involving directing a glare in someone's direction followed by directing the eyes down or across the person's body "which communicates hostility, displeasure, disapproval, or a general rejection of the person at whom it is directed" (Rickford and Rickford, 1976, p. 296). "Kiss-teeth," also called *chups* or *suck-teeth* involves sucking air in through clenched teeth and slightly parted lips and "is an expression of anger, impatience, exasperation or annoyance" (Rickford and Rickford, 1976, p. 303). These are often used together, more often by women in the Afro-diaspora than men, and are considered ill-mannered by the upper classes.
6 The significance of Gaelic (and other) sports for maintaining ethnic identity outside of Ireland has also been widely studied (see Darby and Hassan, 2007).
7 Test matches are a type of first-class cricket organised by the International Cricket Council and played between national representative teams for a maximum of ninety overs per day. Each team is required to bat twice. Malcolm (2013) notes that test match rules, while grounded in a philosophy of equality and fairness are at times arbitrary and advantage one team. It is a source of bemusement to the uninitiated that "test matches are scheduled for up to five days, and they may end at any point before that" (Malcolm, 2013, p. 5). This was the standard form of cricket until the introduction of one-day international competitions in the early 1970s and Twenty20 cricket in the early 2000s.
8 James Clifford (1986, p. 11) points out that senses are hierarchically ordered differently in different cultures and "the truth of vision in Western, literate cultures has predominated over the evidences of sound and interlocution, of touch, smell and taste." Although I use the Western term "observation," I used not only sight in this analysis. I observed with my ears, hips and taste buds.
9 While these authors highlight the role of the participants in the restorying process so that the final story becomes a collaboration, I found that few of the 200 club members were actually interested in the writing, revising and editing processes. I shared the entire manuscript with key informants and particular stories with relevant participants and some helped to morph the stories by providing more details of plot, character or broader analysis; however, few offered many changes. While it is important to offer to participants to be involved in the writing process, the assumption that they are as

invested in the final product as the researcher is naive. In fact, the questions raised by my PhD supervisory committee, external examiners, and manuscript reviewers also contributed to the restorying process.

10 The term "diaspora space" comes from Avtar Brah (1996), though Gilroy (1993, p. 23) draws from Martin Delany to explore "Jewish experiences of dispersal as a model for understanding the history of black Americans." The analysis he offers highlights the contiguous journeys for self-actualisation of different diasporas. The term "disjunctures" comes from Brent Hayes Edwards (2003), who outlines the ever present gaps, mistranslations and power asymmetries in the African diaspora within and across space. He draws from Gilroy's (1993) anti-Afrocentrism and anti-essentialism arguments, but argues more forcefully for exploring black gender, class, aesthetics and national contexts.

1

Community

Diasporas are communities positioned at the interstices of (1) a (mythical) homeland or local community where people are from, (2) the location where they reside, and (3) a globally dispersed, yet collectively identified group. These communities are neither homogeneous nor innate. A sense of community, Brubaker (2004) notes in *Ethnicity without Groups*, is often objectified as a "thing," something always already there that people "have," but "'groupness' and 'boundedness' [are] emergent properties of particular structural or conjunctural settings" (p. 55). Some groups go to great lengths to establish themselves as cohesive and bounded communities. For example, as Brent Hayes Edwards (2001) astutely points out, the term "*diaspora* is introduced in large part to account for difference among African-derived populations, in a way that a term like *Pan-Africanism* could not … it forces us to consider discourses of cultural and political linkage only through and across difference" (Edwards, 2001, p. 64). A key example of discourses of cultural linkages is the pre-civil war collective self-definitions of the Afro-diaspora, which "often treated Africa as a fallen civilisation to be redeemed by African-American Christians. Self-identification as a diasporic 'people' did not necessarily imply claiming cultural commonality" (Brubaker, 2004, p. 57). The boundaries that diasporic groups construct around themselves shift around the multiple identities people express. Flattening a complex history and complex individuals through a focus on a singular identity as a diasporic group prevents us from understanding the ways in which group boundaries are constantly being (re-)made by people who have experienced the uneven trajectories of ancestry, plurilocal homelands and varied ways of construing sameness and difference.

The Afro-Caribbean diaspora is a community fractured by "disjunctures produced by the diverse intersectional experiences of gender, class, sexuality, ethnicity, age, generation, disability, geography, history, religion, beliefs and language/dialect differences" that produce power struggles (Hua, 2006, p. 193). Nevertheless, people who live within these groups develop a solidarity with each other via transportation and communication technologies, economic and social remittances, political rights bestowed upon migrants, and transnational or cultural organisations that permit them to feel close to one another. They conceive of themselves as one community in spite of distance from the homeland or other dispersed group members. Furthermore, their proximity in the place of residence allows for a local sense of community that is not dependent on an elsewhere. This chapter explores the various tactics used by the MCSC members to reify the Afro-Caribbean community, to celebrate blackness and masculinity, and to establish themselves as part of a local community. I delve into their activities before, during and after games that mark them as part of a bounded group.

Liming: creating Afro-Caribbean social spaces and networks

For many of the Mavericks, playing cricket in Canada meant playing in cold weather for the first time. Although their season does not start until May, it might not be more than 15 degrees Celsius at that time of year in Toronto, a big adjustment from the 25–35 degrees Celsius year-round temperatures they were used to. Warlie, a 70-year-old black Barbadian-Canadian, who arrived in Montreal in December of 1968 explains that "In Toronto there's no ocean to jump in, so the black man plays cricket and dominoes. I can be with the fellas and jus' relax all summer. Winters are long an' it's hard to get used to. I tried to skate once, but the ice cracked, so now we don't fight it. We not hockey players. Cricket's our sport." Warlie describes surviving Canadian winters as a struggle; his story of the ice cracking beneath his skates reflects how insecure and isolated he felt when he first arrived in Canada. He enjoys being active and feels imprisoned by cold weather, since he does not participate in any winter sports. Summers, in contrast, are full of physical activity, friendship and opportunities to relax. As he talks with me, he easily slips between the individual ("I tried to skate once") and the collective ("Cricket's our sport") signalling the sense of community and social connections he developed by playing cricket and its associated activities, such as dominoes. Despite the cold weather, every May the men transform an empty field into a distinctly Afro-Caribbean environment. They recreate the cricket environments of their homelands and their youth through *liming*, defined by Warlie as "being with the fellas and jus' relax."

Liming is a uniquely Caribbean expression that captures the practice of socialising, hanging out, relaxing, or partying, which often involves outdoor eating, drinking, dancing, playing dominoes, chatting and spirited rounds of verbal sparring. Known as *the dozens* (United States), *gaffing* (Guyana), *picong* (Trinidad and Tobago), or *keeping noise* (Barbados), Afro-Caribbean men and women tease, heckle and mock each other in a friendly manner with a combination of jokes and insults. This way of speaking is described by Abrahams in his text *The Man-of-Words in the West Indies* as a valued way of expressing masculinity and advancing reputation in outdoor Afro-Caribbean spaces. Rather than the content of their speech, the emphasis on speech using poetry or proverbs, aggressive talk using witty banter, socialising in an antiphonic pattern and using their native patois languages and English accents are keys to communication and characteristic of Afro-Caribbean communication rituals. Patois is not "broken," "bad," or a dialect of English; it draws directly from African linguistic structures in combination with the language of colonisers and many expressions are common enough throughout the Anglophone Caribbean for men and women from different nations to communicate with each other. The use of patois or speaking English with an accent in diasporic settings provides for its speakers a sense of identity. The MCSC members keep their culture alive with every word as they discuss their families, local and international politics, dominoes and cricket. As Madan (2000, p. 29) notes of Indian diasporic cricket fans, in "talking cricket," and "in articulating allegiances and negotiating hybrid spaces, these subjects actually speak their identity as [Afro-Caribbean-Canadians] into existence." Their joking and socialising are the lived social practices that denote the cricket grounds as an Afro-Caribbean homespace.

Language (accent, style of communication and topics of conversation) is one of the primary signals that Mavericks' cricket grounds are spaces set apart from mainstream Canadian society. Carrington has noted of Afro-Caribbean cricketers in England, the movement "to create nearly autonomous spaces are an attempt to resist what might be described as the 'terrorising white gaze' (hooks, 1992) within public spaces … [W]ithin a wider white environment, the cricket club provides many of the black men with a sense of ontological security" (Carrington, 1998, p. 283). Afro-Caribbean cricketers in Canada also create a black space in which they can feel comfortable. The ways they communicate with each other and with visitors from the diaspora while *liming* on and around the cricket boundary and club social events are examples of their negotiations over diverse conceptions of freedom, which, Noble (2008, p. 90) accurately points out, are not situated strictly within "party politics and political nationalist movements that characterised earlier anti-colonial and civil rights politics. Instead they are increasingly being traced out on the intimate contours of the body and the self" for black people. MCSC members liberate themselves by carving out space in Toronto that is just for "their people." Through *liming*, MCSC members are able to renew their sense of local and global community.

As a possible result of their status as visible minorities, ongoing racism in the dominant Canadian culture and relatively small numbers (and therefore lack of ethnically exclusive neighbourhoods), Caribbeans, in contrast to Italians according to a 1991 study, were found to be more likely to use sport to generate an ethnic identity. A statistical analysis of Caribbean and Italian soccer club members indicates that Caribbeans are more highly involved in their clubs as players and as participants in social activities and rely more on their soccer teams "as one key means for sustaining ethnic identity" (Walter, Brown and Grabb, 1991, p. 90). The authors went on to suggest that Caribbean clubs more often encourage "the use of ethnic language or dialect in conversation, and the recruitment of players by members' recommendations rather than by open competition" (p. 90) to maintain the club's ethnic links. With fewer organisations, social networks and material and cultural resources at their disposal than other non-racialised groups, Caribbean people are more likely to turn to a sports organisation to shape their identities.

The MCSC games are not merely sporting activities. They bring together family and friends from throughout the Black Atlantic to *lime* at the matches so they can feel "at home" whether they are in their nations of origin, elsewhere in the Caribbean, elsewhere in the diaspora, or at grounds in Toronto. While some club members emphasise their ways of life and thought as the same as in their homeland – as pure, stable and timeless – this should not, as Hannerz (1997) suggests, invalidate analyses that demonstrate the ways their cultures are creolised and Canadianised. That is to say, they use cricket to maintain black identities, but their status as Caribbeans means they are already embedded in a culture (if not an ancestry) that is a mixture of African, Asian, Indian, European and Middle Eastern. Moreover, their relative permanence in Canada, and in some cases, mixed-race children and families, reveal that their communities are not always so narrowly defined. Nevertheless, in the face of all this mixture, the ongoing naming of MCSC as a black club means that it is used for racialised community making in Canada.

Club members migrated to Canada mainly in the 1970s and 1980s to fill labour shortages and secure an income for their families. While much of their lives were completely transformed upon migration, especially for those who arrived in winter, cricket remained constant. They described joining teams as a saviour in their first months in Canada. In some cases, family members, or friends from work introduced the Mavericks to the cricket community. In other cases, they found work and even family (some cricketers met their wives and reunited with cousins) through their interactions at cricket matches and related social events.

Mavericks, such as Mason, a 72-year-old Barbadian-Canadian, intentionally joined cricket leagues to ease the transition to their new country:

> I went to trials for the Trinidad and Tobago team and I didn't make it, so I say "Let me jus' come to Canada an' start my life." I could have stayed back one year an' everyone telling me "Stay, you'll be selected when you're older." But I just decide I want to start makin' money ... At that time there were so many jobs here. They were beggin' us to come. It's just what you did. Finish A Levels [secondary school exams] and go to Canada or New York or England find work. I get a job and make friends, that's when I found a cricket team to play wit', so it seem everyt'ing work out. (Mason)

Erol, a 55-year-old black Barbadian-Canadian, also found league cricket through the interpersonal networks of a tightly knit Afro-Caribbean community:

> When I came to Canada first, I eventually hooked up with the West Indian community people and they encourage me to you know, come out and have fun with them. So being new to the country I t'ink that was my – I would say – that was one of the focal points of me getting out and start playing cricket. (Erol)

Mason and Erol, through their new friends, set about playing competitive, recreational cricket in Canada and recreated Afro-Caribbean spaces through their *liming* practices at games.

For a new immigrant who felt "lost," cricket offered a sense of familiarity, comfort and security:

> I didn't know that there was cricket played in Canada. I always ask and nobody ever knew ... I lived in a predominantly white neighbourhood. That was Ajax and at the time when I came there was no West Indian store. To get a West Indian store you had to come all the way back into Scarborough ... You see a black person in Ajax it was like "Oh my god!" ... And I remember one day my wife was driving down Baseline [Road] and she saw a big sign, "Cricket plays here" and "Practice on Wednesdays" ... So I went and I was the only Guyanese. All Bajans [people from Barbados] and Trinidadians, but it was comfortable, you know? (Reggie)

For Caribbean men new to Toronto, cricket provided instant access to a broader network of Caribbean people. In a Canadian (middle-class) culture that is focused on "inside life" (i.e., life inside homes, cars, workspaces, restaurants, or arenas), cricket offered Caribbean men a reminder of their (working-class) home life where domestic affairs (including cooking and eating), drinking, socialising and physical activities are performed outdoors. Carrington's (1998) description of a recreational cricket club in England suggests that elsewhere in the Caribbean diaspora, this type of organisation provides the same sense of comfort for its participants, who describe it as "more than a club"; it was significant "in providing a safe space within a wider (hostile) environment for the earlier Caribbean migrants" (p. 284). Upon their arrival in a new country, Caribbean migrants can generate a sense of comfort at the cricket grounds, as they "develop a panethnic Caribbean identity as a result of interacting through these networks with other immigrants from the Caribbean," inevitably giving their "ethnic identity a transnational focus" (Rogers, 2001, p. 181). Reggie, an Indo-Guyanese who felt isolated in a white neighbourhood, shifted his primary category of affiliation from national group (Guyanese) to regional group (Caribbean) and racial group (black) based on his initial lack of access to other Indo-Guyanese people, the mixed nationalities of his first team members and the predominance of Afro-Caribbean people and cultures in the club.

The summers of 2008 and 2009 in Toronto were among the rainiest in recent memory. It rained at least once almost every weekend from May to September. Nevertheless, the Mavericks went out with their friends to play cricket under dark clouds and grey skies; if and when it rained, they continued to play until the captain decided the risk of injury was too great. At that time, they would call off the game and retire to the grassy area outside the boundary, where cars are parked, to join spectators already engaged in the non-cricket aspect of their weekend rituals: *liming*. The fact that MCSC members are forced to park their cars on the grass surrounding the boundary means that occasionally the fête (party) atmosphere is punctuated by the sound of a ball cracking a windshield. Men gathered at their cars were then briefly reminded that they were, in fact, at a cricket match. They turned around, heckled a player or two, and returned to their conversations.

Players and spectators brought out coolers full of food and drink, supplied their own lawn chairs and used their vehicles as a sound system, shelter, restaurant and bar as the occasion warranted. In better weather, more spectators came to the games and stayed longer afterwards; however, regardless of the forecast, every weekend, all summer long, at least twenty-two players and a few dozen spectators occupied various Toronto cricket grounds and contiguous parking zones in their efforts to reconstruct home and regenerate their communities. Werbner (2005, p. 745) points out a paradox of multiculturalism: "in order to sink roots in a new country, transnational migrants in the modern world begin by setting themselves culturally and socially apart." This is the function of *liming* at the cricket grounds. In most sports, a post-game celebration (or mourning) involving food and drink is standard. It is an inherent feature of the sport of cricket – hours of passive waiting for one's turn at bat – that allow the Mavericks to *lime* before, during and after games.

Pre-game *liming*

Before cricket games have even begun or, in some cases, before their turn at batting, some MCSC players and all spectators were already generating a celebratory, carnival atmosphere through pre-game *liming*. Burton (1995) explains "carnival" and Caribbean "street culture" as a social, cultural and psychological complex unique to the Caribbean. As a result of slavery with manual labour of the most crushing and dehumanising kind imaginable, it should come as no surprise that the pastimes of Caribbean cultures would place an extraordinary emphasis on carefree vitality and re-humanising celebrations. On their way to matches, whether on tour in a bus or in their personal vehicles, the Mavericks play and sing along with "oldies," including calypso, reggae and country songs as well as American popular ballads. More recent music styles out of the Caribbean such as ragga and dancehall are not predominant since the Mavericks typically celebrate the music of "their generation."

While travelling on a bus to a game during a tour in England, one player contributed a Frank and Nancy Sinatra CD and a 1960s rhythm-and-blues CD to the ambiance, and players sang loudly the lyrics to "Saying something stupid like I love you.". When Al Green's "Let's Stay Together" came on, Warlie, a 70-year-old black Barbadian-Canadian, stood up in the aisle of the bus and serenaded me. His performance included a finale in which he got down on one knee and sang with outstretched arms (not an easy feat for him owing to his ailing joints). "How do you all know these words?" I asked him. "You haffa born early like me!" He replied enthusiastically as he struggled to stand. When I inquired about the most popular artists they were listening to before they migrated, Warlie and his peers shared their fondness for calypsonians such as Lord Kitchener, Mighty Sparrow, King Short Shirt and Black Stalin. They also celebrated Motown artists including Marvin Gaye, The Temptations, Curtis Mayfield and James Brown. The latter two, Gilroy (2010, p. 105) notes, "brought the political language of Black Power into the centre of the dance floor." Notably, the music the Mavericks listen to is not only of the indigenous calypso, soca and reggae varieties, though these cannot be named as 'purely' indigenous as the stylings of itinerant Caribbean musicians are cross-fertilised by American elements (Gilroy, 2010). They also grew up listening to American music including the explosion of African-American rhythm and blues, soft soul and street funk with its righteous demands for civil and political rights (Ward, 1998). This music helped to cement their race consciousness and is a reminder of their youth and their own Caribbean homelands, despite its American origins.

The Mavericks are committed to celebrating their games (whether they win or lose) with music and dance. This ritual in which real, re-humanising pleasure is derived from consuming and moving the body to a range of calypso, reggae, soca and African-American music reveals a complex dialogue with plurilocal black cultures. As Gilroy states, "for a while, music did occupy the epicenter of black culture in a new and distinctively modern way: as both custom and commodity" (2010, p. 145). The Mavericks' connection to black music, and therefore the Afro-diaspora, is also evident through their commitment to the reggae remix. Michael, a 56 year-old Indo-Guyanese-Canadian, who was also "born early," drove me to several home games in Toronto and insisted on belting out the lyrics to reggae remixes of country ballads by artists such as Willie Nelson. The MCSC's use of music to sing and flirt is an important means of performing masculinity, communicating across gender, and marking the Afro-diasporic space as an explicitly heterosexual community.

On one cold and windy Saturday in May 2008, I had bundled up before I made my way to watch the Mavericks take on another team comprised predominantly of Afro-Caribbeans. I approached a group of three women, wives of three of the players, whom I had seen the week before. They were the only women at the game the previous week and again they had come prepared with lawn chairs, blankets and large umbrellas. I set up my chair beside them and they expressed surprise that I had come back to another game. I told them that I would be at all the games, all summer long, but that I was also surprised at their returning, especially since it had been so chilly and pouring rain the previous Saturday. They acted as though there was nowhere else they would rather be:

> The problem is people, young people these days don't know how to relax. We need time to do these long games and lime or gaff as the Guyanese say. You come early and stay late, just relax … Once you have a West Indian pace of life, this is all you do on the weekends. (Camila)
>
> Money cyaan't buy dis, you know. People wit' money not here an' dey don't know what dey missing! … We don' wan' no shopping or watching TV. That's North American. What we want is lime. That might appeal to our children – walking up and down the mall – but that's not us. (Tayana)

Percelle, the eldest of the group, a 41-year-old Grenadian-Canadian, sat back, adjusted her sunhat (which was unwarranted, but indicated her hope that the sun would emerge) and took out a novel. "That's what's wrong with Canadians." She said, matter-of-factly distinguishing herself as a non-Canadian despite having lived in the country for 30 years. "You're always supposed to be on the go. Here on the weekends (she took an exaggerated deep breath). Aaaaaaaaahhh. Ain't it?" She looked to me for confirmation that spending time at the games is relaxing as she wrapped a blanket around her legs for warmth. I nodded. "*That's the West Indian in us*." Percelle spoke as though she had effectively summed up everything I needed to know: Afro-Caribbean culture involves relaxing. The irony here is that the female partners of male cricketers who are present at the cricket ground are in the vast minority. For many weeks, only three to ten women joined thirty or more men. The majority of female partners were elsewhere, doing unpaid domestic labour or possibly involved in women-only spaces for relaxing such as hair salons (Anthony, 2005), bus shopping trips (Trotz, 2011), or kitchens (Marshall, 1983). The literatures on the lived experiences of Afro-Caribbean womanhood in Canada (e.g., Beckford, 2012; Chancy, 1997, Crawford, 2003; Jackson and Naidoo, 2012) hardly posit "relaxation" as a main tenet. Rather, the intersections of racism, sexism and classism force Afro-Caribbean women to work harder, suffer more abuse and experience more discrimination than the average Canadian. Black Caribbean women compensate for this by creating a persona of strength that allows them to deal with all manner of hardship without breaking down physically or mentally, and diversions allow them to disengage from the realities they face (Jackson and Naidoo, 2012). Claiming a lifestyle premised on relaxation may be one way in which Percelle and her peers combat their lived reality.

Many female MCSC members contrast their Caribbean and Canadian cultures and posit the cricket grounds as "outside" Canada. They "travel" to the grounds to escape a (young) mainstream, consumerist Canadian society. These women arrive early to games, set up their seats, arrange their umbrellas to shade them from the sun (or protect them from the rain), open their coolers full of snacks and alcohol, and set about the business of relaxing. They are proud of their weekends' "West Indian pace of life" and explain relaxing without spending money and "walking up and down the mall" as part of their sense of Afro-Caribbeanness. They claim consumerism is a big part of being Canadian that they do not subscribe to, yet their new clothing (brightly coloured tops and shorts), accessories (big earrings, gold watches, multiple rings and purses to match their outfits) and choices of alcohol (imported beer and expensive cognac) belie their anti-consumerist attitudes. The female club members reported jobs in office administration, accounting, business and education. None of them were retired. Their working- and middle-class, 9 a.m.–5 p.m. weekday hours and adult children permitted them the freedom and motivation to *lime* on the weekends. Some of their peers who were engaged in shift work or had young children were unable to make it to the cricket grounds. However, for men and women who are getting sicker and lonelier in old age, with less disposable income, connecting with their friends and family at the cricket ground and engaging in a celebratory atmosphere was one way of assuaging the emotional and physical pain of ageing in the diaspora.

The focus on *liming* can only partially explain why "young people" (second- and third-generation Afro-Caribbean-Canadians) do not join the MCSC. When the Mavericks competed in England, a few opposing teams boasted Caribbean men from their twenties to their seventies on their rosters. This multi-generational mix, within the same type of *liming* atmosphere the MCSC creates in Toronto, suggests that the local broader sporting culture may be a significant factor in determining whether or not second- and third-generation Afro-Caribbean immigrants are interested in devoting their entire weekends to the club. In England, although football (soccer) is the more popular sport, cricket holds a central place in popular culture even as it is seen as epitomising rural, traditional, elitist, white, Englishness (Malcolm, 2013). In Canada, however, cricket remains marginal, is only beginning to appear in some multi-ethnic high schools and falls far short of soccer, ice hockey, volleyball and baseball in popularity among the adult population (Canadian Heritage, 2013). Recreationally, among second- and third-generation immigrants, cricket is played primarily by South Asian youth in Canada. Although their young people are missing, the MCSC players and spectators see the cricket grounds as a place to recreate Afro-Caribbean communities.

Bishops is a 69-year-old black Barbadian-Canadian supporter who migrated to Canada in 1989, but has been visiting Toronto to work and stay with family since 1962. He umpired for the Mavericks from the time he migrated until he developed cataracts in the early 2000s. Bishops still arrives to every home game at least an hour early. He no longer needs to prepare for the game; rather, he arrives early so that he can "have a drink, or whatever. See who is about … I like being around, so it doesn't disturb my weekend. This *is* my weekend … How long I been comin' here? So long I can't remember (laughs)." Pre-game *liming* has been a regular part of Bishops' weekend routine for 20 years and something he has done in Toronto for nearly half a century. He talks with other MCSC members over the cacophony of rhythms that emanate from multiple car stereos in the parking area. He reminisces about past games, heckles his friends and enjoys a game or two of dominoes. His weakened eyes prevent him from umpiring or driving, but his sister brings him to the matches in the mornings and picks him up late at night, giving him the entire day on Saturday and again on Sunday to *lime* with his friends. This cricket institution is important for his sense of community. Like the older Afro-Caribbean men in England, whom Carrington (1998) records describing the cricket club as "part of their history" (p. 287), a "focal point," and a "shining light" in the community (p. 288), Bishops is unable to imagine what else he would do with his weekends. His entire social circle can be found within the MCSC.

Before games (and before MCSC members were fully intoxicated) were occasions for more serious discussions. MCSC members do not often discuss the negative experiences of racism they have had in Canada; however, they do see themselves as racialised subjects. When asked about challenges at work, transit, or life in Toronto, most players and supporters recounted experiences of institutional or interpersonal racism, such as being turned down for a job for which they were qualified, being reprimanded for infractions that were common among all employees, being stared at in public, or sensing (especially white women's) fear or disgust when alone in an elevator or seated on a bus. Discussions of racism were rarely named as such, but a tacit understanding was shared among players who spoke of whites as "they," and described to me a look or feeling of exclusion they experienced.

Invariably, they relied on a neoliberal mantra of having a "thick skin," getting an education and using hard work and perseverance to overcome racial barriers. Having a close-knit network of friends and family also helped them to survive, especially when they first arrived in Canada. Rogers' (2001, p. 186) observations of Afro-Caribbeans in New York suggest "Racial barriers that block their path into the mainstream make it necessary for these black immigrants to hold onto their transnational ties and the accompanying exit option." The "exit" does not have to be to an entirely different nation-state or homeland, however. MCSC games and events provided a separate space for blacks to share their struggles and create an alternative community. Beyond escaping racial barriers, many of the MCSC members join together because they enjoy each other's company and find it easy to create a carefree social environment at the cricket grounds.

Fête-match *liming*

Every Maverick game featured a celebratory atmosphere, but approximately one-third of the Mavericks games were formally named fête-matches, a cricket match and fête in one. Fête-matches were typically held in honour of a visiting team from Windsor, Ontario; Montreal, Quebec; the Caribbean; or United States. However, one of the biggest fête-matches of the summer was between locals. A Memorial Match is held every July in honour of a Toronto police officer of Barbadian descent who died in the line of duty:

> [The memorial game] is Metro [Toronto Police] versus Barbados Ex-Police. On that day you mus' come early or will not get a place to park anywhere. Many senior officers come ... *Share* and *Camera* [Caribbean-Canadian newspapers] come to do stories on it for the local players. There is no stereo system unfortunately because we don't have a clubhouse but people blast music from their cars. It is something the whole community is involved in. (Winston)

To say that "the whole community" is involved raises the question of how "community" should be defined. There are some obvious constituents of the Afro-Caribbean community missing: those who are lesbian, gay, bisexual, transgendered, queer, between 10 and 40 years of age, Francophones, Hispanophones, Indo-Caribbeans, many wives and girlfriends and non-drinkers, to name a few, are unable or unwilling to join in this celebratory, Afro-Caribbean space. Nevertheless, those who attend the Memorial Match name it as a central feature in the community social calendar.

On the day of the Memorial Match in 2008, I made my way to the grounds early so that I could find a parking place. One hour before the game was scheduled to begin, only a few players and a handful of supporters were present. I wondered if I had gone to the wrong location and asked one of the men I saw relaxing at the scorer's table. "No, dis [Mavericks], dey always startin' late boy! You know 'bout West Indian time?" West Indian Time requires the addition of at least one hour to any game's scheduled starting time. Tettey and Puplampu (2005) explain that members of the African diaspora can adhere to a mainstream concept of time in their workplaces and in dealings with institutions outside their homespace; however, within their communities they revert to African time, black people time, island time or West Indian time, which constitute a form of time that is non-linear or polychronic and does not dwell on schedules. "The fact that they are able to apply appropriate time schemes to particular contexts is an indication of the dialectics of continuity and discontinuity that characterise the *in-between* spaces these communities occupy" (Tettey and Puplampu, 2005, p. 154, emphasis in original). They avoid misunderstandings and tensions because all share a "silent language" (Hall, 1959) and an understanding of MCSC as an organisation that runs on polychronic time. They are hybridised Caribbean-Canadians, who emphasise certain aspects of their identities at particular times.

By one o'clock, the scheduled starting time, the crowd had thickened, but several players were still missing. No one who had arrived on time seemed to mind or even notice that the game did not start promptly. While they waited for the match to begin, some men started to play a game of dominoes. Others were gathered around the trunks of their cars, filling their plastic cups with a caramel-coloured liquid (usually rum or brandy), telling jokes and talking aggressively. Some players were getting into uniform, using the area around the boundary as their changing room with no apparent concern for modesty. They sat on the grass, applied their ointments, bandages and braces in preparation for the game. By the time the game started, I was thankful that I had arrived early because the field adjacent to the boundary had rapidly filled with cars. At the coin toss there were over 100 spectators and close to 200 more joined us by the end of the day.

Throughout the game, the music, alcohol and conversation helped MCSC members to create communities similar to what they (imagine they) experienced at home. Men who were former police officers from Barbados bonded with current members of the Toronto police force, while a popular Edwin Yearwood song, *It Feels Like I'm Home Again*, was featured at the 2009 Memorial Match. The song eloquently captures the mood at the grounds by describing the celebrating, music playing, dancing and "misbehaving" that go on at a Caribbean party. MCSC members use music and other cultural forms to make cricket grounds in Toronto, their nations of origin and elsewhere in the diaspora feel like home.

Early in 2008, the team travelled to the island of St. Lucia for a tournament. At one of those games, a very loud, rusty green jeep pulled up alongside the grounds and Sutara, a 65-year-old Indo-Trinidadian-Canadian woman, announced "Reggae truck come!" as though this was one of the regular features of the match for which she had been waiting. She got out of her seat and was grabbed by her 66-year-old Trinidadian husband, Hussein. They danced at the side of the field even though he was fully dressed in cricket whites, with his pads on, waiting for the next wicket to fall so that he could go in to bat. The sight of spectators and players grabbing women to dance with around the boundary was a regular feature of the Mavericks' fête-matches.

Terrel, a 56-year-old black St. Lucian-Canadian, took great pride in the history of the club and the way in which it brings people together for travel and games every weekend:

> We play an entertaining form of cricket. It is a community t'ing. We all know each other. That is what makes it enjoyable. There are more spectators at our cricket than any other cricket in Ontario because we are set up as a community cricket club … You see there we dancin' an' singin', here, we do a prayer before it [second innings] start. It's not just sport for us. (Terrel)

The prayer and moment of silence among players standing in a circle on the field after the tea break one game demonstrated to one club member, whose brother had recently died in Barbados, that he has the support, empathy and love of his fellow players. By describing their activities as "not just sport," Terrel explained that MCSC provides a resource beyond cricket matches. They are a social community that draws on each other for emotional support. Their friendships are so long lasting (over 50 years in some cases) that some MSCS members consider each other "fictive kin." Afro-Caribbeans are involved in family networks that knit blood relatives and friends across global spaces. Research studies on diasporic families (Bashi, 2007; Olwig, 2001; Sutton, 2004; 2008) mainly focus on women's experiences and roles in maintaining social and kin networks, especially underlining the inclusive nature of the concept of family, including step parents, half-siblings and fictive kin, who are "like family to us" in childrearing and emotional support (Sutton, 2004, p. 245). The MCSC demonstrates that men also preserve communities and develop social capital across the diaspora through the relationships they renew with their friends and family members at cricket matches. This is particularly true for those men who are unable or unwilling to return to the homeland after retirement as they had once planned. Meeting at the local cricket ground with others not only to celebrate good times, but also to share their sadness around ageing (though this is often done through humour); cope with illness, death and grief; and reconcile their physical and emotional alienation from the homeland, helps them to survive in the diaspora.

In cricket, only the batsman and bowler are guaranteed to be engaged in every play. The fielders and the other batsmen spend 90 per cent of the game waiting for their turn in the spotlight, which, for the Mavericks, leaves ample time to drink and socialise with each other during games. One might expect such a relaxed approach to come from spectators, not players, but as a result of the non-competitive ethos and friendly nature of the Mavericks' cricket, being on the field does not stop them from telling jokes, heckling other players and even eating and drinking. At one game, I witnessed Otis, a 47-year old black Barbadian-Canadian fielding at the third-man position (close to the boundary) while drinking rum and coke from a plastic cup and devouring a curry chicken roti wrapped in a napkin. He kept his beverage and lunch just outside the boundary, out of respect for the sanctity of the field; however, in between plays he came over to chat with some of the spectators there while he ate and drank. In his discussion of professional cricket, Burton (1995, p. 91) explains that the "constant and indispensable involvement of the crowd in West Indian cricket can be paralleled in many other Afro-Caribbean cultural institutions where there is no absolutely clear-cut separation between 'performers' and 'spectators.'" For example in Afro-Christian religious worship there is passionate interplay between 'priests' and 'congregation.' In carnival the performers, masqueraders and audience eventually become indistinguishable. Afro-Caribbean cricket can be best appreciated and understood as a similar "collective rite" and "popular fête" where the players and spectators become indistinguishable.

A close examination of the concept of boundaries helps to understand the function of cricket for the MCSC. Hannerz (1997, p. 10) explains boundary as a term that belongs with other geographical metaphors, "frontier," and "borderland"; yet these "are terms not for sharp lines, but for zones, where one thing gradually shifts into something else, where there is blurring, ambiguity and uncertainty." Writings emerging out of or about the US–Mexico borderland (e.g., Kearney, 1996) reject the notion of the boundary as a container for culture in favour of a borderland where multiple, complex and contradictory identities are formed. The boundary marker in traditional cricket is a heavy white rope that encircles the playing field. The Mavericks, lacking in many of the resources of wealthier cricket clubs with permanent establishments, mark their boundaries with pylons spaced approximately seven metres apart. Consequently, an imaginary line connecting the pylons separates the playing field from the spectators' area. This porous boundary marker operates as more of a frontier or borderland, and what happens at the interstices is symbolic of the ways these Afro-Caribbean-Canadian men recreate their ethnic identities. The boundary around their cricket field is a ludic space, a contact zone for the meeting and mingling of people and a metaphor for the national, regional and village boundaries that are crossed regularly by the players.

For the MCSC, the boundary does not distinguish players and non-players, those formally involved in athletic pursuits from those who are there to be entertained and socialise. The supporters are often former players or current Mavericks who are taking a day off from play. They do not allow an imaginary boundary line to separate them. Their back and forth conversations and combining of "serious" sporting play with "frivolous" word play, drinking or eating resists the competitive, serious and hierarchical traditional construction of the Victorian English sport, and is in line with Afro-Caribbean transformations of cricket into a fête or carnival atmosphere where boundaries are made and transgressed. Gupta and Ferguson (1992) point out that the hybridised subject that is produced in borderlands is more normal than exceptional. The spaces on either side of the boundary are not as stable, homogenous or fixed as traditional anthropological work has shown. The diasporic subject, situated within a "transnational public sphere means that the fiction that such boundaries enclose cultures and regulate cultural exchange can no longer be sustained" (Gupta and Ferguson, 1992, p. 19). The laughing, joking, eating, talking and fielding Otis engaged in at the border zone contiguous with the playing field demonstrate the inseparability of socialising and playing sport, and operate as a metaphor for the regular border crossing and hybrid identities of these men of the Afro-diaspora.

To take the metaphor of crossing boundaries further, the Mavericks continue to play cricket with their friends and family members in and from other nations. The imaginary line separating nation-states, such as that between Canada and the United States is also porous. Massey (1994) describes spaces as "extraverted." Local places are grounded in global flows that are unrestrained by boundaries. The modes of belonging to a place (i.e., within the boundaries) are defined by a multiplicity of political, social and cultural practices and procedures in other places (i.e., outside the boundary). Therefore, the players (and their food and drink) that slip through are essential to the creation of a global sense of place and unity among Afro-Caribbean-Canadians. When Otis engaged with his peers – from Toronto, Montreal and England – at the boundary, he demonstrated how the local depends on the global. The making and crossing of boundaries, in multiple senses of the word, is essential for creating this Afro-diasporic community.

Although eating while playing was against Otis' captain's wishes, when the weather is hot and a team is visiting from out of town, some cricket etiquette is abandoned in favour of the fête. Warlie's Barbadian-English brother who came to visit him in Toronto for a few weeks said, "I like this game. It reminds me of when Maple play home all of you keeping noise here." His comparison of the Mavericks in Toronto to Maple Cricket Club in Holetown, one of Barbados' most esteemed clubs, is evidence that the Mavericks have done an adequate job recreating a homeland environment through cricket. The many differences from Maple, including the matting they were playing on, the relative wealth and age of the players, the diversity of the players' nationalities and the level of cricket play were all ignored in favour of emphasising the similarities and the affective sense of home created.

During cricket games, the Mavericks entertain each other with domino competitions and spirited rounds of verbal sparring featuring ribald jokes, witty insults and clever "trash talking" in an antiphonal call and response fashion. "I find that they are very aggressive in the sense of conversation, very noisy, makes a lot of noise. 'Always miserable' I call it (laughs)," Layton, a Barbadian-Canadian joked about his fellow Afro-Caribbeans. The consumption of spirits typically accompanies their socialising, which increases in volume and intensity as each afternoon turns into evening. Outsiders may misconstrue the constant yelling of the domino players, cricketers and spectators as fighting, but, as Otis and Layton explained, friends say what is on their minds and do not take insults personally:

> It's a fun bunch. We have our ups and downs but when that's finished we all family ... When it's done I don't hold it against any person ... You figure a bad fiel' placing, or bad batting order or bad bowling change, these are things that can happen that cause cricketers to get frustrated, but after we leave the fiel' we all one group. Like it never happen. (Layton)

Although Layton was shouting and swearing at (and about) his captain for the better part of 10 minutes, he insists that there are no hard feelings. This means of aggressive talking is a ludic, community celebration of speech, a ritualised conflict that brings men together (Abrahams, 1983). Otis agrees:

> You see, for me I figure if me and you is friends an' I get upset wit' you an' you get upset wit' me I should be able to tell you how I feel an' it should be no problem between me an' you. When me speak me mind we should be able to sit down an' have a drink an' be happy 'bout letting we one another know how we feel ... I don't care how loud it get.

Their demonstrations of verbosity, volume and vehemence are central to performances of Afro-Caribbean masculinity. Abrahams (1983) shows that Caribbean men are socialised to engage in a form of ritualised battle with each other through their words. Language is not used merely for communication; rather, talking with wit, poetry, repetition, creative insults, volume and fluency is an instrument of power, domination and masculine display. Community members join into the antiphony of the argument, creating a celebration of speaking acts enjoyed by all, and subverting the structures and hierarchies of the everyday world (Abrahams, 1983). Highlighting as he does, talking in this way as "play," Abrahams (1983) makes it easy to see that the physical engagement with the sport of cricket is not the only way these men play on their summer weekends. Moreover, those who come to games as supporters and spend afternoons commenting on cricketers' accomplishments (or lack thereof) are just as engaged in cricket play in a manner different from the dominant understanding of the sport. Barbadian diasporic novelist, Paule Marshall (1983) explains that the idiom of a people, the way they use language, reflects their very conception of reality. The Mavericks loudly ridicule each other, take note of people breaking the rules and point out failures, often in a humorous manner, demonstrating the importance of being heard, freedom of speech, justice and reputation in Afro-Caribbean communities.

A popular spark for loud disagreements around the boundary was a differing philosophy about the objectives of the cricket games and tours: recreation and vacation versus responsibility and competition. For example, the umpires for their matches are usually volunteers: MCSC supporters or current players who are taking a rest day typically assume the responsibility. They don a white jacket and hat, carry six stones or marbles to keep track of the legal balls in each over and are not permitted to consume alcohol. Many of the Mavericks are resistant to taking on an umpiring role, especially because if they are not playing that day, they want to drink and *lime* around the boundary with their friends. On one occasion, a few players from the batting team were asked to share the umpiring duties for a few overs each. They refused and an intense argument broke out around the boundary, with the captain yelling about players "Not having any fucking respect" and the players shouting that they cannot be told what to do ("I'm nobody's bitch!" was a phrase that was repeated often). The use of sexist and/or homophobic remarks is commonplace in the community, reinforcing the notion of the cricket grounds as a place to make boys into (hegemonic) men (Carrington, 1998; James, 1963; Williams, 2001) and to perform a particular style of heterosexual masculinity. As a result of their differing philosophies about appropriate behaviour, the games, matches, meetings and post-game parties were punctuated by big disagreements.

When Hussein, a 66-year-old Maverick was bumped from his spot as opening batsman for two consecutive games he threatened to quit cricket all together. The captain had suggested that the seven top Mavericks should remain in the line-up at all times to improve their chances of winning the tournament in St. Lucia. The other players were described as "the walking wounded," capable of bending down for balls, but often unable to get back up. Spectators often called out to the players to remind them that they were "playing cricket, not football [soccer]" because they were constantly using their feet to attempt to stop balls in the field instead of diving for catches as they may have done in years past. Hussein announced to his teammates: "I was around here from the origins [of this team], and he think he can play some fucking "super seven"? You see him? No fucking loyalty! Where would dis masters team be without me? We're supposed to be playing *friendlies*. Raas!" Hussein's swearing and use of the expletive "Raas!" (which translates most closely to "Damn!") demonstrated his anger and sense of disbelief that he was being cast aside in favour of more capable players. The "super seven" were not only the seven most talented, but also happened to be the youngest and fittest of the Mavericks. The blow to Hussein's ego that came with the realisation that he may now be considered too infirm for a team he helped to pioneer erupted in a verbal explosion. However, his "anger" dissipated as quickly as it erupted, as he turned to laugh and joke with one of his older (and even more infirm) teammates, demonstrating that the performance of anger was more authentic than the emotion itself.

In his examination of the linguistic innovations and performances of the black diaspora, Gilroy (1993, p. 85) notes that an "amplified and exaggerated masculinity has become the boastful centerpiece of a culture of compensation that self-consciously salves the misery of the disempowered and subordinated." Taking this concept into a sporting arena, Majors and Billson (1992, p. 30) point out that symbolic displays of toughness defend a black man's identity and gain him respect as an athlete. After a team meeting during which the recreation versus competition issues were discussed at length, amidst a combination of aggressive posturing and cool disinterest, the manager agreed to prioritise recreational rather than competitive goals and give every player equal game time. Subsequently, the "super seven" remained in every game for which they were available; however, Hussein re-entered the line-up as opening batsman for some of the games. This suited him well because once he was out he was free to drink on the sidelines while his teammates chased the number of runs needed to win.

The Mavericks prided themselves on their capacity for drinking and told stories around the boundary, in the pavilion, or at their cars about their purchase and consumption of expensive alcohol, how well they can play when they are drunk and how much fun they had while drunk at parties, on tours or after games. These stories are part of the gender myth making that dictates how they come to know themselves and their community. With their increasing age and declining physical prowess, the Mavericks are forced to emphasise other aspects of masculinity to protect their status. As Whannel (2002, p. 68) notes, "some of the key ingredients of a particular form of sporting masculinity ... being a rock-hard, unsentimental heavy drinker" are of key importance to the view of sport as "a form of masculine proving ground." The Mavericks drink copious amounts of alcohol and their brand choices are both deliberate and symbolic; as I've written elsewhere, they "mark their masculinity, class status and prominence within the group, through the purchase, sharing and consumption of expensive alcohols" (Joseph, 2011a, p. 159). The act of drinking is imbricated with costs, styles and rituals that denote class distinctions. Club members are expected to bring bottles of beer or spirits to the grounds to share among friends. This is over and above the portion of the club fees they pay that goes towards alcohol for the after-parties. Consumption of vodka is not as common as cognac. Anthony adopted a haughty English accent "May I offer me lady a spot of Courvoisier" as he pretended to be my butler and poured generously from an $80, 750-ml bottle. Consuming expensive brands and embodying Englishness are used to signal sophistication.

Consumption of rums, in contrast, signal a commitment to the homeland, transnational travel and working-class roots. Players are quick to emphasise that they "only" drink rums from their homelands (e.g., Wray and Nephew from Jamaica, Cavalier from Antigua), which "not only signals a fixation on tradition for these older men, but it also provides evidence of their nostalgia for, allegiance to, and regular access to home" (Joseph, 2011a, 159). The Mavericks boast about how little they paid when they purchased the bottles the last time they were home. They could possibly buy some of their favourite Caribbean rum brands in Toronto liquor stores, yet they prefer to keep money in their nations of origin, supporting their friends and family who are shop owners and pay local (Caribbean national) prices. Even though the rum was acquired for a low cost it has a high value. When one woman uses Terrel's rum to quell the sting of a mosquito bite she is chastised (jokingly) for "wasting" it. "Ah wah dis t'all? You t'ink I here fe watch fuckin' cricket? I here fe drink! Don't go wastin' me rum 'pon stupidness, you hear?" His mock anger and miserable attitude elicited laughter from all within earshot and this type of behaviour carried on for the duration of most games and well into the after-parties.

Post-game *liming*

A cricket match might start at noon (one o'clock Caribbean time), but many MCSC members do not arrive at the Mavericks' home grounds until five o'clock, in advance of the post-game celebrations that typically get underway by six or seven o'clock. Post-game celebrations are a key motivational factor for MCSC members' participation in this community. Vilroy, a 68-year-old black Barbadian-Canadian, explained to me: "Once the game is out of the way then we party!" Warlie, his 70-year-old compatriot concurs: "The joy of that cricket [with visiting teams] is the socialise after the game. It doesn't matter who win, because we, at our age, we just havin' fun. And it's about R and R. Do you know what that means?" Warlie asked me, with a twinkle in his eye. "Rest and Relaxation?" I inquired, knowing that there had to be something more to this furtive question. "No, no, no, no." Warlie laughed. "R and R is rice and rum! That's the fun part. After the game, we have someone to go cook for us every weekend, an' have food an' drinks." The Mavericks refer to their sport as "R and R cricket," "goat water cricket," "rum cricket," "liming cricket," and "fête-match cricket," which emphasises the priority food, drink, conversation and dance takes in this Afro-Caribbean community. Marshall, a black 58-year-old Barbadian-Canadian, explained that "It is a very social type of game, so what happens is that the game of cricket really starts after the game. The camaraderie, the getting together after the game and having drinks and a few post-mortems and stuff like that makes the game of cricket, what it really is."

Most of the Mavericks' games were followed by players gathering in the changing room (or around the boundary where changing rooms were unavailable) for a slow process of changing out of their cricketing clothes and starting a post-mortem meeting where they discussed the strengths and weaknesses of their performances in the game over a few drinks. After changing, the Mavericks typically enjoyed in a dinner, award presentation, party or dance where alcohol was also a significant feature. Male and female bodies rubbed together to the rhythms of the omnipresent music. The lascivious behaviour increased as more alcohol was consumed, but these actions were not dependent on the outcome of the game: "Win or lose we drink our booze!" was a common mantra.

After the players changed out of their whites (uniforms), they typically had an opportunity to enjoy food provided by the home team. Usually the wife or girlfriend of one member of the team, or a female club member prepared the food. On the Mavericks' tours, the cooks had the advantage of using the kitchens in the clubhouses to prepare meals. Clubhouse kitchens were usually busy all day with at least two generations of women spending the morning preparing tea (a meal of crustless egg, tuna, cornmeal and/or cucumber sandwiches served with hot tea and cold juice) for between innings. They spent the afternoons cooking an elaborate traditional Caribbean meal for dinner. All afternoon the mother–daughter team, sometimes with grandchildren running underfoot, chopped vegetables, seasoned meat and prepared sauces, the aromas of which filled the clubhouse and the grounds, building players' and spectators' anticipation of the meal to come. MCSC members were unable to enjoy this aromatic aspect of the after-party at their home games because the meals were always prepared off-site and brought to the grounds by the caterers in their cars, thus they relished having access to a clubhouse for the fragrant reminders of the homeland it provided.

Those who were able to replicate authentically the flavours of the homeland, by using Caribbean imported ingredients or recipes handed down for generations, were venerated, welcomed back and in all cases paid to provide dinner. Women's recipes are an indigenous knowledge system containing centuries-old information about ingredients, spices and modes of preparation. One MCSC member who operates her own catering company with her daughters was often hired to provide meals. Despite their hard labour, the pleasure women gain from preparing these meals, especially in association with their children, should not be discounted. They created stereotypical Afro-Caribbean dishes: rice and peas, fried or jerk chicken or fish, provisions (plantain, breadfruit, yams), green salad, oxtail and gravy, and goat water or curry goat, with souse (pork hooves, chopped tomatoes, onions and cucumbers in a vinegar sauce) or cassava pone (cake) for dessert. As Schmidt (2008) notes about Caribbean music in the diaspora, the incorporation of many national styles signals a trans-Caribbean presence that opposes mainstream or singular nation styles. The chefs did not shy away from serving Jamaican akee alongside Barbadian flying fish. Trinidadian chicken roti was paired with Barbadian macaroni pie and was usually laid out on a table with servers making up plates for the long line of players, supporters and community members who came for dinner.

The performance of gastro-nostalgia is characterised by continued preference for ingredients, cooking styles and eating practices from the homeland, which reflect a desire to establish bonds of communion with the past and the diaspora, maintain culinary/cultural identities and enact postcolonial resistance against mainstream cultural forms (Cook and Harrison, 2003, 2007; Theopano and Curtis, 1991). Unsatisfied with iconic "Canadian" cuisine, such as Tim Horton's doughnuts, the members require, what Vilroy calls, "proper food" after their games: "Now some of the clubs try to outdo each other with curry goat and t'ing. You know it's a social gathering. After running around in the sun we don't want to just eat a donut, so we have some proper food. West Indian food."

Whether it is the cooking style of barbeque, the African-inspired use of root crops such as dasheens and yams, the partiality for spices such as curry or jerk, the incorporation of fruits such as plantain and okra, or the omnipresent hot pepper sauce, Afro-Caribbean food carries with it regional and heritage markers, and eating it can give rise to an imagined, temporary visit to the homeland and a sense of maintenance of ancestral identifications. Sorrel juice, malt drinks, coconut water, rum punch and a range of soft drinks put thirsty MCSC members at ease with the liquid flavours of home. The global production of some of these products (e.g., Coca-Cola from the United States or coconut water sourced from Thailand) does not negate their association with the homeland for club members.

The foods consumed after games offer a sense of regional if not nation-of-origin identity for the Mavericks. More than the specific food types, for some club members the rituals of eating – including dining in a casual buffet style; sucking, crushing and spitting out bones; and eating until one's belt must be loosened – signal resistance to assimilation to hegemonic Canadian culture and bourgeois propriety restrictions of eating indoors, at a table with a knife and fork, waiting until everyone is served and not talking with food in one's mouth. On one occasion, I lined up for dinner behind a corpulent woman, Beatrice, who was a supporter of a visiting team from New York. She took two plates at the start of the buffet table and asked the servers for two pieces of fried chicken on each plate. This did not seem to be an anomaly because many women, who are always permitted to line up first for food, often get a plate for their children or husbands at the same time. However, Beatrice had neither a husband nor children with her on the trip. The caterer, who knew this, pointed at one of her laden plates and asked, "Who is this for?" With a New York-Guyanese accent she exclaimed, "How you t'ink I get so big an' fat?!" in mock anger. "My mumma tell me don' be too skinny, dey t'ink you poor, so me eatin' fuh two, thank you very much!" she exclaimed with a scowl. After loading up her plates with rice and peas and green salad, she stuck out her large breasts and round backside and pranced away from the buffet table. This comment elicited laughter from many other women in the line and sent a clear message about the social significance of food in this black cricket space.

We do not need to explore Afro-Caribbean communities in depth to discover examples of class-based nutritional inequalities as matters of life and death. Hurricanes, earthquakes and droughts leave many families at the lower rungs of the socio-economic ladder, at risk of experiencing lingering hunger and, indeed, dying of starvation. Although many of the Mavericks demonstrate a high-class status through their alcohol preferences, the food the Mavericks purchase, share and consume represents what Bourdieu (1984, p. 185) refers to as popular, working-class tastes for the heavy, the fat and the coarse. It is interesting to note that the Mavericks do not describe this as central to working-class emphases on the importance of body strength and cheap, nutritious, calorie-rich foods, as Bourdieu (1984) describes. Instead, their emphasis on indulgence and over-consumption is used to mark a higher class status; a big, round bottom and ample breasts for women in particular, are symbols of wealth, health and prestige in this community. Not every woman took two plates, but the servings of food were always generous and seconds were provided without rebuke until every scrap was consumed. Indeed, to pass on dinner was frowned upon. Any of my attempts to decline were met with astonishment, frustration and even anger. My Caribbeanness was constantly questioned and tested, and not eating placed me under suspicion among women. Although the ground might be marked as a men's cricket space, it also provides a venue to perform middle-class, black, older women's Caribbean femininity through food consumption. The overt rejection of dominant North American beauty standards that require a skinny body, flat belly and food portion restrictions reveal the space as outside mainstream Canadian society.

An important corollary of dinner was dancing. Many teams hosted a party at their clubhouse, a street fête, their hotels, or at a rented hall. It is important to re-emphasise here that which team won the game is not important. C. L. R. James' (1963, pp. 197–198) thick description of cricket explains:

> cricket is perhaps the only game in which the end result (except where national or local pride is at stake) is not of great importance. Appreciation of cricket has little to do with the end, and less still with what are called 'the finer points', of the game. What matters in cricket, as in all the arts, is not finer points but what everyone with some knowledge of the elements can see and feel.

James refers to emotions evoked by the players on the field, but his analysis can be extended to the broader cricket environment. What do the spectators see and feel around the boundary, in the clubhouse, or at the parties?

The disparity in the numbers of male and female MCSC members was most noticeable at parties where men only danced with female partners, and many men were left standing at the bar or sitting at tables because all of the women were occupied. Certain players constantly asked me to reserve them a dance, so that I was never wanting for a partner. Reggie, a 52-year-old Indo-Guyanese-Canadian player, remarked "Where you get so much pep?" when another player asked if he could cut in to dance with me, and Reggie, after having danced three songs already, needed to sit and rest. About half of the club members usually remained on the dance floor for the majority of the night. They danced with their hands in the air, "getting on bad" and "wining their waists" (grinding their groins and backsides on their partners), to old calypso and reggae tunes and paraded around the dance floor in pairs to country songs and American ballads until they were sweaty, out of breath and sore in the joints or muscles, at which time they retreated to the seating area to rest, or to the bar to refill their glasses.

Terrel, a 56-year-old black St. Lucian-Canadian, explained that he always has something to celebrate and is proud to be the last one to leave a party, even when he is on the visiting team: "We send home the members, we close up their clubhouse, we like to party as a community. It helps that we always winnin'!" The Mavericks did not, in fact, always win, but their celebrations at the end of each night certainly gave that impression. When the Mavericks travelled, their celebrations typically continued from the after-party in the clubhouse, to the bus, to their hotel. Back at the hotel, female MCSC members sat at tables in the hotel restaurant or suites, chatted with one another, or more often, went to their rooms to sleep, while the men spent hours standing or sitting near the bar, or relaxing in their suites discussing Windies cricket or nation of origin politics as well as the critical moments of the game they had just won or lost: Which over was the turning point? Which bail came off which stump, and why? Was it or was it not a leg bye? Can the umpire be trusted? Should the captain have moved the slip? These questions were critical to players' egos, their impressions of their performances and their anticipation for upcoming games.

One night after a game in St. Lucia, four of the Mavericks and I sat at a table in Lawrence's hotel suite drinking rum and eating his famous curried pork. I asked the players to tell me how they each got introduced to the group and Curtis explained when he first arrived in Canada and had started working at a factory near his home in Scarborough he overheard Lawrence talking at lunchtime. He instantly recognised the white Trinidadian's accent, and although he is a black man from Grenada he felt a kinship between them. Lawrence invited him out to cricket and despite their age difference – Curtis was only 18 years of age when they met and Lawrence was 48 – they remained close friends ever since. Curtis explained that Lawrence was "like a father".

> He help nurture me into a man, you know? ... I was content to keep renting [a house] – terrified actually – of taking on a debt like a mortgage and so. Baby coming the next year and he sit me down and advise me, paying rent is same as paying a mortgage, but if you own property you can get somewhere in Canada, you know? ... He really show me the ins and outs of this place. For that I owe him my life.

To my surprise, Curtis appeared to be close to tears and he reached over to put Lawrence in a headlock before planting a kiss on his cheek. Lawrence replied "I love this guy. Known him near 30 years and I can say I love him" as he hugged Curtis back before wrestling out of the headlock. This type of open, physical affection between men was rare, but an important aspect of the homosocial camaraderie developed through this sport and social club.

Michelle Stephens (2005, p. 14) draws from C. L. R. James' work to discuss the homosocial "routes" transnational Caribbean intellectuals of the early twentieth century followed; they created "a black transnational community as black men travelling in colonial space in a common state of desiring, desiring freedom, language, community – and each other." The space James describes is a homosocial world that permits deep affinities between men, but as Stephens

(2005) and Abdel-Shehid (2005) point out, homosexual affections or attractions are disavowed. As much as they displayed their love for each other, Lawrence and Curtis were both also known for displays of homophobic banter, even later that same night, as another one of the Mavericks, Michael, a 56-year-old Indo-Guyanese-Canadian, joined the party in a pink-and-blue, iridescent, button-down shirt that Lawrence and Curtis felt was a "homo style." Michael was derided and interrogated about what kind of club (gay or straight) he would be frequenting later that night. Homosexual or transgendered men, *queens*, *buggers* and *batty bwoys*, who are a minority but well known on every Caribbean island and in Caribbean-Canadian communities (Crichlow, 2004; Murray, 2012) are said not to exist among the MCSC members; however, it must be surmised that somewhere, in the space of "freedom," post-game *liming* and homosociality represented by the cricket grounds and cricket-related travel, it is likely that some male club members had additional, intimate motivations for participation in men-only spaces. I admit, there were many social spaces, locker rooms and hotel suites that I chose not to or was prohibited from accessing or researching owing to my gender and personal comfort levels; therefore, I was unable to document whether MCSC homosociality ever presents as homosexuality. My questions on this topic were met with denial, abhorrence, or laughter. Nevertheless, the cricket and social club after-parties allow opportunities for some alternative visions of black male intimacy.

This chapter highlights how *liming* before, during and after cricket matches is a means of (re)creating (in) an Afro-Caribbean community. By drawing on Afro-Caribbean cultures, not only cricket, but also verbal play, music, dancing, drinking and eating, MCSC members also hail elements of their ancestry. Though they are from different Caribbean nations, they unite based on their shared cultural roots, shared racial identifications and the creation of predominantly male, trans-Caribbean cultural spaces. People from Antigua, Barbados, Guyana and Jamaica are united as one community in Canada; they can head to their local cricket ground to capture a sense of Caribbeanness while "at home" in Toronto.

If black musical forms can be considered a "counterculture of modernity," supplying "a great deal of the courage required to go on living in the present" (Gilroy, 1993, p. 36), then physical cultural practices, such as black/Caribbean cricket spaces, can also be examined as "deeply encoded oppositional practices" (p. 37) and means of "individual self-fashioning and communal liberation" (p. 40). Mavericks' raucous behaviour at the cricket grounds, antiphonal communication styles and blurred distinctions between friends and family every weekend in Toronto and on trips abroad are functions of the desire to resist their embedment in a predominantly white culture throughout their working week. They rely on diasporic resources including the folk cultures of their ancestors and opportunities for *liming* that allow them to feel that within Canada and the diaspora they are part of a community. What I have described here is generally in line with other anti-assimilationist theories and histories of diaspora that demonstrate how immigrants maintain their cultures in their new homes. This is not to say that the MCSC members are not also deeply influenced and transformed by their stays in the metropolis and visits to other diasporic locations. They are at once members of local, tightly bound Afro-Caribbean communities and transformed by the influence of the mainstream Canadian society and the embodied cultural understanding they gain in the various locations to which they travel. Their routes of travel and the influence this has on a globalised sense of community in the Afro-diaspora will be discussed in the next chapter.

2

Routes

Old Dog Tom

"Old Dog Tom!" a portly, dark-skinned man shouted from across the parking lot. Erol's head peeked up from over the gear bag he was desperately searching through at the side of the cricket pitch. He would be unable to bat if he did not put ointment and a tensor bandage on the knees he'd abused for fifty years. He had heard the call but could not make out the figure crossing the parking lot, although it was clear that the man was beckoning to him. "Tom" had been Erol's nickname in primary school. When he was 7 years old, he'd had a fascination with the illustrations of Old Dog Tom books. He would carry them around with him, trace the images, and beg, borrow, or steal art supplies so he could try to reproduce them. Back then in his village, most dogs were feral, but Erol was the strange boy who wanted a dog for a pet. His friends started calling him Tom and many of his school mates hardly remembered his real name.

When he heard someone in England calling for "Old Dog Tom," he knew it must be someone who knew him from his younger days. At the collegiate they had started calling him Elquemedo after the famous spin bowler, and after that he was known as Shakey, which was related to a particularly boisterous night at the dancehall. As the portly man drew close, Erol began to distinguish his features, a round dimpled nose, skin black as tar and teeth big like a lion. It could be none other than his childhood friend, Chris, whom he had known as Boca, due to his big teeth and the fact that it was the only word he got right on their first form oral Spanish test. They stood in an extended, warm embrace. "My brother, how you been keepin'?" Thirty years apart and it was like they were back again at the Maple Cricket Club grounds in Holetown, Barbados.

The cross-border flows of people and cultures, including a desire to return to origins, are considered defining features of diasporas. Many scholars have shown that return visits to the birthplace are critically important in facilitating the survival, mobility, socialisation and possible repatriation of many migrants. The Mavericks demonstrate that visits to diasporic locations *other than the homeland* are equally important in facilitating the formation of community and identity. "Old Dog Tom" is just one representation of the dozens of reunions that occurred between MCSC members and their friends and family members when they travelled to play and watch cricket. Erol, a 55-year-old Barbadian-Canadian, who co-wrote the above narrative with me on the Mavericks' trip to England explained, "You know who is your close friend because he call your nickname." Hearing that name, especially when it is a surprise because you were not expecting to see an old friend in a new place "instantly bring back all the memories. It's like my whole childhood rushin' back when I look 'pon he face an' he call 'Old Dog Tom.'" In addition to using nicknames for those who were known, club members respectfully referred to each other as "brother," "sister," and "mama," which are names that connote racial connections and family relationships even where none exist. A trip to England is just what this Barbadian-Canadian needed to suture homespaces. This chapter outlines the ways in which community is created beyond the local Toronto spaces club members occupy. Through their physical travel, reunions with loved ones, learning about new places, and multinational emotional and financial investments, club members use "routes" to create plurilocal homespaces and broaden their identities.

Keep on moving: creating borderless communities

In his description of black unity and identity across the Atlantic, Paul Gilroy (1993) refers to "Keep on Moving," the name of a Soul II Soul song that resulted from British, Jamaican and African-American collaborations, as a "fundamental injunction ... [that] expressed the restlessness of spirit ... a new topography of loyalty and identity in which the structures and presuppositions of the nation-state have been left behind because they are seen to be outmoded" (p. 16). The history of the Black Atlantic, Gilroy opines, its continual criss-crossing of black people and the attempt to express cultures that are global or outer-national directly "contrast[s] the national, nationalistic, and ethnically absolute paradigms of cultural criticism to be found in England and [North] America ... [and] provides a means to reexamine the problems of nationality, location, identity and historical memory" (Gilroy, 1993, p. 16). Another "Keep on Moving" song, with lyrics sung by Jamaican reggae icon Bob Marley, is also relevant to black and Caribbean transnational politics. Marley calls out "Lord forgive me for not going back/But I'll be there anyhow" and suggests that even while the protagonist is away, he has ways to make his presence felt at home, but he's "got to keep on movin'." The peripatetic Mavericks could use either song as their anthem. They are constantly on the move, connecting to people and cultures here and there. It is impossible to understand their experiences without following them throughout their Black Atlantic "routes."

As a result of their success in working- and middle-class careers over several decades, many of the club members have several weeks annual holidays and many others have retired. They are thus able to use their leisure time and disposable income to travel with their friends and family members on annual cricket-related trips. When they travel, a group of approximately fifteen players are joined by about fifteen to thirty friends and family members. Their agendas include trips to England quadrennially, to at least one Caribbean location annually and to the United States at least twice each summer. Not every club member takes every trip, but the opportunity is there for them and the available spots fill up rapidly. They also invite teams from these locations to play in their "home" games in Toronto. These various spaces operate as plurilocal Caribbean homespaces; primarily homosocial, they are substitutes for migrants' homelands.

Club members' routes, or travel itineraries, reveal their passion for global imaginings of community, rather than solely local, black, Caribbean, or Canadian ones, and the importance of homosocial relationships. The cricket grounds then, like the seafaring communities of the twentieth century captured by Nassy Brown, Paul Gilroy and Claude McKay, are transnational communities whose "history is a verbal story, whose record lies in an oral and aural culture submerged beneath the national print cultures" (Stephens, 2005, p. 183). The MCSC members, as Cohen (2007, pp. 374–375) notes of black Brazilians, rely "much less on a recovered memory of Africa ... [they] have discovered new circuits of cultural capital that they tap into to augment their sense of modernity and involvement in a global consciousness." He describes these cultural routes as foundational to a black creolisation. More than simply a mixture between the dominant European and subordinate African cultures, black creolisation involves mixtures and borrowings from across the Black Atlantic. The alternative realities of the cricket ground are where cultures are exchanged, memories are re-enacted and masculine diasporic identities formed. The cricketers and spectators are from the same place, and yet not. They are all migrants, but some call Canada home and others are English or American. They are all Caribbean, yet some identify as Jamaican and others Barbadian. They majority identify as black, but some have skin the colour of tar and others café au lait; their ancestry may be African, Asian and/or European. Mavericks and their supporters keep on moving among various nations and cricket spaces, which informs their gendered and racialised, national and diasporic identities.

This chapter suggests that the "routes" of the Mavericks Cricket and Social Club (MCSC) are used to assuage Afro-Caribbean men's emotional longings and needs for belonging. It outlines two significant practices of community making that their routes allow them to access. First, they reunited with the familiar sights, sounds, smells, languages, activities and people of their nation or region of origin when they returned to a homespace. Memories came flooding back and social networks proliferated with every old relationship that was renewed. Second, players and spectators made financial and material investments in various local communities to which they were affiliated when they travelled for cricket trips. They spent their money in Caribbean-owned businesses (e.g., taxi companies, restaurants and barber's shops); made contributions to island-specific and regional cultural organisations and political associations; and left financial and goods remittances (e.g., cash or cricket equipment) to under-resourced sports teams. Through reunions and investments, MCSC members exploit their "routes" to create a global black community. The remainder of the chapter highlights that even without travel, the MCSC members are able to proliferate their international social connections by hosting cricket events in Toronto, and their money crosses borders through the donations they make to help communities and people in need throughout the Caribbean. Last, I dispel the myth that "routes" to the homeland facilitate repatriation. Many of the Mavericks explain that their cricket-related travel helped them decide against returning permanently to their nation of origin.

Reunions

With families and friends dispersed across the Black Atlantic, sport tourism and its related emotional reunions and economic contributions are critical elements in the maintenance of a broad sense of community. Michele Stephens (2005), drawing from Paul Robeson's autobiography *Here I Stand*, notes that "From the very beginning of Negro history in our land, Negroes have asserted their right to freedom of movement … the concept of *travel* has been inseparably linked in the minds of our people with the concept of *freedom*" (p. 240). From fugitive slaves to seafarers to domestic workers to cricket players, Afro-Caribbeans have created identity in multi-national spaces through their cross-border movements. Regular return visits reinforce not only migrants' sense of connection to the homeland, or what Voigt-Graf (2004, p. 38) refers to as the "cultural hearth," but also affirms their sense of citizenship, permanence and connection to people in other nations, referred to as the "diasporic nodes."

In the past two decades, there has been an increasing trend: a growing roots tourism industry where black people have made efforts to return to slave ports in Ghana and Nigeria (Clarke, 2006; Pierre, 2009). Researchers have found that participants use a "common sense" link between blackness and Africanness, based on US black nationalist imaginaries of the mid-1960s: black people, who feel "lost" as a result of the oppressive conditions and dominant culture of whites (in the United States, Canada, Germany, etc.), can supposedly "find" their "true African selves" by embracing African traditions and visiting African nations. Roots tourism is also beginning to be popular in the Caribbean, where tourist boards recognise the untapped potential of the African-American (and Canadian) market. Black visitors to the Caribbean may be less likely to be solely sun-seekers. Instead, some visitors yearning for a connection to the homeland seek out plantations, visit chattel houses as well as other national heritage sites, shop for souvenirs and attend folkloric music and dance shows (Brooke, n.d.; Garraway, 2006; Joseph, 2011b). These tours instil a sense of the legacy of slavery and the indicators of national pride (literary heroes, civil rights activists and cricket celebrities). The Mavericks incorporate tourism into every trip they take. They visit stadia, learn about the distinctive local cultures and connect to their cultural legacies (Joseph, 2011b).

For their 2008 trip to England, in addition to playing eight games over a two-week period, the MCSC shopped at the cricket department of Lillywhites, a sport clothing and equipment store on Piccadilly Circus; joined an award ceremony and reception at the Barbados High Commission, where they dined on traditional Barbadian foods; and attended the annual Barbados Cultural Organisation Charity Ball in London. At each of these locations/events one or more of the Mavericks reunited with old associates and family members – unexpectedly in many cases. Because the main organisers of the tour were from Barbados, many of the events they organised were specific to that nation; however, even men and women from other islands/territories reunited with Barbadians and other people from their nations of origin.

A typical greeting was an exaltation of the player's name followed by "A you dat?!" (Is that you?!). Players often introduced themselves to the opposing team members by first and last name; identified their island, parish or village of origin; recalled the organisations to which they (used to) belong, or described the location of their current extended families. My inability to share this detailed information about my Antiguan heritage when asked marked me as a second-generation outsider. First-generation Afro-Caribbeans, in contrast, shared their backgrounds and sometimes reminded men they met from their village of their nicknames. In the Caribbean, as elsewhere in the Afro-diaspora, few men go by their real names. Nicknames based on something they said or did as youth (e.g., "Shakey" for a boisterous night at a dancehall, or "Boca" for a successful oral spelling test answer), stuck to some men for decades and were a way of expressing an intimate familiarity or long-standing relationship. The Caribbean players on both sides of the Atlantic are of similar ages, from large families (eight children or more in many cases) and small villages (typically less than 5,000 people). Thomas, a 44-year-old Barbadian-Canadian, explained to me the chances of two cricketers from the same area knowing (of) each other were relatively high:

> We had a lot of rivalries between different clubs but I can distinctly remember going to Checker Hall, St. Lucy [Barbados] and playing those guys up in there and … I actually met one of the guys that I used to play cricket against in there [a clubhouse in England] … It was great meeting him again, you know after the competitive sports and after all these years and we still playin' cricket. (Thomas)

One cricketer explained to me that the potential for reunions is an important aspect of why he travels with the Mavericks:

> **Janelle:** I noticed that you ran into a guy last night. Did you know him from back home?
>
> **George:** Yeah, from my neighbourhood and from school … he used to play cricket also … [On these tours] You meet people that you knew before and you're rekindled, you know? I also met a guy at the Embassy, the Barbados Consulate when we went there, that went to school with me and I didn't know he was up here [in England] either, so that's what happens.

George, a 47-year-old Barbadian-Canadian, points out that it is not only cricket, but also the local tourism in which the MCSC members engage when they are travelling, that allows them to encounter their former compatriots.

At one game in England, a fierce game of dominoes in the cricket clubhouse drew more attention than the cricket game on the field. While we stood watching a group of local black Barbadian-English men play dominoes, Warlie clarified for me that the potential for reunions is a strong motivator for travel. When a team visits from out of town, "That's when everybody comes out to see who it is and rekindle old relationships or friendships that they haven't seen for a while. Cricket builds that because you go all over the world and you get to meet people. People that you haven't seen for X amount of years, but you remember."

When I mentioned that I was studying Caribbean culture and cricket, the locals said: "If you want to see a carnival you shoulda been here two weeks ago for the Australian High Commission versus Barbados High Commission game." "There was one hundred cars in the parking lot, [bus] coaches come from all over the country, people set up stalls to sell food." "There was music, big speakers an' thousands of people. The entire back fiel' was full up of people selling their wares." "People drinkin' at their cars an' blastin' their car radios." The scenes they described equate cricket with a Caribbean carnival atmosphere and were an exact replica of the annual Memorial Match held in Toronto.

Rather than travelling to Barbados, Afro-Caribbean-English men go to their local grounds to experience a homespace, "see who it is" and potentially reunite with their former compatriots, friends and family members. Once the English players realised that some of the players on the Canadian team were from their village back home, they were excited to reminisce and the actual cricket match became secondary to the relationships they were able to renew. Constance Sutton (2008) argues that return visits formalised as family reunions allow for the recreation of kin ties, and the development of significant family rituals and public performances of region, nation, lineage and friendship. Reunion rituals are "signifying practices," that is, "expressive performances that call public attention to customs and values and create a consciousness of valued behavior and beliefs, even when these are disputed" (Sutton, 2008, p. 44). The memories that players and supporters exchanged connected them socially and embedded them in a homespace, a space of belonging and shared beliefs. They reminisced about people with whom they grew up: "You know Charles got pancreatic cancer?" "Oh, McKenzie working for the government now. Can you believe he push paper?!" They ruminated over local events "I didn't have TV until 1968. Boy, dat was a real transformation in de village." And they reflected on the successes of the West Indies Cricket team: "We were golden in dem days!" "Unilaterally, everyone can agree [Gary] Sobers was the best all-round!" Rather than focusing on their real homelands, coeval nations *over there*, these first-generation migrants remake their homes *over here*, through sharing memories of the past, home, friends and family with each other.

For MCSC members, travelling and talking with people from their homelands in plurilocal spaces allows them to understand the similarities and differences for Afro-Caribbeans across the Black Atlantic. For example, at one game in England, a discussion about public transit came up around the boundary among the Mavericks and Afro-Caribbean-English players from the opposing team. The pleasures and perils of relying on municipal governments in Toronto,

Canada and London, England were compared. The discussions of fare increases, worker strikes and the complexity (and therefore ease of travel) of the respective systems revealed many differences and similarities, which allowed MCSC members to broaden their understanding of different homespaces. Similarly, discussions of police "stop and search" tactics and the risks of DWB (driving while black) were outlined by Afro-Caribbeans in both London and in Toronto. Learning about each other's communities, as they do when they go on city tours or visit consulates in their travel destinations, cements their identities as plurilocal black men and women.

One of the highlights of the cricket tour in England was the invitation to the annual Barbados Cultural Organisation Charity Ball. Most MCSC members considered this event expensive. At £50 per ticket, they were adamant that the food served "better be delicious" and that the organisers should offer "more than just a dance." The club president reminded them that the organisation does a lot of charitable work in Barbados; nevertheless, most members remained focused on what they would receive for £50. They were not disappointed, especially when they were entertained by an Afro-Caribbean comedian, offered a chance to win door prizes as grand as a trip for two to an all-inclusive resort in Barbados, and had an opportunity to meet the special guest of the evening, Sir Gary Sobers, one of their cricketing heroes and arguably one of the greatest international cricketers of all time. The Mavericks scrambled to introduce themselves, take his picture and thank him for what he gave to cricket and the West Indies. They were "honoured to shake his hand." The elaborate buffet dinner was followed by a dance and a professional photographer set up a small studio in the lobby. While some patrons began to dance others lined up to have their photographs taken. Ten of the Mavericks managed to get a group picture taken with Sir Gary. I ran into Otis and Layton immediately after the photo was taken and they both had stars in their eyes. "Well, this is one trip to the motherland I will never forget!" (Layton). "Dat picture going right in my front hallway, you understand? Front an' centre!" (Otis). The "motherland," England, offered these two Barbadian men an opportunity to meet one of the icons from their homeland. Even men from other islands, such as Winston a black 59-year-old from Antigua, were impressed by the opportunity to be in the presence of cricketing greatness. Winston gushed: "He shook my hand, Janelle. You have no idea what this means to me."

Travelling to England also allowed the MCSC to organise trips to more proximal diasporic locations. Through Barbadians they knew in England, who have friends and family in Boston, Massachusetts, the MCSC members were able to meet other people they knew and arrange annual games. Now they have added Boston to the list of teams they either host or visit every long weekend from May to September. Layton, a 48-year-old Barbadian-Canadian, is responsible for planning the Victoria Day trip, which sometimes coincides with the US Memorial Day holiday.

> We travel every year, wholly and solely the long weekend in May. That's one of the things. The club travels … our trips consists of between Boston; Philadelphia; Toledo, Ohio; Hartford. Once there's an invitation out there we go … We always travel that long weekend. For example, our [club's] 25-year anniversary, most of the group was going to England in 2004 but some of the group was here [in Toronto] and within two weeks we put a trip together to Toledo, Ohio and we had a full bus [45 people]. So nothing stops us from going away that May long weekend. Nothing. (Layton)

The Mavericks are devoted to long weekend travel for conviviality. In addition to the May long weekend, Layton and other long-standing club members have planned annual bus trips for Canada Day long weekend in early July and Labour Day long weekend in early September. Layton explains that the annual bus trips are such big events in the MCSC social calendar that even female club members are enthusiastic:

> Shopping! The women love the shopping in the US … Because we travel on the Friday night, on the Saturday morning you probably don't get to the hotel until two or three o'clock. So the ladies from here will meet up with ladies from there and will probably go shopping somewhere [on Saturday] and the Sunday they are all there [at the game].

Some women, who have been travelling with the Mavericks for decades, have developed relationships with the wives of some of the players from the other teams. In some cases they too have family and friends in the cities the Mavericks visit, so the cricket trip for the long weekend provides an opportunity for them to regenerate family and friendship ties as well as take advantage of the Canadian–US dollar exchange rate, greater bargains, wider selections and lower US taxes on food and clothing. Layton's comments draw attention to the facts that "women and men differentially experience and participate in cross-border networks" (Trotz, 2011, p. 34), and that the Mavericks are a fascinating case study for how men's and women's motivations to make the drive from Toronto to Connecticut, Maryland or Pennsylvania were rarely mutually exclusive and could be combined on the same trip. There is a complex imbrication of economic and social/cultural investments that underlie transnational networks within diasporas–and cricket trips throughout the Black Atlantic are only partially about cricket.

In addition to their long-weekend trips to the United States, the Mavericks travel to the Caribbean for two weeks at least once per year. Return visits to the

Caribbean give club members an opportunity to reconnect with people they left behind, who live in other islands and territories and who now reside around the world. At one game in Canaries, St. Lucia, both Griffith (from Barbados) and Michael (from Guyana) encountered old friends unexpectedly. They both ran into men who now live in St. Lucia that they had known when they attended the Royal Police Training College in Barbados. None of the four men had been born in St. Lucia and all were surprised and thrilled to meet each other at the game. They had intense conversations trying to get caught up on the goings on of the past three decades. The similarity between reunions in St. Lucia and England demonstrate the deterritorialisation of the Caribbean and the potential for diasporas to create homespaces in a variety of locations, including places other than the nation of origin or residence.

Remittances

While the routes to dispersed Caribbean locations facilitate reunions, the MCSC also travels to homelands to make economic contributions. Sending remittances (money and goods) to support those living in the Caribbean is a major source of the gross national product for many Caribbean nations and they have "become the most often-cited, tangible evidence and measuring stick for the ties connecting migrants with their societies of origin" (Guarnizo, 2003, p. 666). Money sent home can have a significant impact on local economies, market development, poverty reduction and economic growth, especially because money from remittances exceeds flows of foreign investment, official development assistance and sales of exports (Mundaca, 2009, p. 288).

The concept of remittance, however, opens much richer possibilities according to Jenny Burman (2002, p. 50): "if we consider the affective content implied by the extended definition of 'remit,' with its many nuances exceeding the act of sending: to surrender, to put back, to withdraw, to set free, to relieve from tension." Money and goods are sent to sites and people left behind out of a sense of responsibility, altruism, attachment, selfishness, guilt and/or reparation; remittances are emotive investments (Crawford, 2003). Their full impact is difficult to measure, especially when goods remittances, including equipment, clothing, food and their associated social remittances, including ideas, identities, cultural practices or status are taken into account. Money and material items delivered by hand are difficult for government statistical agencies to capture, but have a significant impact on many nations' economies, assist in maintaining community organisations and allow diasporas to extend further ideas about themselves and their new places of residence.

The Mavericks diasporic economic transactions are not formalised through non-governmental organisations, banks, or governments. On a more local, individual scale, they give money and donate their equipment in good or as-new condition to cricket clubs in the parishes and villages they visit for friendly games while on tour. In doing so, they mark themselves as benevolent, generous and having "made it" in Canada. Their donations confer them with the status of benefactors and enhance their standing and respect in their home communities, which may even translate into respect for the friends and family members they left behind. Maintaining respect through myths of affluence in Canada are critical components of Afro-Caribbean diasporic identities.

Diasporas can contest and redefine regimes of social hierarchies in their home and host nations, and improve their social position in both locations through the economic contributions they make. Individuals with little status in Canada demonstrated their Caribbean status through affiliation with high powered individuals, such as government officials and local celebrities upon returning to their homelands. For example, a 63-year-old black Barbadian-Canadian, Arnold, introduced his brother-in-law, a Barbadian government minister, to the team as "a big man dis" (this is an important man) when the Mavericks played a local team at the 3Ws Oval in Barbados in November 2009. Arnold assured that his teammates acknowledged his brother-in-law's status and by association Arnold's family importance in the context of the island. A donation of cricket equipment from Arnold or his teammates to the local team then reflected well on him, his wife's family, and in this case, the Barbadian government as well.

A particularly poignant scene occurred at the Dennery cricket ground in St. Lucia in March 2008. Kundell, a 52-year-old St. Lucian-Canadian acted as the liaison between the Mavericks and a local team owing to his social and kinship relations with the latter. During the game, I noticed two young black boys, about 6 and 8 years of age, who began to play a bat-and-ball game just beside the boundary rope of the field. They took turns in bowling to each other and trying to specify in advance where their ball (which was actually an empty plastic pop bottle) would go once they hit it with their bat (which was fashioned out of a broken piece of plywood). Immediately after the game at this ground, the players had a post-game ceremony in which the captains and organisers gave speeches. The captain of the local team offered words of thanks to his Canadian "brothers":

Participation in this tournament contributes to the redevelopment of sport in St. Lucia. We are thankful that you could also find time to come here and play a friendly game with us. Refurbishing the Dennery cricket field would not be possible without the support of players like you from Canada and the UK. We really really appreciate what you do for us.

In response, the Mavericks' captain, Sam, a 61-year-old black Barbadian-Canadian thanked them for the opportunity and a great game:

We are just happy we can come here and contribute. Give back to our local communities. You know we brought our fees to play but we also brought some small tokens to help your club. Please accept these small gifts on behalf of the Ontario players.

At that moment, the Mavericks started digging into their equipment bags and brought out shoes, pads, helmets and bats to donate to the cricket club so that underprivileged youth, such as the two playing with the plywood and pop bottle, could have an opportunity to use real equipment and ostensibly to succeed in the sport. One of the boys was called forward to thank the MCSC. Sam described Dennery, as one of "our local communities," although he is from Barbados, not St. Lucia, thus indicating his sense of a home away from home. At the same time, he specified Ontario as his home, distinguishing himself as an outsider who is "happy to contribute."

As a consequence of the high-quality competition and hospitality that the team offered the Mavericks, Kundell, who had arranged the game, was venerated by his fellow club members. The donations the Mavericks made to that local club resulted in Kundell receiving accolades from his St. Lucian family and friends as well. Diasporic communities such as this "offer a unique context for interpreting individual and collective status claims ... where certain practices, rituals, goods and artifacts have mutually intelligible meanings to community members" (Goldring 1998, p. 173). In this context, where cricket skill and therefore youth development is highly valued, the donation of money and equipment to a local club are prized remittances with long-lasting consequences. Diasporas are interpreted as having done well in relation to those they left behind based on the way they behave or dress, artefacts and friends they bring with them upon return, and their generosity with money and materials. Even if they experience marginalisation in the host country, valorisation among those who share community membership "at home" evinces the importance of place in shifting levels of status within diaporas' transnational social networks. When the Mavericks return to the Caribbean they operate in a liminal space between local and tourist. The desire and ability to afford to give away relatively new items, marks them as wealthy and *from* the islands, but no longer *of* them. They also are able to distinguish among each other who is the morally superior, philanthropic, transnational citizen, who really cares about "his people" and who takes his (relative) wealth for granted.

I commended Ciskel, a 47-year-old Guyanese-Canadian, who told me that he purchases a new bat every year and takes his old one when he travels to the Caribbean because "You know for sure you'll see someone who needs it." He wished he could have been on the receiving end of such generosity when he was a boy. "Doesn't that get expensive?" I asked, since bats can cost between $200 and $400 each. Ciskel explained why he feels an obligation to be generous:

> No, well, in Canada, it's like every man for himself. If I get few dollars I keep it in my bank account. But in the Caribbean it's like, help your neighbour, or at least it should be. It's just … that bat was my contribution, you know? I mean, a boy like that would never play with a solid bat [if] we don't bring 'em down.

Winston, a black 59-year-old Antiguan-Canadian agreed:

> When I was growing up there was hardly any donations. You know, there was hardly any outside source, the school had to raise money to buy gears for the girls and the boys … we wear gears that was probably two, three generations ahead of us. Probably my *dad* used those when he was a boy because in those times we never had help. So if I can help out a school or something, I bring my old stuff down. Why not?

Goods remittances, in the form of cricket equipment, are important elements in the two-week Caribbean cricket tours on which the Mavericks embark. Beyond donating money (which they also do), leaving cricket equipment behind helps to maintain particular (sub)cultures at home, and also maintain diasporic peoples' membership in local Caribbean and racial communities. The Mavericks provide youth with resources to which they never had access and prove that they have not become too middle-class (i.e., individualistic, selfish, obsessed with accumulating wealth), but have become middle-class enough (i.e., with sufficient disposable income to permit regular travel and to give away relatively new items); they have maintained their solidarity and sense of obligation to those left behind and to a broader community. Their apparent benevolence and resistance to an individualist philosophy reveals some of the ambivalences and contradictions of postcolonialism, as they certainly benefit individually from purchases of new equipment that they make for themselves in preparation for leaving their old equipment behind. They mark a middle-class status through their consumption, sartorial styles and new equipment. Importantly, though, they marked themselves as communitarian and despite Winston's comments about helping out a school, their donations were mainly to private cricket clubs instead of schools and therefore primarily benefited boys in their homelands and not girls.

Analysis of their financial and material contributions must also be set within their discussions of the decline of the West Indies (Windies) team and the lack of youth interest in the sport.[1] To get "their boys" on the Windies team back on top, development of youth cricket is often heralded as the second most important factor, after rectifying the West Indies Cricket Board (Griggs, 2006). Ironically, all of the Mavericks describe having to grow up without the use of pads and helmets as especially good for their cricket development: they had to be brave, learn how to control the ball and how to protect their shins and wickets with a bat made from a coconut branch (see Chapter 4). Now, in addition to remitting professional grade cricket bats, they also remit what Levitt (1998, p. 933) refers to as "normative structures," that is values, ideas and beliefs about the importance of proper equipment. Not only for bodily protection, but to become accustomed to using the best tools so that when they join league cricket or elite ranks, they will be able to compete with the rich boys. In their minds, donating proper equipment allows poor youth to improve their games and makes a small contribution towards the improvement of Windies cricket. When MCSC members donate cricket materials they "rally 'round the West Indies," and consummate the lyrics of the calypso song by David Rudder they so often listen to around the boundary at their games. Rudder sings about the difficulties of the West Indies team to produce runs; however, he predicts that with enough support, "the runs are going to flow again like water." In order for the West Indies team to regain supremacy, young boys in the region need the tools necessary for success.

Cricket remittances establish the Mavericks as successful emigrants, improve their status and the status of their friends and family members and, in the hands of particular talented boys who have dreams of one day playing at the professional ranks, the Mavericks' donations make connections to home and to the future of Caribbean cricket concrete.

Hosting return visitors

Not every diasporic Afro-Caribbean can afford to or desires to travel regularly to reconnect with the plurilocal homeland and compatriots now dispersed all over the world. Travelling may assuage the desire to return permanently, but it is not an option for the Afro-Caribbean-Canadian who faces domestic obligations, economic hardship, or restrictive work schedules in Canada. Furthermore, many do not see it as necessary, especially when their own city is the destination for others. For those club members who do not travel, attending home games in Toronto against teams visiting from abroad is one means of maintaining their transnational networks. When the Mavericks are the hosts, they show their guests a good time by recreating a carnival atmosphere. Most invitations to matches in Toronto are for July and August to take advantage of the blazing heat, the "best weather for cricket" according to the Mavericks.

They welcome teams from the north-eastern United States, Quebec, southern Ontario, England and the Caribbean. One team from Barbados makes an annual trip to Ontario, playing games in cities around Toronto including in Pickering, Scarborough, Woodstock and Cambridge before making its way across the border to Boston, Massachusetts. Terrel boasts that the MCSC "was the first team to bring U.S. cricket teams here to play" in the 1980s, but this history is missing from Canadian sport history. These cricket grounds "undoubtedly mark the where and how of black geographies ... [and] are just one example of how a specific, seemingly contained, place is made meaningful by invoking disparate connections in order to undermine and map an absented presence" in Canada (McKittrick, 2002, p. 32). The welcoming of visiting teams can be understood as a political act that abjures geopolitical boundaries on communities, yet places them firmly within the Canadian nation-state.

The reciprocal visits they make to play against north-eastern US teams carry symbolic racial significance. This is made clear through the names of the awards for which they compete: the "Throughway Trophy" and the "Railroad Cup." Canada is symbolised as a place of liberation in dominant narratives of the Underground Railroad, the route and series of safe houses enslaved Africans who had escaped with the help of allies used to cross the border from the United States to Canada in the nineteenth century. The route from the United States to Canada remains as a symbol of freedom, commemorated in the names of the cricket trophies and the speeches made when delivering them to the winners of the games with visiting teams:

> We want to thank our American brothers for coming up to Canada to share this weekend with us. We're delighted to have you here, but sorry to have to beat you like that but ... I think we proved once again that Canada is the best place for a black man to be (laughs) ... No seriously, we love having you here to carry on the traditions of everything this [holds Throughway Trophy in the air] stands for. (Sam)

These games are politicised cultural interventions used to acknowledge difference from the dominant groups in Canada, keep racial identities salient, celebrate black freedom and to acknowledge the shared racialised history of black people in the United States and Canada. Yet, these Afro-Caribbean-Canadian men also use cricket spaces to differentiate themselves from African-Americans and have adopted dominant Canadian discourses of Canada as safe for black people and less racist than the United States.

The Mavericks do not openly discuss the ways that Canada was not free of racism during the period of the Underground Railroad. Blacks in Canada were limited in their freedoms and excluded from belonging both by the Canadian government and by African-Americans working to establish the National Association for the Advancement of Coloured People in 1905 in Fort Erie, Ontario (Walcott, 2003). Nevertheless, in the taunting style of Muhammad Ali, Sam and his peers assume the characteristics of what Grant Farred (2003) refers to as "vernacular intellectuals" who "combine their 'intellectual elaboration' with their 'muscular-nervous effort'" (p. 8). Farred continues, "Because it is a form of recreation, its preoccupation with pleasure rather than recognisable political concerns obscures and undermines its capacity to articulate resistance … cultural politics constitute a politics that is not conscious of itself as a political practice" (Farred, 2003, p. 132). While cultural celebrations by ethnic groups have been demonised as dangerous distractions to the anti-racist struggle (Hesse, 2000; hooks, 1990), the two are not mutually exclusive. The Mavericks do not dwell on the horrors of slavery, turn of the century racial exclusions, or ongoing anti-black racisms, but they acknowledge their shared black histories and struggles even as they turn to a celebratory ethos. Their diasporic physical cultures are political acts.

Layton points out that along with taking bus trips, hosting visiting teams is a highlight of the summer, but he laments that the Canadian summers are too short. "Sometimes we have too many offers to hold one weekend so we really have to set aside time for certain clubs. We have a club that comes every Caribana weekend from the U.S."[2] New Yorkers fill a bus with fifteen players and close to thirty supporters to drive overnight to Toronto to socialise with their friends and family from Toronto and elsewhere and to enjoy festivities associated with Caribana. The MCSC also welcomes visitors from Montreal and England as many members of the diaspora use the festival and the cricket match as an excuse to descend on Toronto. They usually arrive on Saturday morning and attend the Caribana parade or a cricket game on Saturday afternoon, the Mavericks' dance on Saturday night and/or a cricket match on Sunday before they depart on the Monday. One black Antiguan-American player from the New York team referred to his first trip to Canada as "such a good party. Could hardly believe we were in Canada. So many other West Indians came [to watch the game]. The music, food, the weather even! I told my boys we gotta come back. We been coming back each year since 1981." These long-standing travel traditions are central to the making of communal memories and deep transnational friendship networks.

The atmosphere at Caribana and the Mavericks games and dances are similar. These homespaces offer:

> a kind of social therapy that overcomes the separation and isolation imposed by the diaspora and restores to West Indian immigrants a sense of community with each other and a sense of connection to the culture that they claim as a birthright. Politically, however there is more to these carnivals than cultural nostalgia. They are also a means through which West Indians seek and symbolize integration into the metropolitan society, by coming to terms with the opportunities, as well as the constraints, that surround them. (Manning, 1990, p. 35)

The Mavericks experience increasing constraints, especially as they age and face the social isolation and economic restrictions of retirement, reality of physical degeneration and illness and the passing away of their friends. The celebratory atmosphere of the games and transnational connections they make, however, allow them to escape those hardships, if only temporarily. Nurse explains that the "merriment, colourful pageantry, revelry, and street theatre" of diaspora carnivals "are born out of the struggle of marginalized peoples to shape a cultural identity through resistance, liberation and catharsis" (1999, p. 662). The Afro-Caribbean spaces created in Toronto through carnivals and cricket act as a bond within the diasporic community, that is, among migrants dispersed throughout the Black Atlantic and with nationals who remain at home in the nation of origin. They shrink the distance between non-contiguous nations and provide spaces that focus on the capacities, not limitations, of the body.

Terrel, a 56-year-old St. Lucian-Canadian reminded me that "if you are a member of [Mavericks] you have a friend in every country." Sitting in the open trunk of Terrel's van for an hour gave me a chance to hear him recount the history of the club and their activities of the past 30 years. The connections MCSC members who choose to stay in Toronto make to Afro-Caribbean people elsewhere are both social and financial. Terrel clarified for me that MCSC board members decide to invest a certain percentage of funds each year in local charities, organisations and people in need in the Caribbean and the African diaspora. For example, because they share a history with other people of African descent who are at greater risk of developing sickle-cell disease, the MCSC raises funds to contribute to increasing public awareness:

> It's not only involved in cricket. We do whatever we are called on to do, charitable activities, Scarborough Women's Shelter, Sickle Cell Association. We donate to them every year. It would be a different amount each time depending on our budget ... We give equipment to different groups in Barbados. We now have an application in to support a health association in Jamaica that's not being supported by the government. We also give support to sick individuals within our community who need financial help.

The MCSC is a unique type of hometown association in that its members are not linked to a single nation-state. The charitable funds it donates to a wide range of local and foreign organisations and individuals come from fundraising initiatives such as dances and walkathons, philanthropic contributions from certain individuals, support from government institutions such as the Consul General of Barbados, sponsorship from companies for which some of the Mavericks work, and MCSC membership fees ($100 per year). "There are over 100 families included in our membership," Terrel explained. "Some members are even in the U.S. and a few are at home in the Caribbean as well." Foreign MCSC members are typically once-local members who have moved away or people who are related to local members and travel to Canada regularly in the summer and participate in MCSC events. For example, Terrel addressed a man who came over to his van to get some ice: "This guy here is from Montreal, but he comes to all our big events." The Mavericks rely on members from near and far to contribute their membership fees, to buy $15 tickets to the dances they organise, which raise between four and five thousand dollars each year, and to raise money and attend the annual 10-km walkathon at Milliken Park in Toronto.

The activities that the Mavericks engage in to raise funds are always "fun." I received an email advertising a "Fun Raising Dance in Aid of Their 2010 Australia Tour" that made me question whether the Mavericks team manager had made a typographical error. Sam, a 61-year-old black Barbadian-Canadian, assured me that he wanted to emphasise the "fun" time that would be had by all as a result of the door prizes and the excellent DJ they had hired. Another player hosted a domino tournament at his home and asked for a $20 donation from each participant to help to pay for the bus for an upcoming trip to Philadelphia. I thanked him for the invitation and when I told him that I do not play dominoes, he convinced me to come anyway. He claimed that someone would teach me and that even if I did not play, many of the female MCSC members enjoy sitting and talking or dancing in his living room. MCSC members also organise fundraising trips to casinos and fifty–fifty draws.

Fundraising initiatives are imperative for diasporic community building because they facilitate the making of connections with other dispersed Afro-Caribbeans, the purchase of "authentic" Caribbean food for the after-parties, paying a DJ who can spin Caribbean music, and the creation of a carnival-like homespace environment for the games. More importantly, fundraising allows club members, many of whom grew up in working-class homes, to give back to those in need. Terrel, a black 56-year-old St. Lucian-Canadian, takes pride in his ability to give back to the less fortunate "within our community" in Toronto and "at home in the Caribbean." In 2005, the club was able to generate $10,000 in support of rebuilding two schools in Grenada. In 2008, they donated $4,000 to a woman in Jamaica who needed reconstructive surgery. Every year, they fund a scholarship for a Caribbean-Canadian student pursuing a criminology degree at a Canadian post-secondary institution. These types of financial donations demonstrate a commitment to the Caribbean community at home in their nations of origin and at home in Toronto. The MCSC members also donate goods to people in need, in many cases, without leaving their place of residence.

Assimilation hypotheses suggest that the longer immigrants remain in a country, the better able they are to navigate their environments and the less they should be actively involved in the home country. The findings of this study echo those of Portes et al. (2007, p. 260) and Guarnizo et al. (2003, p. 1229), who discovered that because they have resources of time and money to dedicate, it is older, better-educated and more established immigrants who are, in fact, more prone to participate in transnational ventures. For example, a Canadian passport enables transnational travel without restrictions, and migrants with secure jobs or retirement pensions can afford to make charitable donations.

An analysis of Afro-Caribbean migrants' "routes" provides evidence that a bi-nodal diaspora framework (the study of movement, donations and social contacts between the place of origin and Canada) is insufficient to describe the cross-border social and financial connections important to the formation of the Afro-Caribbean diaspora. To fully comprehend the complexities of their embodied transgressions of geopolitical boundaries, a multi-nodal analysis of diaspora that takes account of ethnicity as well as race is warranted. Their deterritorialised identities and practices are formed through travel from Canada to their home nation and other Caribbean countries, as well as to Afro-Caribbean spaces in England and the United States. Accepting visitors from abroad and throwing a fête in Canada is an additional means of strengthening their community networks and self-definitions as black, Afro-Caribbean and as Canadian. Unlike some diasporic groups, such as Indo-Fijians, that retain only a symbolic connection to the "cultural hearth," (Voigt-Graf, 2004), first-generation Afro-Caribbean-Canadians maintain strong links to their nations of origin.

Repatriation

One other critical dimension of their routes is the role of travel to the nation of origin in the repatriation after a few years or decision-making process. Nearly all MCSC members described leaving their nations of origins with plans to repatriate after a few years or upon retirement. However, as a result of their regular return visits to their homelands, where trips were riddled with disappointment owing to a mismatch between their expectations and the reality of the security, familiarity and delight that home is supposed to provide, few maintained this plan. Kundell was particularly eager to show his friends a good time on his native island of St. Lucia. Before we departed he spoke to me at length about the places the team would visit, including his favourite restaurant, The Lime, in Rodney Bay. He desperately anticipated tasting that home-cooked cuisine again. After the first game in the tournament, Kundell was awarded "man of the match" honours for scoring 84 runs in a winning effort. With this honour also comes the "reward" of buying the first round of drinks. He accepted both prizes and directed all of the MCSC members to The Lime for a big celebration. When we got there, we found it was under new management and renovations and were directed to a lower-quality pub across the street. Kundell's disappointment was palpable. He had looked forward to the "oxtail with rice and food (plantain and yams)" for weeks and was already salivating. He was shocked and disappointed at how much things had changed. This "third rupture," James (1993) explains (the first being the rupture from Africa and the second being the rupture from the Caribbean), is the result of a nostalgia that paints an idealised, static picture of home. When the migrant learns that home no longer exists as he or she remembers, it can be disorienting.

Kundell's disappointment extended to his actual performance after his illustrious start to the tournament. He initially thought a tournament at home in St. Lucia would be the ideal location. In fact, he had been integral to the organising efforts. He eschewed the team hotel in favour of returning to his childhood home and paying a visit to his elderly parents. Nevertheless, he ensured that the Mavericks brought business to a hotel his friend managed. He had looked forward to playing matches with friends and family in the audience and against some of his old mates on grounds he had accessed as a child. However, after the first week, he started to feel as though playing cricket at home featured too many distractions and obligations. He did not have enough time to visit all the members of his extended family whom he felt compelled to see and bestow with gifts. Arranging matches against local teams became stressful, owing to the laissez-faire attitude, of some of the locals. He explained that sleeping in his childhood bed was uncomfortable and led to his inability to concentrate on the sport. His cricket performance suffered as a result. He went out without scoring a run in half of the remaining games and vowed not to return to St. Lucia any time soon.

I described this experience to Riddick, a black 54-year old, who related similar stories of disappointment upon return to his homeland, Barbados.

> I've been here [in Canada] 30 something years versus the 16 I spent in Barbados so I guess I feel more Canadian than Barbadian. When I go home I'm ready to come back after two or three weeks. Here you have the theatre. There you get tired of the beach ... I go to Barbados every year and visit my family and play cricket. It's real relaxed there. No pressures. But it's not like when we were kids. There's nothing to do. (Riddick)

Unlike Kundell, who experienced too many obligations and not enough time, when Riddick takes return trips he cannot fill the time. In Toronto, he enjoys watching plays, eating Malaysian food and having reliable internet access. In Barbados, he feels relaxed, but socially restricted.

Marshall is disillusioned with his homeland as a result of the rude behaviour he so often sees on the streets – behaviour he insists was unconscionable when he lived there 34 years ago.

> **Marshall:** I don't understand why people have to be so ignorant. Last time I went home this one pregnant woman was taking her time crossing the street. I wait for her in my car, but she was *really* taking her time. Finally she gets in front of my car and I say "you're welcome" kind of sarcastically, but she really taking for-*ever!* Then, can you believe she has the nerve to cuss *me* out? And not just a little cussing. She went up one side of me and down the other with swears. I see it all the time when I go home now. People just too ignorant!
> **Janelle:** Maybe you're too Canadian now? You're too polite?
> **Marshall:** Maybe that's something like it. Either I changed or they did, but I'll tell you something, it makes me want to change my mind about retiring there.

Marshall's interaction with this woman rudely interrupted his nostalgia for a homeland where "proper manners" are a priority – especially for women. He acknowledged that a change had taken place but could not pinpoint its locus.

This analysis requires a reading across the Atlantic as well as across class and gender dimensions.

Locals might also share MCSC members' admonishments of (especially) young females who curse, roll their eyes and kiss their teeth (expressions of frustration). Indeed, Belinda Edmonson's (2003) description of public femininity in the Caribbean explains how women who do not conform to respectable public performances are positioned as "anti-women," who undermine social, economic and political nationalist projects. To mark the boundary around his own middle-class black masculinity, he had been taught to create notable distinctions in habit, speech and style from working classes and from women. To see a woman "cussing" outdoors in the way he and his peers do was unacceptable because she was drawing from, in Wilson's (1973) terms, a masculine reputation system. Moreover, for over a century the respectable classes have not tolerated the "wantoness" of young black women associated with the streets, yards and dancehalls because they have been perceived to threaten to reverse the gains of the black middle-class, who seek to be recognised as civilised (Edmonson, 2003). The fact that the working-class woman Marshall encountered was pregnant was not lost on him. She represented the future of his homeland, Barbados. As civilised, middle-class local men and also as Canadian returnees, some migrants reject some aspects of the indigenous cultures in which they grew up.

Jared, a black 57-year-old Antiguan-Canadian intended to build a home in Antigua to live in for half of the year after he retired, but after visiting for one cricket trip and seeing how homes that are not secured can be looted or destroyed, he quickly changed his mind: "If I come back, it's got to be permanent. I'm not interested in leaving my house empty for six months for these vagabonds. I'll probably just rest my bones in Canada. It's a lot of headache. It's just a real headache now." Duval (2004) has pointed out that return visits can facilitate the process of repatriation. The reports of these cricket tourists suggest that their "routes" can facilitate the decision not to repatriate.

Visiting the homeland forces members of the Afro-Caribbean diaspora to see home not as the idyllic utopia they remember, but as a dynamic site, and the change may be for the worse, in their opinion. Nostalgia, despite its private, sometimes intensely felt personal character and psychological manifestations, is a deeply social emotion that connects us to others, a connection that can be sharply broken when forced to face a reality that does not match with one's memory. Nostalgia is "a longing for a home that no longer exists or has never existed ... a sentiment of loss and displacement ... a romance with one's own fantasy" (Boym, 2001, p. xiii). If they stay "at home" in Canada, they can create the homeland environment they desire and associate with people who they perceive as sharing their values.

Some Afro-Caribbeans' desires to connect with people and cultures of the Black Atlantic are fulfilled through their affiliations with a cricket and social club. The MCSC travels various routes to Caribbean and diasporic locations to facilitate emotional reunions and economic investments. Their charitable donations of money and goods help to improve the lives of the poor and infirm locally and across the Black Atlantic, the potential of the West Indies cricket team, and their status both here and in the Caribbean region as morally upright, benevolent, and generous members of the diaspora. Moreover, when they use funds to augment their own cricket experiences (e.g., to pay for authentic Afro-Caribbean food, well-kept grounds, professional umpires, or trips to diasporic Afro-Caribbean cricket spaces or to their Caribbean homelands where they can play with their friends and family members), they are able to replicate the cricket they played at home and reconstruct the homeland. However, their routes also reveal that they are unable to remake the idyllic past, forcing them to draw on nostalgic memories of home for pleasure. In the following chapter, this idea of travelling to the homeland is discussed further, but rather than focusing on actual geographic travel, it is shown how cricket-related nostalgic storytelling is an essential means of creating gendered and racial identities for older Afro-Caribbean men.

Notes

1 The Windies is ranked eighth of 10 teams, above only Bangladesh and Zimbabwe (December 2015).
2 Caribana is the colloquial name for a festival now officially called The Scotiabank Toronto Caribbean Carnival.

3

Nostalgia

Ninety-nine not out

You see dis bat? I use dis to score more hundreds playing friendly cricket than I ever did back in Guyana or in de Toronto leagues. I guess you could say I really came of age in de last two decades. Once I had my feet wet, initiated in de leagues, dere was no stopping me. Oh, one tour we went on in Barbados, you know against, what he name? You know, Marcus Jones' cousin dere. Ah, yes, Dighton. I was facing him and make ninety-nine runs. Game nearly finish and me, I need one run to make a hundred. That would be eight centuries for me in friendlies. So I standin' guard like dis. I waitin' for one las' ball, an' I see he talkin' talkin' to de captain. Next t'ing I know, he bowl wide. Wide! Dat ball come all de way out here so. Wide! You ever see anyt'ing so stupid? Raas! Me cyaan't believe dat captain tell Dighton bowl wide so me cyaant make me hundred. Wide! Dem noh want give a man a hundred against dem. So I was ninety-nine not out dat day, boy.

Ninety-nine? Ninety-nine? I neva woulda do dat. But you know, dat how t'ings go today. Everyone competition competition. Dem no care 'bout honesty, 'tegrity, or sportsmanship like we learned in before times. What?! When we were boys, we would play morning to sunset an' no matter you win, lose or draw you always show de other guys respec'. You noh bowl wide. Back den every little nook and crevice we found, like dere, just three square feet, as a likkle chil' we would play cricket right dere. And de ball would seldom go into de water or go over de fence because we were force' to control it. I control my ball see. If I bowling or batting, I control it. We make up our games, wit' whatever we could fin'. A tin can for a wicket, an orange for a ball. I play every day and dem always respec' me cause I do it all. Given the opportunity, I made my centuries. I was good. Bowl, wicket keep, bat. I neva had a bat like dis in dem days, but still, I could lash!

Stuart Hall provides astute advice concerning the cultural practices of filmmaking in the Afro-Caribbean diaspora: rather than "thinking of identity as an already accomplished fact, which the new cultural practices then represent, we should think, instead, of identity as a 'production' which is never complete, always in process, and always constituted within, not outside, representation" (Hall, 2003, p. 234). We must question, what are those acts of production and representation? In addition to "routes," that is, cross-border travel, the Afro-Caribbean diaspora is produced through emotional experiences and represented through storytelling. Important to Afro-Caribbean storytelling is the style of oration: boasting, using verbal repetition for emphasis and nostalgic monologues. The above narrative, "Ninety-nine Not Out," weaves together the stories told to me by three spectators at a home game one afternoon. The narrative captures the MCSC member as a man-of-words or, more specifically, the "sweet talking" man (Abrahams, 1983). The interlocutors conveniently leave out the part of the experience that describes failure (e.g., the inability to produce runs with the final ball offered after the wide ball). Stories instead demonstrate sophisticated language, bravado and grandiloquence in service of illustrating prowess and potency. In the space of the cricket ground, where reputation (as opposed to respectability) is valued, men spend their entire afternoon and evenings for the entire summer engaged in embodied, stylised, creative, sport-related storytelling to affirm their racial and gender status. Remembering is a political act; the past may or may not have existed as it is remembered, especially as club members age, their memories fail and their stories merge with the stories of others. Their current inability to produce (in cricket, labour, financial, or sexual terms) can be masked with stories of past potency. Facts about the homeland transform into fiction, but the memory becomes more real with each renewal, especially as such memories are shared.

Longing for the past

The sharing of collective memories is an attempt to recreate, memorialise and relive the past. Afro-Caribbean migrants nostalgically reminisce about cricket experiences. They passionately recount and in some cases, imaginatively recreate their career highlights and lowlights. They often use props, including T-shirts, score sheets and cricket equipment (such as "dis bat"), to help tell their stories and prove their previous athletic prominence. Their stories involve friends and family members who were there, such as "Marcus Jones' cousin," indicating the importance of interpersonal relationships to their participation. Their recollections are always acted out, told with gestures, pointing "out here so" (one metre away) to replicate the original events in order for a new audience to bear witness. They also emphasise how different things are today in Canada, in comparison to "when we were boys" and "before times" back in their homelands. Their desires for and stories about other places and other times tie them to plurilocal homelands and to each other. Although men's talk has been highlighted as a key feature of Afro-Caribbean blackness (Abrahams, 1983; Wilson, 1973), not enough attention has been paid to the particular way in which older men express themselves in these storytelling circles. Their wealth of experience (seven decades in some cases) provides them with a plethora of past experiences from which to draw. This chapter examines the ways in which older men's storytelling is nostalgic and recreates a spatial and temporal sense of home as a racialised and gendered space.

MCSC members reflect on three different types of nostalgic stories through which the values of the community become known and shared. First, they discuss how poor they were as children and the ingenuity they deployed to create equipment for the bat-and-ball game that sustained them throughout their youth. They link stories about making balls, inventing drills, risking punishment just to play cricket, and playing alongside future national heroes, to their own sporting prowess and to the achievements of the West Indies (Windies) team in a bygone era. Second, by sharing their memories of the Windies cricket supremacy in the 1970s and 1980s, MCSC members are able to demonstrate their sport and political knowledge, and revel in the pride they once felt for their nation, region, gender and race. Even their discussions of their former poverty and the current Windies failures contribute to understandings of the homeland and exhibit the (dis)continuities of the immigrant experience. Third, in addition to the various routes the Mavericks travel in order to reconnect with their kin and kith, their *stories about their travels* to places in the Caribbean and Caribbean places in other countries appease their longing for the past and an elsewhere. They regenerate what they have lost and confirm their belonging to a Black Atlantic interpersonal network through their travel stories. They become conscious of their black culture as a result of their "out-migration and subsequent return [which], along with tourism, have precipitated an unprecedented degree of cultural self-awareness, canonization of tradition, and pride" (Matory, 2008, p. 950). Around the cricket pitch, the Mavericks use a "wide ball" or a spectacularly hit "four" on a cricket trip as the impetus to recall personal and broader social histories, and deal with the pain of temporal and physical displacement.

Nostalgia, from the Greek *nostos* (return home) and *algia* (longing), is an important dimension of the production of Afro-Caribbean identity and community. Nostalgia, once portrayed as a private, pathological, physical illness characteristic of those forced from their homes or unable to return to them (i.e., soldiers, slaves and refugees), evolved to be considered a normal collective emotional state (Davis, 1979, p. 14). Today, nostalgia is no longer regarded negatively and is not only connected to pining for a geographical home. It is seen as a "bittersweet" emotion of wistful longing for the past and recalling or reliving "the way things were," combined with the recognition that return is impossible. Emotions such as nostalgia are not merely individual. Emotions, associated with signs, objects and the power of language (Ahmed, 2004), can be collectively felt and expressed (Ritivoi, 2002).

Men's stories told around the boundary, in their changing rooms, and at their hotels, parties, dances or meetings narrate the past: how it really was, how it may have been, and how they knew it was not, but hoped it would be. The truth or accuracy of nostalgic memories and stories are not as important as the bittersweet feelings they evoke (Fairley and Gammon, 2005, p. 185), and why and how these memories emerge and are used (Wilson, 2005, p. 46). Diasporic communities are characterised as having fragmented identities and lacking of a sense of belonging as a result of leaving behind a first home and language, a familiar environment and a previously unacknowledged sense of security – especially for racialised subjects in their new, inconsistently welcoming homes. In postmodern, globalised societies, Wilson (2005, p. 8) points out, there are a number of threats, distractions and obstacles which prevent the construction and maintenance of a coherent, consistent self; "the acts of remembering, recalling, reminiscing and the corollary emotional experience of nostalgia may facilitate the kind of coherence, consistency, and sense of identity that each of us so desperately needs." Even if migrants are unable to make a physical trip to their place of origin, they can access the homeland and the past through shared nostalgic memories. As Stephens (2005) writes of one of Claude McKay's black diasporic literary characters, "community is enacted in the act of telling and listening to a story, not by official categories of race and nationality" (p. 202). A good story is neither journalistic nor concerned with representing ideology. The sharing of collective memories recreates and memorialises the homeland and the individual and collective past.

An excess of time for conversation and reflection increases nostalgia according to Boym (2001, p. xv). At cricket games when men are *liming* – sitting around the boundary watching the game or waiting for their turn at bat, standing in the field waiting for a ball to fly or roll in their direction, or leaning against a car parked on the grass, waiting for their thirst to be quenched and their bellies to be full – they have ample time for conversation and reflection, or what they call "keeping noise," that is, joking, socialising and recounting their histories. The anecdotes of one become the yarns of many. Their nostalgic stories, including island- and region-specific verbal and physical vernacular expressions, paint a picture of a nurturing past/other place that helps them to mediate longing for and belonging to plurilocal homelands. They transcend local communities and are welded into a common culture with other members of the Afro-Caribbean diaspora.

Davis perceives nostalgia as a strategy to resolve the tension between the search for continuity and the threat of discontinuity, a tension noted by Stuart Hall (2003) in his description of the process of postcolonial Afro-Caribbean identity formation. Hall explains that there are at least two different ways of thinking about cultural identity: a sort of collective "'one true self' ... with stable, unchanging, and continuous frames of reference and meaning" (p. 234) contrasts sharply with a sense of rupture from heritage or homeland. Gadsby (2006, p. 18) describes the discontinuity as potentially crippling for migrants who experience "a type of exile that at the same time separates one from place of birth as well from the new society encountered." At once homesick and possibly sick of home, diasporas create identities that depend on both estrangement and longing, and both remembering and forgetting.

Memories of childhood cricket

Stuart Hall (2003, p. 235) draws on what Edward Said once called an "imaginative geography and history" to describe an important component of the identity of postcolonial peoples: the "imaginative rediscovery" of "hidden histories" offers a way of "imposing an imaginary coherence on the experience of dispersal and fragmentation." Hall emphasises that Afro-Caribbean people's sense of continuity, oneness and similarity is not discovered through archaeological unearthing, but grounded "in the *re-telling* of the past" (p. 235, emphasis in original). In retelling their childhoods, the Mavericks affirm their values and pride in their (sporting) heritage. Their stories spill into tales of poverty, creativity, perseverance and community cohesion. Hall reminds us that the past is "always constructed through memory, fantasy, narrative, and myth" (2003, p. 237). The Mavericks' stories of their pasts may not all be true, but they are detailed, numerous and similar, regardless of the specific Caribbean territory in which they grew up.

When I asked how long he had been playing cricket, Vilroy, a 68-year-old black Barbadian-Canadian, exclaimed that he was "born with a cricket bat in hand … When I was a boy we would play morning to sunset. Cricket was a religion!" MCSC members often described how poor they were as children and provided dozens of examples of ingenuity they deployed to create equipment and play the game. Helmets were deemed unnecessary until the late 1970s even for professional cricketers, so it is no surprise they were not a concern for the Mavericks as children in the 1950s and 1960s. Even gloves, shoes and shin pads were all a luxury they hardly considered until they were adults. However, bats and balls were a necessity. When the cost of one bat and one ball was more than the combined weekly income of some of their parents, boys came up with innumerable strategies to gain access to the equipment they needed. Regardless of which island or territory they were from, all of the Mavericks were familiar with the terms "coco bat" and "rubber ball." In group discussions, MCSC members would laugh at each other's stories of the lengths they would go to obtain cricket equipment and each man had an elaborate description of his particular technique.

Their bats were especially treasured because they each made their own and lasted much longer than balls. Generally there were only two means of fashioning a bat, with woodworking equipment or with a machete: "I liked making [my bats] from wood because I loved working with wood and a saw, so I cut my bats out myself with wood and a saw. I used a plane and planed them out and stuff like that. But that was later on" (Marshall). Later on, when Marshall was an adolescent, he had access to wood and carpentry equipment. However when he was a child, like most of his peers, he would make his "willows" from coconut branches. The instructions were simple and echoed by nearly every player I talked to: We would find "a coconut branch from a coconut tree, and wait until it dry, and then we shape a bat out of it with a machete" (Warlie). Every Caribbean territory has its share of coconut trees and this was the dominant strategy boys used to make bats.

To make cricket balls, however, there were nearly as many instructions as there were cricketers. At one of the Mavericks' practices in the batting nets, the players lined up behind the batsman to await their turn. I sat by the entrance charged with the task of ensuring that each batsman would have his 12 minutes at the crease. As each player finished his turn, he came to sit with me and tell me about his ball-making technique:

> We would make our own balls by melting down rubber we could find, for instance, the casing around a ham was good, or we would smash up a milk tin until it was round. (Warlie)
>
> [To make knit balls] what you needed was something round in the centre … we've used a rock inside there or a seed … and then we took cloth and wrapped it around and kept it round. [At] Easter, we flew kites, then after Easter there was lots of twine around and that's what you knitted the balls with. (Marshall)
>
> A rubber string ball … is actually made from the inner tube of a bicycle [tyre] so you cut it into strips six to eight millimetres in width and it's just like

an elastic [string] … so you have to get enough string to wrap around a piece of wet newspaper and you actually form it into the shape of a ball … it's black when it's finish' and the rubber gives it the good bounce and the paper makes it hard. (Robert)

We would tape up the orange [and play with it] until it explodes then we would get another one, we would start with a bucket of oranges and you know when we'd run out of tape we'd just throw the oranges at the batsman just to play. (Kundell)

A few of the MCSC members with economic privilege came from families or attended schools that provided equipment; however, the majority grew up poor and cherished one particular ball-making technique.

The MCSC members enjoyed showing me the wounds they received from playing cricket with improper equipment. These wounds act as objects of nostalgia. They are embodied artefacts that have no inherent meaning, but are imbued with the power to act as symbols of creativity, perseverance, courage and racial and gender pride when they tell stories about them. Every male member of the MCSC could describe an injury, superficial scrapes as well as deep lacerations, with which he continued to play cricket as a boy. At times, they built on each other's stories, interacting without any probing questions from me, and sharing their similar experiences, facts and myths despite different nations of origin and even class backgrounds. Afro-Caribbean men in the diaspora use their bleeding shins, foreheads, elbows and the resulting scars to attest to how serious and passionate they once were – and in some cases, still are – about the game. The dangerous situations they put themselves in, especially in the 1970s as ferocious fast bowling became a marker of Windies pride, also attest to their bravery, a marker of Afro-Caribbean masculinity.

Roland, a 51-year-old black Guyanese-Canadian, explained to me that they had to be prepared with nails and a heavy rock to use as a hammer at the cricket grounds because "if the bat would split we would nail it back together … [unfortunately] sometimes nails would fly out (laughs). Oh yes!" Projectile metal caused many of the scars Kundell and Marshall lay bare:

We used … Carnation milk cans … as a ball when we didn't have one … By the time you've hit that around a few times it's pretty round … and obviously when you miss … and you get hit with the corner? Ooooh! I've got lots of wounds on my shins to attest to that. (Marshall)

What we did was we would burn up a whole heap of plastic nylon and … when the plastic is soft you put it in the coconut shell, roll it around and then it becomes the shape, and then you have a cricket ball, but it is as hard as a rock you know (laughs)! If dat catch you [hits your shins], wow [it hurts]! (Kundell)

The Mavericks acknowledge that they were forced to use these strategies to make equipment and accept the scars that resulted because they were unable to "put a few pennies together and buy one ball" (Roland) much less purchase a bat. Nevertheless, they have found a way for their lack of pennies to be a source of pride. Their testimonies about living in poverty, their ball making techniques and the resultant wounds demonstrate Wilson's (2005) and Ritivoi's (2002) findings that informants can recall in vivid detail a tragic experience, yet regard the experience with humour or positive feelings.

Ahmed reminds us that scars are traces of injuries that persist in the healing of the present: "a good scar allows healing, it even covers over, *but the covering always exposes the injury, reminding us of how it shapes the body*" (2004, p. 202, emphasis in original). Their tales contributed to the healing; putting a positive spin on their former life circumstances, according to Ahmed (2004) and Davis (1979) allowed them to feel better about many of the injustices that have shaped their lives. Nostalgic sentiments are almost always positive; framing disappointments in an "it-was-all-for-the-best attitude," or creating a sharp contrast between the "triumphant past" or idyllic other place and a "lamentable present" is nostalgia's rhetorical signature (Davis, 1979, pp. 14–16). The lamentable present includes their physical decline and the concomitant decline of their favourite team: The Windies.

Today, their equipment bags are not only full of bats and balls, but also the hip pads, gloves and helmets they want, together with the bandages, ointments and bifocals they wish they could do without. Their previous economic distress, which they rationalise as integral to their skill development, has disappeared along with their physical prowess. Kundell explained that "playing without equipment is a good way of developing your skill." Because the only thing between him and "busted shins" was his bat, he trained to use it as a defensive weapon. Roland also noted: "You learn to avoid getting hit on the shins. Because, if it hurt enough you'll find a way to avoid it … Yeah so that helped our technique quite a bit." Warlie added: "We made do with what we had. The grounds were not that good, but we produced lots of good cricketers in those early days." The Mavericks and their peers are confident that they made the best of a bad situation, created by the powers of global capitalism, colonialism and racist exploitation. Though they had very few resources at their disposal, colonial oppressions did not achieve total domination. They used their creativity, the blessings that nature provided and the refuse others discarded to transform material lack in the 1950s and 1960s into exceptional skills in the 1970s and 1980s. They are quick to note that their contemporaries, boys from underdeveloped nations who grew up using the same (makeshift) equipment and playing on inferior grounds, ended up conquering the world in international cricket. They do not long for another *place*; rather they long for the *time* when "their team" ranked number one in the world and they felt physically able to face any threat. These days the Windies consistently ranks in the bottom third of international teams and the Mavericks' own bodies are beginning to betray them.

Stories of Windies supremacy

The Windies have not been consistently successful since the mid-1990s. Nevertheless, MCSC members continue to support them through mediated access to their games, actual visits to their international test matches, and sharing memories of their past triumphs with each other. They are as passionate about celebrating prior successes as they are about critiquing the minutiae of today's Windies players' lacklustre performances. The personal attachment so many Afro-Caribbean men have to professional cricket has not changed in a century. In 1963, C. L. R. James commented, "There is a whole generation of us, and perhaps two generations, who have been formed by [the cricket ethic] not only in social attitudes but in our most intimate personal lives, in fact there more than anywhere else" (1963, p. 41). He continued:

> All of us knew our West Indian cricketers, so to speak, from birth, when they made their first century, when they became engaged, if they drank whisky instead of rum. A test player with all his gifts was not a personage remote, to be read about in papers and worshipped from afar. They were all over the place, ready to play in any match, ready to talk. (1963, p. 62)

The small populations of the various Caribbean territories, the centrality of past Windies team members to the Mavericks' personal social circles and their ongoing social exchanges around the boundary suggest that what occurs at the professional cricket ranks and at an international scale remains central to some Afro-Caribbean-Canadian men's identities and narrative exchanges at the local scale. James' (1963) examination of Windies cricketers showed the passion with which fans attended to every success of Learie Constantine, George Headly and the three Ws: Worrell, Walcott and Weekes. The Mavericks' attentions are directed not only to them, but to the superseding generation of men – Gary Sobers, Vivian Richards, Desmond Haynes, Michael Holding and Courtney Walsh – with whom they grew up in Barbados, Jamaica and Antigua. The

Mavericks memorised and memorialised these heroes' record-breaking performances, artful mastery of bowling and breathtaking strokes.

When they recount and celebrate the Windies achievements, the Mavericks are not engaging in romantic or wilful nostalgia, imagining success where there was none. A striking number of the world's best-ever cricketers come from this tiny region (Garfield Sobers, Vivian Richards and Brian Lara to name a few) and from 1980 to 1994, Wilde (1994) documents, the team won an unprecedented 79 per cent of all tests played, 16 of the 24 test series, and comprehensively beat the English team, winning all five tests in England in 1984, all five tests in the Caribbean in 1985–86, and four of five tests in England in 1988. The Windies team enjoyed an era of supremacy that has been matched in intensity and longevity by poor performances since the mid-1990s. In the *Toronto Star* newspaper, Garry Steckles (2009) asked a question on which the Mavericks ruminate regularly:

> For decade after glorious decade … [the Windies] ruled imperiously with style, with panache, with the sort of swagger that no other cricketers, no matter how talented they were, could hope to match. It was called Calypso Cricket … How could one of the greatest teams in the history of sport – any sport – go from a swashbuckling, world-conquering dynasty to a pitiful and pitied basket-case in just over a decade?

The Windies dramatic deterioration leaves the Mavericks and their supporters longing for the heyday of their younger years. Their own physical decline and inability to perform as they used to are mirrored by the Windies' failings on the international stage.

Kundell, a 52-year-old St. Lucian-Canadian, eloquently described for me his passion for cricket and pride in "his team" despite its now predictable lack of aptitude and negative attitude:

> **Kundell:** I give up on them every game but the next game I think the interest is just the same (laughs). Yeah, every game they lost and I [say] "Ok that's it, these guys are worthless!" and then I can't wait until the next game (laughs).
> **Janelle:** What is it for you that keeps you coming back?
> **Kundell:** I don't know it's, I guess, my love for cricket and being a West Indian … I followed the West Indies team when they were at their strongest and I always … admire teams that play cricket at that level and the West Indies team, as they did during that era, were the toughest team around and nobody could beat them … not even England!
> **Janelle:** Can you describe the feeling of beating England? What did that mean for you?

Kundell: Yeah it was always a joy to beat England, you know. I think it goes back to colonialism because we felt a little oppressed by the English, so every time we beat England it was like a moral victory. We beat the white boys again, and we beat them, and we beat them to the ground! It was a Caribbean victory, not just for the West Indies team or for the eleven players on the team, but the whole Caribbean enjoyed beating England. Even in 1980 when England toured the Caribbean, or was it '82? And the tour manager had a heart attack ... There was no sympathy for them at the time, even with the tragedy.

Janelle: He died?

Kundell: Yeah he died of a heart attack. There was no sympathy throughout the Caribbean over that because it was the West Indies causing the pain!

Kundell paints a vivid picture of the links between cricket success, political "moral victory," and racial pride so often described in the Windies cricket literature (which many club members have read and lent to me for my research) and by so many male MCSC members. The black *man* as a particularly gendered symbol of race power, citizenship and domination began during the decades around the turn of the century and were directly influenced by American and Victorian notions of national strength and gentlemanly behaviour (Stephens, 2005). By the middle of the twentieth century, black power was symbolised by a man in cricket pads wielding either a bat or a ball as his weapon of choice. Players and supporters take the opportunity around the boundary to compare the best-ever players and their weapons, recall their favourite games and discuss their cherished moments in the Windies archive. These stories often have a racial element as they discuss how "surprised those white boys were," or recall the pleasure of beating "the English bastards."

In the twentieth-century Caribbean, St. Pierre (1995, p. 112) explains, non-whites aimed to out-perform whites in all facets of European culture: "There was the dress, the speech, the culinary habits – and there was cricket! The thirst for recognition produced non-white cricketers superior to white cricketers in every department of the game." The impact of spending a childhood prior to national independence, when white British and light-skinned black people held all the positions of power, cannot be underestimated. Until 1957, the Windies team was captained by a (near) white and the game of cricket mirrored life in general in Caribbean society where those with light skin were represented in the top echelons of society out of proportion to their small numbers in the population (St. Pierre, 1995).[1] It was common knowledge that white privilege had allowed many of the planter and merchant classes to play for and captain the

West Indies team in preference over talented, darker skinned players. When, in 1960, black Barbadian Frank Worrell was chosen to captain the West Indies side on a tour to Australia, it became clear that the challenge to British authority and white racial supremacy within the game and within the nation(s) were parallel (Malcolm, 2013, pp. 82–83). The Mavericks, growing up in the 1950s and 1960s in the Caribbean, witnessed a profound shift in social and political power out of the hands of upper-class whites and cricket best exemplified that social mobility and meritocracy was possible for black boys and men. Given that the debates concerning whether or not the Caribbean region was deserving of independence hinged on questions of the nature of Afro-Caribbean masculinity (Stephens, 2005), and that the international Windies team comprises the region's best men, it is with a specifically gendered lens that MCSC members take pride in their national and cricket accomplishments. Slowly over the coming decades the majority of Caribbean territories claimed their independence from European colonisers, dark-skinned governments replaced light and black (and Indian) cricket-playing men replaced white men.

Windies cricketers from the 1970s and 1980s are described as embodying their frustrations with the unequal power structure in Caribbean society and releasing violence in the forms of long run-ups and ferociously fast bowling, big swings and tremendous centuries.[2] According to Kundell, the Windies players were so powerful they were even able to cause the pain of England's assistant team manager Ken Barrington, who died of a heart attack in 1981 at 50 years of age. Success in cricket and even the death of a white English sporting figure were a means for black Caribbean men, including those already living in the diaspora, to feel proud and united since they were forced to carve out an alternative path to hegemonic success, given the strictures placed on their advancement.

Jared described embodied black pride in this way: "You probably can't really appreciate this because it was before you were born, but you know, it was like *anything* was possible back in those days. *Any*thing." The Mavericks impassioned memories of the time when the Windies was supreme are significant, because this period coincides with a time of transition, hope and pride. It overlapped with the granting of political independence to their nations and the period when the rumblings of the US civil rights and black power movements reverberated across the Caribbean. It was an era when beauty, power, knowledge and accomplishments of black people finally began to be valued in the public sphere. And for some, it coincided with their migrations out of their tiny islands and territories and the start of their adult lives.

Like C. L. R. James (1963), who insists that racism in sport "was in its time and place a natural social response to local social conditions [that] … sharpened up the game" (p. 58), the Mavericks saw their achievements as a response to the challenge posed by whites who did not believe in their intellectual and physical capacities. In *What's my name?: Vernacular Intellectuals*, Farred writes that "[t]alented batsmen and bowlers gave voice, through their cultural actions on the cricket oval, to a black (male) agency that colonialism denied the colonized" (2003, p. 134). The Windies provided a rich source of accomplishments to draw from for gendered, racial and regional pride. The accomplishments of black male professional cricketers provided an empowering vision of self-determination and made the Mavericks believe that they too were capable of greatness, that anything was possible. Furthermore, the supremacy of the Windies in the 1970s and 1980s coincided with some of the Mavericks' migrations to Canada, their hopes for educational and economic success, the birth of their children and their dreams for opportunities and achievements beyond what they were able to access in the Caribbean. These decades were also a time when the Mavericks were at the apogee of their own physical prowess; they were dominating cricket leagues in southern Quebec and Ontario. Today, both they and the Windies are in decline.

The losses of the Windies and black power movements, along with personal strength, ability and control suggest that Mavericks' stories about a previous time are examples of what Boym (2001, p. 55) refers to as *reflective nostalgia*: "a form of deep mourning that performs a labor of grief both through pondering pain and through play that points to the future" (Boym, 2001, p. 55). Boym contrasts *reflective* and *restorative nostalgia*. *Reflective nostalgia* dwells in *algia*, in longing and loss, the imperfect process of individual and collective remembrance and dreams of another place and time. In contrast, *restorative nostalgia* "puts emphasis on *nostos* and proposes to rebuild the lost home and patch up the memory gaps" (2001, p. 41). Other than through the material donations they make to their nations of origin to invest in cricket for boys, there is little hope for the Mavericks to restore the power of the Windies, of their bodies or of the Black Power movement.

Gilroy, in *Postcolonial Melancholia* (2005), draws our attention to nostalgia as the process of mystification and mythification of societal transformation; our memories of purportedly great eras when our people were the most powerful in the world always ignore less favourable elements of the era, and are tied to the aching loss of racial and gender power. The MCSC members' memories are called upon to do important cultural work, that is, to recall a time when they felt powerful. This is connected to both gender and race, since traditional markers of hegemonic masculinity decline with age, and living in multicultural

Canada they see that the dreams of living lives free of racism – dreams they initiated during the US civil rights movement and after their nations gained independence – have not come true. Their naive expectation of increasing hospitality and power in Canada is countered regularly when police target them, they receive passive hostility or micro-forms of aggression in public spaces, or they encounter structural and everyday racism in their workplaces. To counteract these negative experiences, they invest significant energy in recalling more positive times.

Charles, a black 67-year-old Jamaican-Canadian who is a passionate and long-standing Mavericks supporter railed against the West Indies Players Association (WIPA) that went on strike (in July 2009) because the players wanted more money. In "his day," Windies players would "never strike" because they knew how "privileged they were" to have risen above their humble beginnings and be selected to represent the region at the highest level. He had a vituperative exchange with a number of players around the boundary because the West Indies Cricket Board decided to "put in the second-string guys [to] play agains' Bangladesh an' they lost!" His interlocutors mentioned:

> They should fire all a dem, pay dem for their stats. Den you can see who shows up for work, who really wants it, who has skills.
> They pay so-and-so this much money and he ain't bat thirty-five. You can put any one a dese ol' men on the fiel' right now into dat line up an' dey can bat thirty-five!

Charles continued: "Lose to Bangladesh?! What kin' of bullshit is dis?! Black people everywhere should feel shame! … Players today are no talent, selfish SOBs. WIPA is a fuckin' joke!" Charles' complaints reminded me of the literature that documents decades of condemnation of the West Indies Cricket Board. Half a century ago C.L.R. James wrote letters of complaint to the Board over their censure of Gilchrist, a fast but unruly bowler and hero to the people. The Board ignored James' advice and the people's wishes. He notes, "This was not the first time that I had had doubts of the inability of the Board to understand the age in which it was living" (1963, p. 236). Obviously, complaints about the West Indies Cricket Board are enduring. The racial pride of Charles and his friends is linked to the success of the Windies team, which Charles believes is actively prevented by the "stupidness" of today's Board. His displeasure with losing to Bangladesh can also be examined in relation to local and historical Indo-Afro ethnic antagonisms (see Chapter 6). He explicitly equates the Windies' previous successes with a sense of racial accomplishment not only for people in the Caribbean, and not merely for the Afro-Caribbean diaspora, but for "black people everywhere."

Watching the Windies' successful performances at international games, at home, or more likely, in sports bars in Toronto, offered a diasporic resource for MCSC members. The images themselves, as well as the opportunities for socialising professional games presented, helped to unite geographically dispersed black men. In contrast, the Windies' failures denote racial shame.

Charles' "reflective nostalgia" (Boym, 2001) assuages *algia*, a longing for the past or home. His longing is not for a specific place (Jamaica) or region (the Caribbean) or a time (childhood, or the era of the Windies' supremacy). Rather, like many young Afro-Caribbean men of the generation that witnessed their countries' independence from British rule, he longs for a social space of black power and pride he felt in the 1970s and 1980s. The Windies' success provided proof that blacks can, in fact, compete against the best in the world, that being from "little" islands, the "third world," and "the periphery" did not equate to little achievements, third rate performances, or peripheral status. During the era of supremacy, the West Indies Cricket Board (WICB) and the Windies players, finally managed and captained by blacks, showed promise and unity. Since then, however, Hussein, a 66-year-old Indo-Trinidadian-Canadian, notes the WICB has "fallen apart":

> Before times, we were this powerful black team, like you see how the Australians see themselves as all white and all Australian. After they [British colonialists] realised they couldn't hold us down we were really like one black nation. These days there are more internal rivalries between the islands, no cohesion or team work.

The signature nostalgic move, according to Davis (1979) and Wilson (2005) is to compare then and now, "before times" and "these days" and to look for culprits to explain why things have gone downhill. Among the Mavericks, discussions of the dysfunctional Board spill into more general discussions of internal rivalries among Caribbean nations, the fractures within regional and national politics, and widespread political corruption and individual failures. Charles explained: "These days, when people think of Jamaica, all they think of is gun violence in (Toronto suburbs) Scarborough or Jane and Finch. Even our people. They don't know about [Michael] Holding or Courtney Walsh!" Charles may have overlooked contemporary Jamaican sporting heroes, such as Usain Bolt who, in 2008 were synonymous with Jamaica for "our people" – Afro-Caribbean-Canadians. Nevertheless, his point remains that the Mavericks are fearful that, especially among second-generation Afro-Caribbean-Canadians, the knowledge of the prowess of former Windies players and its associated regional and racial pride, will soon dissipate. Losing to weak teams such as Bangladesh certainly would not be of help. Concomitantly their own accomplishments will soon be forgotten as the number of MCSC members decrease as they age, retire and, sadly, die.

The positive emotions associated with the era of Windies supremacy tell us about a deep history. Ahmed (2004, p. 202) helps us understand that emotions "are the very 'flesh' of time ... Emotions show us how histories ... of colonialism, slavery and violence shape lives and worlds in the present." Rather than focus on current failures, the Mavericks enjoy reminiscing about momentous events in Windies' test match history that they witnessed and their own cricket accomplishments of the past. This "ethnic myth," as Paul Gilroy (2005) calls it, allows for a one-sided construction of the past. The Mavericks' own mythology surrounding the 1970s and 1980s allows them and their country*men* to emerge as heroes and ignore the embarrassing elements of the era, including sexism, pigmentocracy, ethnic conflicts, class wars and homophobia, to name a few of which they were both victims and aggressors. The pattern of melancholy for the lost past "has become the mechanism that sustains the unstable edifice of increasingly brittle and empty national identity ... it is around sport that more habitable and ... more modern formations of national identity have been powerfully articulated" (Gilroy, 2005, p. 106). The Mavericks are able to use sport and nostalgic sport-related stories to retain a racial identity.

Narratives of club travel

In addition to stories of their childhoods and Windies' supremacy, MCSC members share memories of their travels to regenerate their race and gender. When the MCSC travels, members inject into their trips meaningful, commemorative, heritage practices such as cricket games, picnics, city tours and dances. The trips club members take and, importantly, their stories of their experiences, often prompted by artefacts of nostalgia (e.g., plaques, pictures), reinforce the idea of cricket trips as about much more than sport; they are diaspora "heritage practices," which permit the consumption of other spaces and other times (Joseph, 2011b). Their practices within the rituals of the games and tournaments and other activities they enjoy while abroad resemble what Boym (2001) calls "restorative nostalgia," which stresses *nostos* and a remaking of the past/home. Notably, the "home" they remake is not necessarily their nation of origin. As I have stressed throughout this book, members of the MCSC are attached to plurilocal homelands.

Memories the MCSC members share about the trips they have taken reinforce each other's nostalgic recollections, the identity of the community and their longing to return again. As Fairley and Gammon (2005, p. 192) note: "When repeat trip participants come together to take part in a trip, memories of past trips become particularly salient ... [N]ewcomers become aware of the activities that are important to the group to the point where they are able to relive past trips vicariously."

MCSC members constantly compared their current activities (playing cricket, drinking, dancing, or playing dominoes) to spectacular experiences they had in other times and places. When I told Erol, a 55-year-old black Barbadian-Canadian, I had never before visited his homeland of Barbados, he assured me that there is no better way to see the island than on a cricket trip:

> You come wit' us an' you see the whole island. We play games every part and we have fun. You go fish fry, you see all the stadiums. You get to really party ... *Every* tour we went to Barbados [we had] coolers pack up with ice, drinks, Barbados rum, Guinness. Dem bring fish cake, dumpling, food [plantains and yams], everyt'ing! We drink an' play. What?! Play and drink same time. No matter what you drink you never get drunk. You jus' relax. Go beach for conch salad. Jamaicans brings jerk chicken, Barbadians brings sweetbread, rice an peas and this is every day! They had police escorts, security to protec' we and our bus pack up wit' drink! You will see.

This description of an all-you-can-drink-and-eat affair is Erol's idea of paradise. Sport is a marginal element of the way he describes a cricket trip to his homeland and stories such as these are repeated to entice others to join the team on their upcoming trips.

When I introduced myself as being of Antiguan descent, most players had a story about a great trip they had to Antigua that involved watching or playing at least one game of cricket. Wesley, a black 57-year-old Jamaican-Canadian spoke longingly of the beautiful weather and challenging games he played in Antigua when he travelled there with a masters' team in 2005. In fact, he was wearing the team shirt from that trip the first time I met him and he used the shirt as a prop in a story he told me about the loss they suffered in the final game in that tournament. Wesley's detailed explanation of how his team had been on a pace to win and ultimately gave away the game is paralleled by his intricate description of the parties they attended on that trip:

> I still wear dis [shirt] with pride even though we lost that tournament. De guys tryin' to show off. Against my advice, I might add. Dey gave up de wickets slowly, by not running and waiting instead fe see if balls dey hit mek it to de boundary.

"What you standin' dere for?" I was yellin' at dem ... "Take t'ree [runs]! OK, take two!" Not even one? Dem t'ink the ball a go out so dey waitin', waitin', den it just drop an' roll deep square leg [fielding position near the boundary] an' him pick it up an' t'row (shakes his head). So *den* dey decide fe run. Ah (pause). We end up losing' by t'ree runs (holds up three fingers and shakes his head) ... But you know we were in beautiful Antigua, so I cyan't really complain. Dey say 365 beaches, you know. Wow. Dat sand was beautiful and white, white, white. Dey really know how to party. We went to one fête on the beach an' dey was playing some sweet calypso an' reggae. I t'ink we party till sun come up. I don't t'ink I did dat since I was your age but we had some fun in Antigua, boy!

That game obviously meant a lot to Wesley who can recount every detail of the final moments three years later. He was disappointed and embarrassed by his teammates' failure (or inability) to run and their resultant second place finish in the tournament, but he contrasts this with one of the goals of the trip they managed to achieve: to party all night long. Repeating "waiting" twice and "white" three times is an Afro-linguistic strategy that adds emphasis (McLaren, 2009). He recites the Antigua and Barbuda Department of Tourism's official line of "365 beaches" and encourages others to travel there as well. Staying up all night partying on brilliant white sand is a strong motivator for cricket-related travel. Players transport each other back to the event or place through their artefacts and stories of great parties and even sad defeats. Although he is Jamaican, Wesley longs for a return to Antigua and wears his T-shirt from that trip as a reminder of the experience.

For most tours, the cricketers create a new uniform with an embroidered team name, and sometimes the date and location of the tour. Trophies, plaques, flags and pins are all exchanged between teams to commemorate the games. Statuettes or plaques engraved with the date, location and names of the teams involved are given to the man of the match and/or captain of the team to honour his contributions. When they return from their trips, some of the Mavericks display in their homes the plaques and trophies they have received among team pictures, old uniforms, balls (which they had hit for a century), framed newspaper articles, photos of them playing or receiving awards, or posters advertising their matches and dances that took place in Toronto, elsewhere in Canada, the Caribbean, the United States and the United Kingdom.

These metonymies of plurilocal homelands represent who these men are. They are irreplaceable artefacts that "anticipate and provide material support for a state of mind. They offer a vantage for creating a retrospective story, which not only aspires to record a past event, but also purports to immortalize it" (Ritivoi,

2002, p. 131). It is clear that particular objects and the nostalgic stories told about them become "sticky or saturated with affect ... language works as a form of power in which emotions align some bodies with others, as well as stick different figures together" (Ahmed, 2004, p. 194). The objects on the walls or mantles from previous cricket games and trips are made and displayed specifically to help them remember; along with their scars from cricket injuries, the objects, material aspects of myths, prompt discussions among the Mavericks that reify experiences, unite club members, commemorate loss and celebrate past visits to Caribbean spaces.

At one meeting held at the home of Reggie, a 52-year-old Indo-Guyanese-Canadian player, I noticed a picture on the wall of uniformed cricketers arranged in two lines. A few players and their wives gathered around the photograph, which, in my view, did not feature any overt indication of when or where it was taken. Based on which MCSC members were present, the uniforms they were wearing, and the characteristics of the cricket field in the background of the photograph, it didn't take long for those who had been there to figure out that it was from a tour they had gone on six years prior: "No it couldn't be Grenada because Hussein was having heart surgery that year so he didn't go, remember?" "Oh yeah, then it must be Barbados. You see the crest [on the players' shirts]" "Yeah, yeah, we really gave it to 'em dat game, boy!" Individual recollections intertwine with collective memories weaving a tapestry of emotions that allow meaning to be generated.

The pictures they took, at cricket matches and also at tourist sites such as Derek Walcott Square and Castries Market in St. Lucia, Piccadilly Circus or Lillywhites department store in London, or the Mount Gay Rum Factory and Sunbury Plantation House in Barbados, serve as reminders of their national, regional, racial and ancestral histories, and their enjoyment of various Afro-Caribbean spaces as holiday destinations. When Hussein shared his photo album from the most recent Barbados trip at the meeting, he fused his experiences with the memories of others who were on the trip and the fantasies of those who could not make it. The Mavericks' exchanges continued over drinks for over an hour after the meeting had formally ended. Wilson (2005, p. 36) reminds us that "nostalgia may be experienced collectively, in the sense that nostalgia occurs when we are with others who shared the event(s) being recalled. In this way, nostalgia might be used as conversational play and as a strategy for bonding." Ahmed (2004) also suggests that individual subjects come into being through their alignment with the collective. Collective memories are how groups pass on traditions, rituals, culture and group history.

As the Mavericks age they incorporate an increasing number of 'heritage cricket tours' into their lifestyles. While this is certainly a result of more free time due to retirement, fewer parenting obligations and more disposable income due to paying off their mortgages and their adult children leaving home, one cannot ignore the impact on their memory making of their decreasing levels of performance, increasing illnesses and injuries and impending sense of mortality. These factors also amplify a desire to connect with another place and time through storytelling about the past. As Boym writes of reflective nostalgia, what is most missed during exile "is not the past and the homeland exactly, but rather this potential space of cultural experience that one has shared with one's friends and compatriots that is based neither on nation nor religion but on elective affinities." In other words, analysis of the Afro-diaspora also requires mining of stories about friendships. As men age, and the folds in the fan of memory multiply, collective memories shared between friends mediate between the past and the present, self and other.

Any discussion of memory, especially among older immigrants, necessarily raises questions of "truth" and the relative value of verification for the social scientist. This chapter is based on the notion that imaginative, narrative or collective truth (based on relationships, emotions, values and interpretations) may be just as important as, if not more significant than, historical truth (based on facts that can be verified). Salman Rushdie (1991, p. 10) writes, "imaginative truth is simultaneously honourable and suspect." The meaning of a memory is more complex than simply resurrecting events. Rushdie (1991) uses the metaphor of looking though a broken mirror: only fragments of the past can be recalled due to the mistakes of a fallible memory compounded by quirks of character and of circumstance (e.g., alcohol consumption). But he values the broken mirror because it shows that every truth is fractured. As their memories fade, older adults rely more and more on the stories they tell each other, which are crucial in generating gendered and racial pride, showing their class status and preserving their version of the past when their stories of recreational cricket are forgotten or ignored by national (both Canadian and Caribbean) historical sporting archives. Boym explains that rather than "recovery of what is peceived [sic] to be an absolute truth," the focus of reflective nostalgia is "on the meditation on history and passage of time ... shattered fragments of memory ... [and it] can be ironic or humorous" (2001, p. 49). This type of nostalgia "does not pretend to rebuild the mythical place called home," Boym continues (p. 50). The storyteller is aware of the gap between the real and imagined homeland, but the "defamiliarization and sense of distance drives them to tell their story, to narrate the relationship between past, present and future" (p. 50) and averts their sense of alienation, loneliness and uprootedness; assuaging the "ache of temporal distance and displacement" (p. 44) said to be characteristic of diasporas. When the historical "facts" are insufficient, Afro-Caribbean peoples turn to oral narratives that are often shared in the kitchen, at a community meeting, or around the boundary of a cricket match.

The memories of home that the MCSC members choose to share simultaneously mask the experiences they would rather forget. When reflecting on their youth some players who attended their islands' top grammar schools, where they were first introduced to formal team cricket, do not highlight the class hardships they experienced as the scholarship students (admitted because of top grades, not family income). For example, Jared, a black 57-year-old Antiguan-Canadian, told me of his simultaneous disappointment and joy due to not being invited to social functions with his school and cricket mates. He was disheartened because the upper-class boys did not want to associate with him, but joyful that he would not have to attend parties in his school uniform (the only nice clothes he owned). When reflecting on their homelands, the Mavericks also do not focus on the hurricanes, volcanic eruptions and earthquakes that damaged their villages on a semi-regular basis. When pressed to discuss this Tayana, a 46-year-old black Guyanese-Canadian, recalled flippantly, "Oh, well of course, every few years you feel a strong wind, the sky turn dark. You see a metal roof flying down the road ... You know a hurricane coming and you rush inside." Her simplistic description of living through hurricanes obscures the fact that some of the MCSC members' homes and communities were severely damaged in hurricanes Baker (1950) and Donna (1960) when they were young. More recently, hurricane Ivan (2004) caused fear for the safety of their loved ones remaining in the Caribbean who were left without homes, electricity, water or sewer services, and the club raised money to spend on hurricane relief efforts. Many MCSC members fail to acknowledge the feelings of insecurity and trauma imposed by Mother Nature – not to mention colonial powers – in favour of remembering their homelands as beautiful places to live, holiday and play cricket. Like their nostalgic memories, their selective forgetting of various aspects of the homeland forms their identities.

Afro-Caribbean-Canadians, as is the case for other Canadians, may yearn for another time or place as a result of the postmodern condition; that is, the industrial, urban, capitalist culture that creates a sense of alienation and fragmented identities with a dizzying array of possibilities for creating the self (Featherstone, 1991). Alternatively, like other elderly people, their physical decline and impending mortality may be the reason they look to the past with such fondness. Older adults reminisce about past successes to maintain their self-concept through the lifespan and memories are validated through dialogue with others (Radley, 1990). Additionally, the observation of the deterioration of Windies performances, with no evident hope for restoration, combined with the fact that many of their dreams of black liberation remain unfulfilled both in their nations of origin and in Canada, may cause older Afro-Caribbean Canadians in particular to reflect on better times in the past and the narratives they construct may act as vehicles for facilitating the continuity of their diasporic identities, and boosting their national, regional, racial and gender pride. Regardless of the reason, their active memory making allows them to remain connected to each other, their homelands and Afro-Caribbean spaces around the Black Atlantic.

This chapter shows how the Mavericks, who have been playing cricket together since at least the 1980s are unable to recreate history, but they come close to capturing the past through stories about their childhood cricket games, memories they indulge in about professional cricket supremacy, and narratives of previous cricket trips they tell and retell. Through these linguistic strategies MCSC members hold on to "the way things were." Collective memory is an important aspect of group identity and solidarity, and is especially significant in shaping the social life and communal consciousness of diasporic men as they use *selective* group memories and fable formulations of sport-related events to portray themselves, their pasts and their homelands.

The nostalgic object of longing for many men of the Afro-Caribbean diaspora or the Black Atlantic, is not necessarily the nation of origin and not always a place called home; rather, they long for the past, for a time when creativity and perseverance were precursors for success, when a child with "nothing" could still achieve greatness on a world stage, and when they could associate their racial pride with the achievements of Caribbean athletes. The older, racialised, male diasporic subject turns to meaningful, locally available resources, including his own sport memories and those of his peers, to reconstruct what Rushdie (1991) calls the "imaginary homeland." Older Afro-Caribbean-Canadian women, in contrast, are less likely to tell sport stories about the past. The following chapter explores the experiences of women, including the wives, lovers and friends of male players and supporters in this sport and social club. Their gendered experiences reveal some of the disjunctures of the Afro-Caribbean diaspora.

Notes

1 In 1957, black Barbadian Clyde Walcott was vice-captain under white Barbadian John Goddard (St. Pierre, 1995, p. 107). This fact is often overlooked as the accolades of the first black West Indies captain normally go to Frank Worrell in 1960.
2 During the period between 1974 and 1994, the black West Indians developed an aggressive, intimidating, fast-bowling playing style far removed from the White-determined, English traditions of the game. The fact that this was in keeping with racist ideologies of black physicality and violence led to the vilification of the team at the time. Nevertheless, black people across the Caribbean celebrated their team and the wins their aggressive style allowed them to accrue as evidence of Black Power and support for the assertion of West Indian 'national" identity (Malcolm, 2013, pp. 83–85).

4

Disjunctures

Scholarship on black diasporas has notably excluded, disregarded and marginalised women and subordinated attention to the politics of gender. Scholars such as Carole Boyce Davies, Hazel Carby, Constance Sutton, D. Alissa Trotz and Jacqueline Nassy Brown have attempted to redress these oversights by showing "how particular practices (such as travel) and processes (such as diasporic community formation) come to be infused with gender ideologies (or become 'gendered') and how such gendering effectively determines the different positionalities men and women can occupy" (Nassy Brown, 1998, p. 301). Male players and supporters mainly occupy the Mavericks Cricket and Social Club (MCSC), but their gender performances and the function of the club depends on women, whose experiences are explored below.

In seminal black diaspora texts, such as C. L. R. James' *Beyond a Boundary* and Paul Gilroy's *The Black Atlantic: Modernity and Double Consciousness*, women are often left out of the story, portrayed as non-agents, and erased from the history of black politics and Caribbean travel, not to mention sport. A gender analysis of James' work by Hazel Carby, in her book *Race Men*, explains that for James the connection between sport and politics "was seamless precisely because ideologies of masculinity, whether conscious or unconscious, were already shaping his understanding of the performative politics of cricket *and* his idea of how colonialism should be opposed" (Carby, 1998, p. 120, emphasis in original). James' fictional writing, including *Minty Alley*, examines working-class people and relations among women, but "[w]hen James abandoned fiction to write about revolutionary politics and revolutionary heroes, he also gave up trying to write about women" (Carby, 1998, p. 125) and rendered invisible the ways in which gender, including women's experiences and relations as well as performances of multiple masculinities and relations among men, shaped the practices and ideologies of sport and politics.

Where women's experiences are invoked in analyses of the Afro-diaspora, women are often used, according to Michelle Stephens (2005), to represent the past, home, stasis, domesticity and heterosexual captivity, whereas men are described as creating the diasporic future through their transnational, itinerant and homosocial activities. Stephens draws on the work of Carole Boyce Davies to explain the invisibility of women of colour in narratives of nationalism, post-colonialism and diaspora: "it is because she is 'somewhere else, doing something else' in less territorial transnational spaces" (Stephens, 2005, p. 17) that the wife, mother, or girlfriend is ignored. Violet Showers Johnson found of "West Indian" cricket in Boston in the early 1900s, that girls and women were critical to club functions in terms of organising entertainment, food, fundraising for purchase of uniforms and sports equipment, catering and supervising the tea breaks, a sine qua non for any cricket match. The same activities "within the periphery and in the traditional domestic arena of food and entertainment" (Johnson, 2006, p. 61) prevail for the female Afro-Caribbean-Canadians in Toronto 100 years later, but the complexities of their roles, and particularly their relationships with each other, deserve far deeper analysis.

When we examine the different positionalities that women occupy compared to men, and the ways in which gender performances (such as flirtatious overtures and macho heterosexualities) are relational in the space of a cricket ground, different diasporic stories emerge and we begin to understand more fully the formation of Afro-Caribbean diasporic communities. Following Carrington (2008, p. 424), in this text:

> "I examine the extent to which sport provides a contested arena through which competing definitions of race, gender, sexuality, class, and region are articulated. Or, to put it more succinctly, how are different versions of what it means to be black confirmed or challenged within particular sporting locales?"

Many migrants may feel a sense of community where differences are minimised and communal cultures celebrated. To focus solely on the masculinised world of the cricket ground and men's community building, however, would be to trade in fictions that deny the reality of the ways in which this community is fractured. We see through the lens of women's experiences the fallacy of any notion of a universal diasporic experience, the reinforcement of the patriarchal gender order within Afro-Caribbean diasporas, and women's agency within Afro-diasporic and sporting spaces. None of the female club members play cricket, yet exploring their stories is essential in order to reveal the disjunctures of the Afro-diaspora.[1]

A Taste of the Candy Apple

"De first time she come, she flounce outta that car, fly across de grass and she win' up falling into Michael's arms. You know Michael is a real catch. He's got a nice body, always wears tapered clothes. He's clean, you know? Den she come on the scene an' contaminate him. She drove everyone mad. All a dese men, fighting for a taste of the Candy Apple. All de women throwing darts with dey eyes. Look she deh."

I turned in the direction my sister was pointing and saw a round woman in a skin-tight, low-cut, bright red halter top crossing the grassy area by the scorers' table. Her backside and belly battled each stitch of her oh-so-tiny yellow jean shorts. Her personality was even louder than her outfit. "Good afternoon. Good afternoon!" She called to greet everyone within earshot as she waved her three-inch-long, air-brushed, acrylic nails. She walked around the boundary and shook the hands of all her friends, sure not to leave anyone out. "How's your Pops, Kaneisha? You feelin' better Mr. Weste?" She reached a group of four men standing around a table top specifically designed to fit on top of the city's one-metre-tall recycling bins found at the park. They were playing a game of dominoes. One of them must have said something hilarious, but all we could hear was Candice screaming, "Oh lawd, stop!" as she doubled over in laughter, held her belly with her left hand and slapped her right hand on the chest of the man standing next to her. She needed him to stop him the joke he was telling while she caught her breath.

"You see me?" My sister chimed in, showing that despite 30 years in Canada she had not lost a touch of her Bajan speaking ways. "You would neva, eva, ehh-hhh-vaaahh catch me wearin' somet'ing like dat in public. People will talk. It's like, someone need tell she, leave a likkle to de imagination, nuh?" Leaning in and in a lowered voice she offered, "You know she won a worker's compensation lawsuit for an injury she claim happen at her job, but she look disabled to you? She just scandalous." My sister had a way of kissing her teeth, shaking her head and rolling her eyes at the same time that made you feel as though whatever she was thinking about was dirtier than a cigarette floating in a sewer. As this was my first time visiting Toronto in 10 years, she felt she needed to fill me in on all of the gossip. "Imagine, Erol tell Layton an' Layton tell me dat she spend all dat lawsuit money on dat car! Look it deh." I was sure that all the pointing around the boundary was going to have that woman in our faces sooner rather than later. I stole a glance at the sparkling new white Lexus luxury SUV parked on the grass beside the cricket grounds. Compared to the practical Honda Civics and Dodge Caravans of some of the other players and supporters her vehicle was conspicuously out of place. "And you see how she park it so, under dat tree. Notice all de other cars all de way down deh so. Wait. Just wait. She t'ink a tree can protec' she? When one a dese ol' men hit that ball over deh, dat windshield is toast. Just wait."

If a ball could decimate her car, none of us were safe just a few metres away, were we? A hard cricket ball could cause serious damage to an unsuspecting spectator, couldn't it? I had no intention of returning to Connecticut with a broken jaw, arm or anything else for that matter. "Should we move over?" I asked her. "We too close?"

"We just need to keep one eye on de ball." She quipped. "I tell Layton over and over de club needs to apply to de city to make dis a proper ground. Get some bleachers, maybe a washroom in here. Den maybe some more wives would show up for dese games. And definitely, we could have a parking lot across de road away from dis nonsense. I been tellin' him for years. I know I'm just gonna have to do it myself. Do you know who to call about that? Maybe Candy Apple can help. Here she come." My sister turned a snicker into a smile in a heartbeat as Candice approached us. "Well hello there!"

"A Taste of the Candy Apple" was developed through conversation with a Torontonian and her group of sisters who had travelled to Toronto from Connecticut for the Labour Day weekend, 2008. I shared a version of the story with the sister who lives in Toronto the following week and she highlighted several different dimensions of female MCSC members' experiences that vary based on their relationships to men and commitment to the club. We rewrote the story to identify four different 'types' of women associated with the Mavericks: widows, gossipers, lovers and supporters are described below.

This chapter investigates what the experiences of women can tell us about gender and race in the Black Atlantic and Caribbean diaspora. There are the women who do not "show up" to games either because there is nowhere to sit, they have no interest in the sport, or they remain elsewhere in waged labour or in charge of childcare and domestic duties. These women, whom I call "widows," may occasionally attend club trips, dances, picnics, or banquets with their husbands, but they "lose" them every weekend through the summer. Their absence from the regular weekend games is essential for the creation of a homosocial space.

Those who attend games regularly are typically connected to male club members through marriage or romance and use the grounds as they would the beauty salon or the kitchen, as a place for women to get together and share stories and experiences. This group of women I call the "gossipers" barely notices that a cricket match is happening. They sit with their sisters and friends at the periphery of the cricket grounds, talk to and about each other, delineate issues of morality and make the values of the community known. They also come to the grounds to observe and police their husbands' and boyfriends' on- and off-field performances and other single women's behaviours.

A woman who is flirtatious can easily transform herself into one of the Mavericks' "lovers." This is a small group of women who are not married to the Mavericks, but accompany them to most games, some dances, and on certain trips providing romance, friendship and support. They remain close to the Mavericks, alongside them at their domino games and on the dancefloor, rather than in the respectable, peripheral zone occupied by most wives. They are the source of much of the gossip at the grounds and play an essential role in creating a heterosexualised, masculine space.

The women I refer to as the "supporters," like the male supporters, invest their time, energy and money in the on-field performances and the functioning of the club. In addition to providing (grand)childcare, they cheer when the players perform well, heckle those who play poorly, cook food for the post-game celebrations, sell tickets to dances and fundraisers, score keep, *lime* with the male spectators and perform administrative duties such as lobbying the municipality for funds. The club could not operate without them. The widows, gossipers, lovers and supporters are not mutually exclusive groups. Some women perform one or all of these roles in distinct times, spaces and contexts, but all are essential to the club function and the homespaces the Mavericks are able to create.

The MCSC claims to be family oriented. Terrel, a 56-year-old black St. Lucian-Canadian reminded me, "We are not only men, because this is a cricket and *social* club, so we include families." Between 10 and 30 per cent of the crowds at most games are women: daughters, friends, girlfriends, lovers and wives of the players. Sometimes this amounts to only two or three women.

Widows

Approximately 60 per cent of the Maverick cricketers are currently married to women, so one might expect to see more women out to support the male players, but the social environment of the cricket grounds was a deterrent for many women and fewer than half of the players' wives ever attend cricket matches. Kundell, a 52-year-old St. Lucian-Canadian, explained that his first wife "wasn't a cricket fan. She came to one game and that was it. In 1989." The culture evident at the cricket ground sometimes included men's loud talking, swearing, spitting, scratching of genital areas, misogynist comments and boasting of their sexual or cricketing prowess. As they use the cricket ground to perform black Caribbean masculinity, they often mark the space as not for women, if not anti-woman. Maintaining homeland cultures in the diaspora can also mean preserving gender hierarchies and exclusions; Davis and Upson explain that women were actively prohibited from watching an India–Pakistan cricket match at the South Asian Friendship Center and Bookstore (pseudonym) in Chicago "because it just wasn't safe for them" (2004, p. 638). Among the Mavericks some women might also not feel safe, especially at the players' after-parties. One of the players wore a T-shirt created by the club in 2000 stating that he was a member of "a drinking team with a cricket problem" extolling his true objective at the grounds. Another's shirt stated "Me nah eat nuttin' me cyan't put hot pepper sauce on!" alluding to his alleged disdain for cunnilingus and appreciation for spicy food. These behavioural and sartorial performances effectively marked the space as hyper-masculine and were a turn-off for many female club members, including myself.[2]

Belinda Edmonson (2003), drawing on Wilson's (1973) respectability/reputation thesis, describes the domestic space as the traditional, "respectable," appropriately feminine space for Caribbean women, in contrast to the masculine public space of "reputation" where men of the oppressed classes are expected to endorse the values of the outdoors including talking, swearing, infidelity, drinking and staying out late. These are ways in which men establish a reputation among their peers. They may move into and out of the respectable home space, but theirs is the outdoor, public domain. The cricket ground and its environs, including the grassy area around the boundary where men sit, talk and socialise at their cars, are experienced as public places primarily for men. Meanwhile women are expected to place their loyalties in their husbands, hope for honest, sober, responsible behaviour and wait for them to come home. This dichotomy is found in the families of many MCSC members and is captured in the above vignette. Women were actively excluded from on-field participation with the Mavericks, and most female club members did not attend games. Edmonson (2003, p. 2) states, "crossing of the boundaries by women from private to public space must be interrogated and assessed as either a proper intervention that preserves the woman's femininity, or a social violation that masculinizes or otherwise pathologizes her." Socialising alongside men even at their domino tables is to enter the profane, "reputation" space. Although there were always a few women to spend time with, and respectable ways to behave at the periphery of the cricket grounds, most female club members preferred to simply stay away from games.

Kundell's first wife, who came to only one game in 1989, saw her husband's obsession with cricket as giving her the freedom to do as she pleased every weekend in the summer. While she attended dances and annual club functions, her interest in other weekend activities surpassed her interest in cricket and the masculine space created at the grounds. Not every woman who refrains from joining her husband at the grounds is miserable at home without him. Some women's absences are a form of resistance to sporting cultures, to routine sexual harassment of these men-only spaces, or to engagement with the diaspora.

Tayana, a 46-year-old black Guyanese-Canadian, explained that there are so few women at the grounds because most wives have "too many other things to do than sit 'pon de grass all day Saturday wit' a bunch a men." This short statement elucidates two significant points. First, few of the local clubs have been able to mobilise the funds or municipal support to build a proper clubhouse, which forces spectators to stand, bring their own seating, lean on trees, or sit on the grass, something that many older, middle-class, Afro-Caribbean women find uncomfortable. A clubhouse might make the space more inviting for women who are concerned about staying warm and dry while they watch the games and socialise. On the surface the cricket ground appears to be a loud, friendly Afro-Caribbean space that is "not only men ... we include families" (Terrel). However, without amenities such as chairs and washrooms, the cricket grounds on which the Mavericks play are not very appealing places for many women to spend 16–20 hours on a weekend. Unlike black clubs in England, which have benefited from shifts in government spending to leisure facilities as a means of trying to placate inner-city tensions (Carrington, 1998, 1999), the Mavericks have been unable to convince local governments of their need for permanent cricket structures.

Second, having "too many other things to do" highlights the unpaid domestic labour that many women do on the weekends, which indirectly supports their husbands' sport. In her text, *Mother's Taxi*, Shona Thompson (1999) demonstrates that doing laundry, cooking, driving and raising children unaided, as well as emotionally supporting their husbands and abandoning their own sporting pursuits, are characteristic of wives of recreational athletes in Australia. The wives of MCSC members also perform these tasks in addition to massage, healthcare provision and attending to their (grand)children's needs, which allows their husbands the freedom to spend time at the cricket grounds and cricket-related social activities every weekend from May to September. Thomas (2007, p. 114) observes that "Contemporary diasporic resources, while potentially drawing people together – materially or symbolically – in ways that are useful to them at particular historical moments, are never innocent of the broader conditions of power that shape their availability in specific sites at specific times." Afro-Caribbean-Canadian "widows" are unable to use cricket as a diasporic resource for a number of reasons related to their subordination within patriarchal societies and nuclear families.[3]

The widows' husbands are occupied with cricket for the entire summer, but for them it is not enough. Erol, a 55-year-old Barbadian-Canadian complains that they "only have this three months in a year": "In the summer, we only have cricket twice a week. We practise Tuesdays and Thursdays at [a Toronto] ground and then we play Saturday–Sunday. And if a holiday fall on a Monday we play that day too, Canada Day, Labour Day weekend we play a game also, but that's it." He minimises his participation, describing it as only "three months in a year" and only "twice a week," when he, in fact, practises twice each week and then plays two or three times each week. Moreover, the cricket season lasts from early May to late September, which is indeed five months. Some of the Mavericks drive over two hours – from London, to Mississauga, Ontario – for two-hour practices. Combined with hours of playing and socialising they could easily spend over 30 hours away from home each week, burdening their wives with domestic and (grand-)childcare responsibilities. Some of the wives who attend games bring their young (grand-)children with them. In my own experience, cricket games were a family event until I reached 8 years of age. Once my younger brother and I began weekend sport and dance programmes of our own, and preparing a picnic and activities for us to do at the cricket grounds for a whole day became more of a hassle for my mother than a joy, she stopped attending. My father, on the other hand, was able to continue playing for another decade without those family obligations.

Many women describe the impossibility of supporting both their partners' and their children's sporting pursuits. Eunice, a 46-year-old white English-Canadian woman, explains:

> I haven't been going to the games much since [Sandra] is getting older, since there's always something to do on the weekends. But when she was a baby or before she was born I used to [keep] score ... In fact, when they went on the trip to Jamaica I was pregnant with [Sandra], so I guess we took her to all the games back then ... But now at times they practise twice a week and then they play Saturday and Sunday so I don't see much of him so my friends say "Oh you're a cricket widow for the summer!" ... After they finish playing [cricket] they play dominoes, and that's when it takes even longer ... But over the years I've grown to live with that ... I'm usually the one that ends up taking [Sandra] to basketball. He misses out.

Jean, a 48-year-old black Jamaican-Canadian, explains that her son Jamal is now her first priority.

> I'm usually with [Jamal]. There's no choice any more. I'm usually with him, I mean before when he was much younger, yes we were at every game whether it be Saturday and Sunday we were always there ... and when he got into his baseball more competitively less and less we would go to [my husband's cricket] game, because somebody has to be with [Jamal].

Eunice and Jean do not experience attending their children's sports games instead of their husbands' as a choice. They "live with that" because "somebody has to" care for their children. Eunice did not grow up indoctrinated into Caribbean "respectable" femininity; however, some mores of motherhood (and patriarchy) are cross-cultural. These women's sense of responsibility to their children and domestic spaces are immutable.

Many of the Mavericks were pleased with the fact that their wives and girlfriends give them the space and time they need to enjoy being a MCSC member. Thomas, a 44-year-old Barbadian-Canadian commented:

> I used to think about it every once in a while. Like, "Why doesn't my baby come and watch me every once in a while?" You know, it's OK. I have no problem with that … [My wife] is definitely not a cricket fan. I guess for her it's like being idle … She would prefer to do something else with her time … [but] she's the type of lady that, you know, it doesn't bother her that I'm with the guys … For me, to be able to play cricket every day, let's say on the weekend, among friends, I love that … for my wife to give me permission to go … That's one thing about that side of her personality I love. To me that is very attractive … Every cricketer needs a wife like that. (Thomas)

Roland, a 51-year-old black Guyanese-Canadian, also echoed these sentiments. He has a wife who gives him his "freedom":

> **Roland:** When we start having children she choose to stay home and she understands cricket was in my life before her. And I love her, but cricket is still (pause)
> **Janelle:** The first love?
> **Roland:** Well, if you want to put it that way. It was there before her and she understands that … You know I get home and I'm very sore and limping and stuff like that and she'll look at me and say "You're enjoying the game aren't you?" and I'll say, "Shut up, you know I'm suffering." She will make me beg for a back rub (laughs). But I beg. And I get one.

Their wives "give permission" and "understand" that cricket is important to the Mavericks and facilitate their play, especially because cricket was in their lives first. Roland sees his wife's decision to stay home as a "choice." She was away from the games caring for his children, and now that their kids are adults she continues to perform labour in the form of massage (and cooking, cleaning and laundry) to enable his sports participation. I wondered if there was an activity in her life before him. If there was, it probably remains firmly in the past, since she must devote herself to domestic work while her husband revels in the camaraderie, memories, homosociality and conviviality of the Afro-Caribbean diaspora at the cricket grounds.

Approximately 40 per cent of the male club members are single and, of those, all but one were once married, but are now divorced or separated. While I cannot be sure that cricket played a role in the demise of their marriages, husbands and wives who are still married both expressed the critical importance of a woman's acceptance of the role of cricket in a man's life – even if that means "losing" one's husband for 20 hours or more each weekend in the summer. If *liming* is essential to recreating Afro-diasporic masculinity and men need women to grant them the freedom to do so without jealousy or feelings of possession, widows play an essential role in this community through their absences. As Sylvanie, a 60-year-old black Antiguan-Canadian told me: "I have no desire to interrupt his fun with the boys. He does his thing and I do mine."

Female club members described several differences between watching cricket in the Caribbean and in Canada. In their homelands, they had the option to bring their children to games. Alternatively, they had nearby family members to call on to help with childcare, or left their children to play in the neighbourhood. In Canada, they are limited in their ability to reproduce feminine Afro-Caribbean homespaces and to access sport, even as spectators, owing to a lack of support resources and discursive tools available for assistance with child-minding and domestic duties. Dominant middle-class Canadian discourses dictate that children must be supervised until 13 years of age, preferably in an arts or physical activity programme dedicated to their enrichment. All of the mothers I spoke to indicated that they do not have as much free time as their husbands to socialise on the weekends:

> At home [in the Caribbean], there's always someone to watch the kids. You can just say to the neighbours, "Mrs. Charles, I'm going into town," and she know that means she mus' keep an eye on the kids. Or else we would just go along with our parents to cricket, but here you can't do that. The kids get bored there all day, and besides you don't even know who your neighbours are half the time … So I just usually say let [my husband] go an' I stay home to watch them, pick up around the house. You know. That stuff has to get done. (Jean)

Nassy Brown (1998, p. 298) asks: "how do power relations within the diasporic space of particular black communities determine participation in the transnational space of diaspora that Gilroy calls the Black Atlantic?" In the case of the MCSC, patriarchal relations prohibit many women from full participation in community activities. The cricket grounds, and to a lesser extent, cricket trips are constructed as homosocial gathering places. Masculine mobility is important to the "routes" men aim to create, while their womenfolk "seem to represent everything good about 'black home' and its attendant values, domesticity and heterosexuality," as Stephens (2005, p. 146) writes of the black/Caribbean characters of Claude McKay's novel, *Home to Harlem*. While I do not wish to reinforce a strict home = respectability/street = reputation divide – as there are examples of men and women in the MCSC who defy this binary – it is clear that among MCSC members the distinct value systems described by Wilson (1973) for working-class Afro-Caribbean women and men still apply to the middle-class Afro-Caribbean Canadians. Women are functionally excluded or choose to stay away from the "reputation" value system of the street (or cricket field). This stricture on widows' participation in the club is further limited by Canadian mores, neoliberal structures and a culture that demands women's unpaid labour in a nuclear family setting.

Constructions of the black diaspora emphasise the ways in which Afro-Caribbean men's social institutions free them from nationalisms (see Edwards, 2001; Farred, 2003; Gilroy, 1993), but we must also consider the ways in which they are also freed from domesticity, childcare and women (Joseph, 2011a; Stephens, 2005). Widows surrender their men to the sport. These women's absences during cricket matches allow men to use the space as an arena for male bonding, the experience of which would be negatively transformed if their wives were there by their sides.

For the reason that participation in MCSC activities was as much about *liming*, talking and playing dominoes around the boundary as it was about actual cricket play, respectable women who chose to attend games were expected to navigate carefully the area around the boundary. Female club members were aware that their place at the cricket grounds was not beside their husbands, but at the periphery, with other women, thereby creating a segregated space for gendered reproduction of the Afro-diaspora. Women who did not conform to respectable ways of dressing, talking and occupying space were punished through gossip and social exclusion.

Gossipers

Of the few women who attended games, most admitted to caring little about the sport. I wondered why a woman would bother coming to the grounds and ignoring the game. Percelle, a black 41-year-old Grenadian-Canadian enlightened me about one reason for abandoning cricket "widow" status: "Wives who stay at home don't have a clue what's going on down here. There are a lot of women who would love to distrac' our husbands." She acknowledges that there are a number of chores she "should be doing" at home but while she is "working at home, another woman will be *wukking* the game, you know what I'm sayin'?" Her use of the word "distract" and play on the term work/*wuk* has been well rehearsed in the indigenous Caribbean music form, calypso. Lyrics use *wuk* to refer to sensual dancing or sexual intercourse and *work* to refer to domestic or industrial labour. The suggestion is that a woman can easily distract a man (i.e., get his attention) but must *wuk*/work hard to keep it. From Percelle's perspective, it is a wife's duty to regulate her husband's attention. A woman who is present at the grounds, but segregated from the male crowd can use her "absent-presence" to keep an eye on her partner. Percelle's husband, nearly 20 years her senior, is a "catch" that she is not willing to let slip away. Any woman who misses her cricket-dedicated husband has only one choice according to her: "If you can't beat 'em, join 'em! ... Let me tell you, for five years I was miserable, complaining. He's out all weekend, comes home late, too sore to do anything. Now I come out, find someone to chitchat with, have my drink an' my fun."

Percelle's expression, "now I come out" is significant in a Wilsonian understanding of Caribbean gender relations. Relegated to the home and inside spaces, she was a "respectable" widow, but lonely and burdened with caring for her young son on her own. Her efforts to constrain her husband's activities were futile. As the Caribbean calypso has long opined, a woman who tries to imprison a man in the home or yard is scathingly denounced for threatening a man's power and reputation. Percelle's only option to overcome her "miserable" condition was to enter the cricket ground space of "reputation," but in a limited way: making friends of her own to *lime* with and bringing her son along. He ran around with other children or when he was the only child (as was often the case) a male spectator chatted with him or threw a ball to him so that he could practise batting with his father's cricket bat. Given the lack of local opportunities for young children to play organised cricket in Toronto, and the popularity of sport for young boys, it is likely that her son will pursue another sport as he ages. Percelle has not yet experienced a conflict between her husband and son's schedules and easily made the transition from widow to what I have termed "gossiper."

Unlike male club members, who seem content to stand while they watch the game, or lean on a tree, rubbish bin, or their cars, female MCSC members always travel with canvas folding chairs or blankets to sit on. They bring coolers (insulated boxes) full of coolers (sweet, carbonated alcoholic beverages), ice, wine, beer, spirits and soda to drink. They also pack potato crisps, meat patties, pastries and fruits on which to snack, and novels, crosswords, Sudoku puzzles, knitting and crocheting to occupy their time. These women are marginally concerned about their husbands' on-field performances. Percelle told me "When we come down here we don't have a clue what's going on in the game, but we cheer when they cheer." For the most part, it is only an "expensive" over (when players score a lot of runs), that turns their attention to the field. Instead, the majority of the female MCSC members who attend games congregate around the periphery of the boundary to talk about retail sales, politics, fashion, childrearing, menopause, finance, romance, family members dispersed throughout the diaspora and a number of other topics pertinent to their lives. They discuss whose daughter is "in the way" (pregnant), who is sick with "the cancer," who is sending or refusing to send money home to their families, who is preparing to retire and who recently brought their parents up to live with them. Through these discussions, the values and concerns of the female members of the Afro-Caribbean diaspora become known.

A central topic of conversation revolved around club members' appearance and behaviour. Gossipers were quick to disparage unkempt women who should "know enough" to wear a hat or headscarf "with nappy hair like that," or men who are so intoxicated that they can't walk straight: "You know he smile 'cause he see four breast 'pon you!" Another favourite topic of conversation was the "shameless" single women who attend MCSC games and dances looking for love in all the wrong places. I was warned against appearing to be one of those "loose" or immoral women who wears skimpy clothing and befriends male club members in addition to being directed against appearing too "mannish."[4] When I cut my long, locked hair into a faux-hawk style and attended one game in a pair of cargo pants and a T-shirt without the make-up or earrings I usually wore, I was admonished by a few cricketers and many of the women at the grounds for "looking like a guy." I was told "You so tall, min' dey don' tek you for a man!" "Now I *know* you look like a boy." "Lawd! What happened to your hair? She look like Mr. T (laughs)!"

While changing my appearance was not an intentional ethnographic experiment, it offered insights into the gender dynamics of this sporting space. The female MCSC members made it clear that a masculine appearance is not acceptable for a woman, drawing lines around "proper" gender and sexual orientation at the same time. Percelle's explicit advice to bring a male partner to the ground to appear unavailable, and to be sure to "always wear long earrings wit' short-short hair" like mine also sent me a message that to gain the respect of these women, I had to perform middle-class, conservative, heterosexual, monogamous respectability. A double standard exists, however, as many male MCSC members, whether married or not, exhibited polyamorous behaviour and used their body and verbal language to mark themselves as "available." Their access to a reputation system that accrues status with each additional conquest, girlfriend and child made it in their best interest to be flirtatious.

When I asked Teresah, a black 58-year-old Jamaican-Canadian woman, about her friends in the club, she explained that at first it wasn't easy to make friends because "a lot of West Indian women don't talk fact" about the men in the club:

> You see dese Bajan women, dey out to destroy you. Dey call you an' say dey saw your man huggin' up so-and-so. Cha! (kisses teeth as an expression of disgust) When is real, people hush, hush, hush. Dat's why I told [Michael] "Do not give out our home number!" Me noh want none a dese petty women callin' me!

Teresah reinforces the idea that within Afro-Caribbean diasporic spaces, an unfaithful man can have a mistress without his wife's knowledge because the community is "hush, hush, hush"; that is, silent about the infidelity around his wife. She also notes that having a philandering husband, or more specifically a community that gossips about it, can "destroy" a woman. Implicit in this is an understanding that a man's reputation would survive such accusations. Her comments also draw attention to another of the disjunctures of the seemingly unified Afro-Caribbean diaspora. While women from her native Jamaica are often targets of abusive stereotypes in the Canadian context, she marks herself as not Bajan (from Barbados) and revolts against the spreading of rumours, half-truths and full lies, a characteristic she attributes to Bajan women. Inter-island rivalries and making boundaries around national identities were as common as coolers among women around the boundary.

Gossipers often distinguished themselves from "those blacks" who are constantly bringing shame to the Afro-Caribbean community. Some Bajan women explicitly reprimanded young black Jamaicans and lower-class (or "classless") black people, whom they described as "bad parents" who "don't control their children." Nearly every club member personally knew someone whose son was, as Jean described, "about to take a trip in the back of a cop car or a hearse." Though some club members engaged in the victim blaming so common in mainstream Canadian anti-black discourse, more common in this community were alternative stories of black youth success and good parenting (individual, neoliberal ways of understanding crime avoidance), as well as explanations of the structural limitations that hamper opportunities for success for many Afro-Caribbean people, young black men in particular.

Some Jamaicans distinguished their adult children from the stereotypes of the gun-toting gang member or welfare-abusing single mother by talking about their children's academic, employment and financial accomplishments. They were sure to share stories of their children choosing a university programme or earning a scholarship, purchasing their first home, or making money in the stock market. They discussed the after-school sport and martial arts programmes in which they enrolled their young children to teach them discipline and respect, as well as the tough love they doled out so that their teenagers would not grow to be lazy or foolish. There were a few gossipers who admitted knowing of "good people" who had "raised their boys right," but couldn't keep them away from "bad influences" such as drugs and criminal peers in their low-income neighbourhoods or secondary schools. Some of the mothers pointed out that Jamaicans commit only a small percentage of the crime. Jean, a 48-year-old black Jamaican-Canadian, defended her heritage, saying: "You see nowadays is not only Jamaicans. The Guyanese, Grenadians, I know they come up here and they can't find jobs. They move into a certain place and bam (claps hands). Trouble." That "certain place," club members were aware, referred to Toronto Community Housing, known to be high-crime and highly racialised locations.

These women noted the intersections of poverty, anti-black and anti-immigrant employment discrimination, and the lure of the criminal life for young black Caribbean-Canadians. Although the structural limitations can target black groups equally, the women's comments, and particularly efforts to distinguish themselves from "those Jamaicans" and "lower-class blacks" reveal that the stereotypes of Jamaican incorrigibility and lower class criminality that pervade mainstream Canadian society are also embraced and resisted by some people of Afro-Caribbean descent. My time at the cricket ground revealed that these stereotypes have prompted a crisis of identity among some middle-class Afro-Caribbean-Canadians and Jamaican-Canadians in particular who are under an imperative to prove they (and their children) are not dangerous, uncivilised or undisciplined.

In another example of drawing boundaries around particular Caribbean nations, a black Jamaican-American woman, Beatrice, who had accompanied a cricket team visiting for the weekend from the Bronx, New York, commented that they were missing the Caribbean Festival in New York on that Labour Day weekend, but she did not mind because the "Trinidadians an' dem always win." A discussion ensued comparing the New York and Toronto Caribbean festivals and the coup led by the "Trini organisers" in both cities. This discussion conjoined non-contiguous spaces as Caribbeans from Canada and the United States expressed their shared experiences. Non-Trinidadians claimed what was once a diasporic celebration of unity, emancipation and inversion, has become divisive, imprisoning and a replication of the status quo of the national politics of the Caribbean. They claimed people from the smaller islands, such as Antigua, Grenada and Nevis are unable to have their voices heard, their music played, or their achievements honoured. A few women mentioned that they stopped going out for Caribana events a long time ago, because, as Camila, a black 59-year-old Barbadian-Canadian put it:

> You go to a dance, and all you hear the whole night is calypso, soca ... Where you see Bajan [dance] is gonna be a little more mixed in the sense of they like the same kind of music [as Guyanese do], soul, slow, good music ... They would like the reggae an' stuff like that, right, and the dance music, but Trinidadians is mainly soca (laughs)! You get soca from the time you walk in until you get tired of it, you get a full diet of it.

There was resistance from one Trinidadian club member who claimed "Not true! All o' we mix up," meaning that Trinidadians are a hybrid group composed of many ethnicities with multiple musical preferences. Trinidadians rely on the metaphor of the callaloo and what Puri (1999, p. 17) refers to as "the language of 'multiculturalism' in attempts to manage difference by projecting an image of nonconflictual diversity ... Haunting all of these assertions is a recognition of the fragility of the 'we' of the race- and class-divided nations." Despite efforts to name Trinidadian and pan-Caribbean unity, "All o' we mix up" is not reflected in all of the gossipers' exchanges. Instead, they provide evidence that "[r]acial and nationalist discourses in the Caribbean ... offer contradictory instances of tearing apart and stitching together the people" (Puri, 1999, p. 17). The women who share their opinions, stories and experiences around the boundary of the cricket field provide innumerable examples of national hierarchies, discrimination and exclusions. The disjunctures of diaspora they reveal are reminders of Clifford's (1994) observation that nationalisms (or, for that matter, local hierarchies and conflicts based on class, village, or family politics) do not merely disappear, although we discuss diasporas as though they were unified entities.

Nassy Brown (1998, p. 298) points out a "serious elision in Gilroy's work"; that is, "the possibility that actors may assign mutually contradictory meanings to the black cultural productions they appropriate." Regarding American hegemony in British conceptions of blackness, she demonstrates the lopsided nature of Afro-Caribbean transatlantic cultural exchanges has resulted in antagonisms within the seemingly unified black community. The antagonisms in the Afro-Caribbean diaspora studied here include discourses of anti-Trinidadian hegemony. Because "almost every major city in North America and Britain has a Caribbean-style carnival that is in large part modeled after the one found in Trinidad" (Nurse, 1999, p. 661), some Trinidadian nationalists have gone to great efforts to claim the carnival's masquerading, calypso, soca and steel pan as "theirs," even in the face of great hybridity, cultural transformations and challenges from other Caribbean nations. The gossipers reveal more could be done to unpack Trinidadian privilege and honour the concerns of people from more marginalised Caribbean territories.

Trinidadians' version of imagined community conflicts with some Bajans' and Guyanese's more inclusive constructions according to the latter groups. Given that carnival has operated as a mechanism "for inverting, subverting and deconstructing the moral and philosophical bases of societal strictures, conventions and power relations, if only temporarily and symbolically" (Nurse, 1999, p. 665), it is no surprise that some members of the Afro-Caribbean diaspora see Caribana, or rather abstaining from the parade and associated dances, as sites to resist Trinidadian hegemony. These expressions of anti-Caribana sentiment are complicated by at least two other factors. The increasing restrictions in Toronto about how to engage in Caribana, for example the erection of physical barriers between revellers and audience, and changing of the parade route to a more peripheral location in the city, have emptied the parade of much of its meaning as a practice of freedom on the streets, especially for those who remember how it used to be in the early 1970s. Additionally, the ageing members of the MCSC are less and less able or willing to stand in the audience or walk the long parade route each year. Issues of age, local politics and national rivalries coalesce in understanding the reason for the declining participation among the MCSC members in this iconic Caribbean diaspora event.

Reggae is not soca, Jamaica is not Trinidad, and though music forms flow across national boundaries, they remain discursively linked to national identities. People from some Caribbean territories have more power than others, as a result of their population size and longevity in the diaspora, mobilisation as a group, class privileges and historical stereotypes. In some ways, the gossipers reproduce class, race, gender and nationalist systems by which they have been marginalised, as they put down certain groups within the Caribbean community in order to define themselves. They assert themselves as "proper" black women by pointing out the improper ones. "Gossipers" conversations demonstrate the fissures, rivalries and hierarchies of the Afro-Caribbean-Canadian community.

Lovers

Another group of women, the "lovers," regularly visited the cricket ground upon the invitation of certain male club members. Married and single men flirted openly, glanced at their bodies, lingered in their handshakes, and generously offered to drive them places, show them the city or take them to dinner. Flirting with women is a gender performance that is not necessarily expected to result in a romantic or sexual liaison for men in the Afro-Caribbean diaspora. Some single and married men flirt with and proposition women to disavow homosexuality, and demonstrate that they have "still got it" (sexual prowess) or could "still get it" (a woman's affection). The repudiation of male lovers allows for the categories *black, male* and *heterosexual* to become equated in this community.

Relatively young, attractive and/or scantily clad women can expect to be the greatest recipients of the Mavericks sexualised banter. In some cases, the Mavericks' flirtatious overtures were more than frivolous; rather, they were part of a plan to seduce interested and available women. On several occasions, I was asked for dances, dates and to be a girlfriend and even a wife! Though most of these flirtatious advances were not serious, in some cases my inability to feel comfortable or safe when alone with some participants led to curtailing our interactions (see Joseph, 2013). Some MCSC members carefully walk the line of in/fidelity when they are away from their wives at home games and when they travel for cricket. Angrosino (1986, p. 69), in his analysis of Afro-Caribbean masculinity, notes that even married men are expected to seek their "extra ginger" with "outside women" at one or more points in their lives. Furthermore, he is expected to brag of his sexual conquests, one of the great themes of the indigenous musical art form, the calypso, and a key feature of the Afro-Caribbean reputation system.

Although Wilson (1973) describes "reputation" as a value system engaged in by those lower-class men without access to the resources necessary to access "respectability," middle-class MCSC members also define themselves through this system at certain times and in certain spaces. Similar to Jack Alexander's (1984) findings on the Jamaican family, the behaviours of the MCSC members suggests that middle-class black men are embedded in two value systems simultaneously. They access "respectability" (coded as white, upper-class, stable, honest and oriented towards delayed gratification and family), by committing to a marriage, family and work and maintaining a primary home during the traditional work week. They may operate as principals, engineers or police officers, gaining the respect of the mainstream populace. On their weekends and cricket trips, however, they also access "reputation" (coded as black, lower-class, transient and oriented towards display, and for some, infidelity and deceit) whereby they maintain relationships with lovers. Historically, a black Caribbean sense of masculinity was forged in a liminal space between lower-class black slaves and the upper-class white British plantocracy, allowing the Afro-Caribbean (diaspora) middle-class to straddle both sides of what Wilson (1973) presents as a reputation–respectability dichotomy. Wilson's schema, while not omni-explanatory, is useful in demonstrating their related yet conflicting cultural practices.

On several trips, a few players left their "widows" at home and travelled with their girlfriends instead, clearly indicating another reason why players appreciate their wives' absences from cricket-related spaces. At one game, I sat with two women who pointed at male MCSC members around the field and adjacent area where spectators congregate. They indicated which married men had multiple partners and which women have been romantically involved with more than one of the Mavericks:

> Everyone knows he married and he sometimes bring his wife to big functions like a Christmas dance, but his girlfriend goes everywhere else with him. Watch, he introduce her by name, "This is [Sheila]." He doesn't say, "This is my wife," so most people assume she's his wife but she don't come to cricket. I knew his wife from back home. He's been with her for 20 years and the girlfriend for 15. (Teresah)

I asked the women if they would ever tell a wife about her husband's infidelities and they were vehement that such an intervention would be inappropriate because, first, it is "not their business" and second, "she must know." They exclaimed, "How could she not know?" "For 15 years (kissing teeth)?" "You see me? I'm not gonna be the one to rain on that parade!" "All she would have to do is come down here [to the cricket grounds] *one* afternoon. Just one. But in 20 years I never seen her so ..." Trailing off, Percelle suggests that a widow who "chooses" to remain uninvolved in her husband's affairs (e.g., hobbies and social circles) can expect that he might have an affair (extramarital relationship).

It is possible that a wife might be blissfully ignorant, but what is more likely is that a wife whose husband has "extra ginger" understands herself as in the superior relationship. I was told that some women are satisfied with their husbands' affairs as long as their husbands continue to provide for them and never embarrass them. While I never spoke with any woman who confirmed this as her personal experience, the gossipers were convinced that as long as a wife is enabled to maintain her respectability, her husband can access the polyvalent meanings associated with his gender. "Some men have very abundant *needs*, you know (winks)," Percelle quipped as she laughed. She suggested that a woman who can satisfy her husband sexually will not have to worry about him becoming a philanderer at the same time as she hinted at the fact that a wife might be thankful that she will no longer have to respond to all of her husbands' sexual or companionship desires.

Especially as Afro-Caribbean women age and experience menopause, what they want out of their marriage may shift. Indeed, they may be seeking their own "extra nutmeg" in their husbands' absence. Such an analysis is ripe for development based on future research that examines the intersecting relationships between ageing, heterosexuality, family and gender performances in the reproduction of race and culture in the Black Atlantic. To my knowledge, recreational sport (and its related social events and travel) has not been explored in depth as a significant factor in extramarital relationships. The commitment of some of the men to flirting, dating and consummating relationships with lovers they meet through a sport and social club sheds new light on the concept of the Afro-Caribbean diasporic family and the role of sport as one way in which "outside families" are created and maintained.

As women strive to reproduce their national and regional cultures in the diaspora, the gender performances linked to those identities are also reproduced. Gossipers do not criticise philandering men; rather, they point to lovers and wives as symbols of im/proper femininity. The lovers are easy to notice owing to their interactions with certain men, proximity to the playing field (and men's *liming* areas), or presence at certain times of day (or night). Gossip about lovers marks the boundaries of morally acceptable female sexuality and behaviour. "That woman knows about his wife. They used to work together. [She has] no class." They mark themselves as smart (un-dupable), classy women by their presence at the periphery of the grounds and long-term, (supposedly) monogamous relationships. They rest assured that no other MCSC member would be gossiping about them.

As single women passed by the Mavericks sitting around the boundary or at their hotels, some men called out, asked for a name or a phone number, whistled, or described what they liked about what they saw. One of the lovers, Bethany, a white Scottish-Canadian 45-year-old woman has been supporting the Mavericks for decades. She has had relationships with two of the players and openly flirts with many of them. For example, one afternoon Vilroy, a black 68-year-old Barbadian-Canadian was wearing a T-shirt with "Niagara" branded across the chest, purchased at his most recent trip to Niagara Falls with his grandchildren. Another player, Marshall thought it said "Viagra," and that Vilroy was advertising a pharmaceutical sexual stimulant. He began poking fun at Vilroy, questioning his virility, when Bethany astutely noted that if Vilroy was taking Viagra it would be beneficial to advertise, because a woman who might not give a man in his late sixties a chance might reconsider. Vilroy recommended that Bethany come to the games if she wants to see what his "bat" can do. Vilroy's metaphorical reference to his sexual organ continued the sexual innuendo but made it clear that he was not interested in her. This type of implicit/explicit sexual banter that women and men engage in at the grounds makes some wives suspicious of single women's intentions (suggesting that their husbands' intentions are always already known). Unlike Bethany's flirtatious advances, those by other women were well received by club members.

Yalancy, a black 49-year-old Barbadian-English woman attended a game in England and, after only a few hours at the cricket ground she had made a suitor out of one of the Mavericks. Although I had seen Oliver chatting intimately with her at the game while on tour, I was unaware that this relationship had fully blossomed until I arrived at a cricket game back in Toronto a few months later and ran into beautiful Yalancy in the woman's washroom at a plaza close to the cricket grounds. I recognised her face and was shocked to see her because in England she had told me that she did not care much for cricket and was only at the game because a friend had begged her to attend. Her friend knew that few of the players' wives would make it to the grounds for a weekday game and was desperate for some company. Yalancy wore a low-cut, floor-length summer dress and spent the majority of that game sitting in the clubhouse. She described the game as "dead boring" but had a happy consolation: "I met [Oliver], so I guess I got something out of it! (laughs)." She came to Toronto to visit her new lover for four weeks. Oliver received copious accolades for having such a beautiful woman cross the Atlantic to be with him and support him at all his home games. After he was late for one game and then got injured when a ball hit him in the lip, other players teased him that he had not had enough rest that Yalancy was too much of a distraction, and that if he could not handle such a voluptuous woman, he should give her up. Yalancy's quick wit typically tamed Oliver's peers. Nevertheless, this type of banter and joking, which objectifies many of the Mavericks' female lovers, reveals the power asymmetries among club members and among men and women in the Afro-Caribbean diaspora. Sexualised joking is an essential part of the relational performance of heterosexual masculinity in the Afro-Caribbean diaspora and in sporting spaces.

Another place the lovers are prominent is not at cricket fields, but at the Mavericks' social events, most of which involve drinking, music and dancing. As a person with a particular passion and talent for Caribbean dance, I often found myself on the dance floor at many of these events either on my own (and therefore being watched by club members) or partnered with one of the club members. If, as Walby (2010) asserts, the interview encounter requires reflexive analysis of moments when a researcher is sexualised by respondents, and the ways verbal and bodily responses to sexualisation influence meaning-making processes, surely the dance encounter warrants equal analysis. I observed many players and their lovers "getting on bad" on the dance floor. That is, they danced in a style known as *wining*, which involves circular motions of the hips, typically with bodies pressed close together. Elsewhere, I wrote:

> I wondered if the movements on the dance floor foreshadowed what would occur in their hotel rooms later. I remarked that they placed their hands on these women's lower backs, hips, or shoulders gently guiding the pace and the women complied with movements laden with cultural knowledge. (Joseph, 2013, p. 14)

and knew they might be thinking the same thing of me as I performed on the dance floor. I wanted to be seen as a cultural insider and friend to the players and knew that an authentic style of dance, an appropriate performance of blackness and femininity was essential for me to get inside this predominantly male club. However, I needed to walk a fine line with those men who also wanted to get inside me. I adjusted my distance and hip movements with different club members and over my time in the field. I was not interested in being one of the lovers, but through getting sweaty and exhausted on the dance floor, rubbing bodies with this ageing group of men, drinking, laughing and staying up into the wee hours of the morning with many of the players and their lovers, I gained credibility among participants and insights into the attraction of travel and the joy lovers bring to club members.

Acknowledging the fact that male club members rely on women to show themselves to be macho and heterosexual men forces one to think about the relatively undocumented sexualised histories that are part of the project of the Black Atlantic and the role of sport therein. Some of the flirting or relationships with female lovers may serve as a cover for homosexual affinities. Male lovers are conspicuously absent from these sporting and social spaces.

Supporters

"Supporters" are women who used to be "widows," may be "lovers," and occasionally join the "gossipers," but always invest their money and time in the club. Supporters come out to the Mavericks games to cheer for (or heckle) the players or to help the club with fundraising. They spend their time score keeping; cooking, serving and eating food; playing dominoes; drinking alcohol and travelling alongside male supporters. Layton, a black 48-year-old Barbadian-Canadian, explains, when the Mavericks "host touring teams … [or] go on a trip, that's when a lot of wives and girlfriends and friends comes out." At the second game of the tournament in St. Lucia, I was still new to the MCSC. I sat in the stands with one of the supporters, Teresah, a black 58-year-old Jamaican-Canadian. I asked her if she regularly attends the Mavericks' home games. She told me I would probably not see her in the summer because she does not usually attend home games. In fact, her husband is heavily involved in the organisation of the club but she prefers to remain uninvolved – unless he is going on a tour. Then she is a chief supporter of the club. Many women join the Mavericks' trips because they prefer diasporic tourism (i.e., sightseeing, relaxing, shopping, discovering heritage, or visiting their relatives) over watching cricket (Joseph, 2011b). Teresah has travelled around the world with the Mavericks, and in addition to touring new cities, one of her reasons for making the trips is "hotel security ... I trus' him, but I know how these fellas can get. I'm glad I'm here to keep an eye on him." She explains that her husband needs "support" in order not to drink excessively at the hotel and after games. After decades of trial and error, the couple learned that the best way to regulate Michael's behaviour was for Teresah to remain close by. Other than policing their husbands' behaviours, the majority of female MCSC supporters attend fundraising events, picnics, parties and dances because they remain dedicated to socialising and helping the club.

Hussein's wife, Sutara, joins him at most home games and on every trip. The 65-year-old Trinidadian-Canadian got to know the players in the 1980s, learned to score keep and stays involved in all the club events. Sutara acknowledges that the games are long, but says she has to "find some fun in it" and would not rather be anywhere else on the weekends. She travels with the club whenever they go to the Caribbean and sits in the makeshift stands to enjoy the sunshine and the company of friends. Eunice adds: "I used to play badminton, but then I learned to score keep to keep busy at the games. Now I'm just a spectator. I know how the game is played and I know exactly what's happening so once you understand that it makes it more exciting."

Approximately half of the women at the games are knowledgeable scorekeepers and this is an important way to be involved, and in some close games, the most important way of becoming involved in a game you are excluded from playing. There is usually one scorekeeper for each team and they constantly communicate with each other, the umpire and often unruly fans. I was encouraged to score keep early during my time in the field. I had to quickly learn the rules of the game and a technique for tracking the play. I also learned that one missed wide ball can mean the difference between winning and losing, and the difference between being inundated by the appreciation or anger of dozens of MCSC players and fans. It was also extremely difficult for me to observe and record the field of play and the cultural milieu at the same time. After a few games, I opted to focus my attention on the culture of the club by sitting in the spectators' area and declined the invitation to fulfil this feminised supporting role. However, the experience allowed me to understand how valued the scorekeepers are and how quickly the day can pass in this role.

Other than score keeping, some female MCSC members support the club by preparing traditional Afro-Caribbean food for the after-parties. Typical dishes included rice and peas, fried chicken or fish, provisions (plantain, breadfruit, yams), green salad, goat water or curry vegetables. They also sold tickets to the dances and helped to organise fundraising walkathons and banquets. At one game, Sheila, a black 52-year-old Jamaican woman impatiently watched her husband roam around the boundary, asking club members to buy a raffle ticket to support a fundraising initiative for a school in Trinidad. Sheila interrupted him because she felt his pressure tactics were insufficient. "Look, you goin' buy dis ticket, alright? It for helping children back home. You so selfish you noh want support kids? It don't matter what the raffle for, jus' give 'im de money! $12 for two tickets, alright?" Sheila took over the ticket selling and was sold out within an hour. When I asked her what the prizes were she admitted to me that she had organised some donations, but had yet to receive them. In fact, she was leaving the game at that moment to meet with a few retailers before heading to pick up her children from a party. Sometimes female club supporters are so busy with this unpaid labour, they are unable to attend games in their entirety, which is disappointing for some. Nevertheless, they continue in their subordinated roles because, as Sheila succinctly put it, "the men need help." For both nations and diasporas, Gilroy (2000, p. 83) attests that "the bodies of women provide the favored testing grounds for the principles of obligation, deference, and duty." At home games, the time of the afternoon was directly proportional to the number of women present, and there could be no doubt when it was six o'clock, as half of the women present for any game arrived at that time. They were there either to watch the last few (arguably the most exciting) overs of the game; set up the tables of traditional Caribbean food for the post-game meal; enjoy dinner; chauffeur their husbands, boyfriends, or fathers home; or all of the above. There could be no club without the sporting labour of the male players, but women's supporting labour is essential to creating the cricket ground as a comfortable homespace for all to enjoy.

Afro-Caribbean-Canadian women do not seem to spend much time reflecting on the "good old days." The majority of female MCSC supporters are not Windies cricket fans. They cannot name the current players and have no knowledge of where the most recent test matches took place. For the most part they have never played the sport and do not care much for professional cricket, yet this chapter has shown that the Mavericks entire sporting event really depends on their labour and (absent-) presence. Supporters keep the club running smoothly, maintaining a sense of authentic Caribbeanness as they adhere to gendered expectations of the community and preserve relationships across plurilocal homelands.

Although male and female MCSC members may be subsumed within the title Afro-Caribbean diaspora, "solidarities are sutured together, of course, by power inequality" (Hua, 2006, p. 193), and the overriding patriarchal structures in which they live enable and constrain male and female member's participation differently. Male cricketers depend on women for their performances of masculinity and are supported in their efforts by women. Women's verbal exchanges at the cricket ground reveal how they use sport spaces to bring their families and communities together at times. When Afro-Caribbean women kiss their teeth, use a gossiping mode of communication, express vernacular language such as patois, or touch each other as they talk, they transgress Canadian borders, dramatise the ideals of the group, and maintain a subconscious connection to their Afro-Caribbean roots and each other. In some cases, they espouse a philosophy of "one people, one nation, one destiny" (Guyana's motto), and express "a resolutely *postcolonial* moment of resistance to the bourgeois/western and traditionalist gender norms" (Noble, 2008, p. 123) of Canada, representing a cohesive, black community.

However, Hall (2003) and Gilroy (1993) point out how the boundaries of difference within diasporas are continually repositioned in relation to different points of reference. A seemingly carefree, cohesive community can never be entirely hierarchy-free, as our sport spaces are never free of the normalising pressures of the broader society. With closer investigation, the ways Caribbean people tear each other down and build up boundaries around their nation, sexual orientation or class group enable differences within the Afro-Caribbean diaspora to take on greater importance. Edwards' (2001, p. 64) use of the term décalage suggests that any articulation of the black diaspora is "inherently décalé or disjointed by a host of factors … diaspora can be discursively propped up (calé) into an artificially 'even' or 'balanced' state of 'racial' belonging. But such props," and the disarticulations they occlude, he continues, "must be considered a necessary haunting" (2001, p. 65).

To state that cricket is a diasporic resource for the Afro-Caribbean diaspora is to suggest that the sport is useful for both men and women. The cricket, the food and the convivial atmosphere provide a link to the culture and people of plurilocal homelands, and promote a black sport experience in a predominantly white nation. Yet, in many cases women are haunted by their exclusion from, or subordination within this sport and social club. At the same time, men's cricket games offer room for Afro-Caribbean women to interact with other women, speak freely in their native vernacular and demonstrate a sense of control over their circumstances. To say that women provide the labour and men reap the pleasure is overly simplistic. Many women enjoy sharing their culinary prowess with the group and must be understood as agentic subjects, especially when they create new fusion recipes or healthier versions of traditionally fat- and sodium-laden dishes. Nevertheless, female MCSC members' describe and enact class, sexuality and nationality hierarchies within the Afro-Caribbean-Canadian community, which reminds us to guard against celebrations of unity, hybridity and syncretism in the Afro-diaspora.

Diasporic community-making ventures rely on both unity and disjunctures. In the Caribbean context, any analysis of disjunctures must raise the question of Afro-Indo relations. Though MCSC is predominantly black, racial identifications do not exist in a vacuum. Race is situated, performed and understood as a historical and contemporary relational identity. In particular, at cricket grounds where black and brown bodies abound, the boundary around the Afro-Caribbean-Canadian community is propped up through comparisons to South Asian and Indo-Caribbean experiences. The following chapter explores what encounters with these diasporas also tell us about how the Afro-diaspora is décalé.

Notes

1 Only one woman, Maria, ever played cricket alongside the Mavericks. She was selected for the team that toured England based on her long-standing friendships with many of the players and her outstanding record in women's cricket in the Caribbean and Canada. For the eight-game event, she only participated in two games (in one she batted and fielded, in the other she was "twelfth man" meaning she dressed in uniform and would have substituted for any injured player). She became ill and sat out all remaining games. Maria was nominally treated with respect and a degree of reverence. She was always singled out during post-game speeches – even after games she did not play in – and her prior accomplishments in women's cricket were applauded. Although her official position as a team member marked her as "one of the boys," the homosocial nature of the team and constant reference to her role in *women's* cricket marked her as an outsider. Owing to her gender and, ultimately, her illness, she was relegated to lime with the female supporters in the pavilion.
2 As a female, feminist researcher, I could not help but be "turned off" by some of the men's rowdy and inebriated behaviours and comments, but exiting a research environment when participants' behaviour was detestable limited my capacity to collect the

very data I set out to find: on masculinity, Caribbean cultures and the makings of the Black Atlantic. This type of fieldwork, where sexist jokes are common, pressures to consume alcohol are tacit and overt, and participants are often intoxicated late into the night raises a number of questions regarding ethics and knowledge production. I have detailed struggles over how to document research findings of inebriated participants, when to leave a research setting, and how to protect participant and researcher safety in a heteronomative, sexist environment elsewhere (see Joseph, 2013; 2015; Joseph and Donnelly, 2012). It should suffice to say here that my choices of when and where to stay and go were informed by my desire to continue my research and my understanding of the masculine/feminine reputation/respectability divide in Caribbean homespaces as articulated by Wilson (1973). In order to continue to be welcomed into the community of predominantly male players as a good person to talk to such as a trusted friend, daughter, or granddaughter, I had to maintain a performance of Afro-Caribbean feminine "respectability." That is, to enter the men's "reputation" world and stay too late, drink too much, or worse, be paired romantically with one or more of the players, could ascribe the role of groupie, girlfriend, or mistress; a bad reputation; and, in my estimation, severely limit the data I hoped to collect in future. While I was unable to report on certain ways the players made boundaries around their masculinity and blackness at some cricket after-parties, I did this at the risk of protecting my safety and reputations as a respectable person, a researcher, and a woman.

3 Other reasons for disinterest in the sport could include the fact that few Caribbean female club members were encouraged to play cricket as youth and never developed an affinity for the sport. Additionally, many of the Mavericks were married to or dating women who were not of Caribbean descent and unfamiliar with cricket or the Afro-Caribbean masculine traditions of "sitting 'pon de grass all day.'" Still, they contribute to the making of an Afro-diasporic space with their absence.

4 This creates a conundrum for a young researcher, whose fashion choices in comparison to an older woman might be perceived as "skimpy" and who aims to befriend community members in order to have (in)formal interviews as part of the data collection process. In another study (Joseph, 2013), I explore the difficulty of performing Afro-Caribbean feminine respectability while carrying out research with men in marginally respectable spaces.

5

Diaspora space

This Is Not Cricket!

Listen son, you cyan mek your own choice. But I will never again play with those people. Let me tell you why. The round-robin tournament begin too early. It should come as no surprise, operating on Island Time as we do, that our game not starting on time. Most of us there by 9 a.m., but by the time we each had on our ointment, bandages, gears and whatnot, it was already 9.30. We batting first, so it not so bad that we still waiting on Otis and Sam, at 10 a.m. But they called to say they were on their way. We easily won the first game without them even batting. I think the opponents underestimated our skills. We ol' but we not frail! It was only 20 overs. We finished and on to game two of the tournament by 11.30.

Most of us West Indians playin' with a few Indian and Sri Lankan police officers, so I cyan't say I really shocked when there was trouble, but I had hopes for the best. I knew there were only two things the fellas needed to play well: sunshine and golden juice. You know what I'm sayin'? I had a cooler with plastic cups, ice and a Gatorade bottle full of Courvoisier. I know technically we were playing on the team that represented Law and Order, but a few sips of the good stuff is all we needed to get through the afternoon. And it was hot! You cyan't expec' all we dry out in the sun. Once Layton had a sufficient amount of what he called "blood thinners," he said he could easily bat his age. Yeah, he 48 but that's his reputation. He nearly did it too! We poured from the Gatorade bottle and sipped out of Tim Horton's mugs. No one had to know what we were up to.

Since the first innings of the second game, the smell of curry flooded the air so we knew lunch comin' up. At 2 p.m. we were finished. Victorious again. But by the time we made it to the food marquee, there was nothing left but the dregs of butter chicken and a few scant grains of basmati rice. The red oils pooled at the bottom of the chafing dish mocking us with the memory of the departed tandoori chicken.

Let me ask you this: was it merely a coincidence that the organisers forgot to save some food for the only black team in the tournament? Our opponents got. Everyone else got. What we got? Nothin! Charles, always known for speaking his mind, call out, "They probably figured we wouldn't eat that shit anyway!" They probably figured he was rude as he finished his third beer and threw the empty water bottle at the fence, near, but not in the garbage can. Charles went with the police team captain, Prasham, to Popeye's Louisiana Kitchen and returned with spicy fried chicken, biscuits and french fries. That fried chicken was delicious, see?. I'll take it over that tandoori nonsense any day.

Then get this. After lunch, they say the umpire slated to work our game busy on another field. That game was still at least one hour away from being finished, so the organisers tried to replace him with an umpire who was the opposing team captain's brother! They t'ink all we stupid? That's a conflict of interest! We got into it with the umpire and words was getting heated when he finally refused to work our match, calling us "a bunch of drunks." Can you believe it? Us? Drunks? Not a t'ing go so.

Marshall call out, "Indians organise and you see which games on television, who gets the good fiel' and the umpires!" And Erol screaming, "They forget all we lunch and all we umpire?! I don' need to fucking sit around and watch this jackass steal outs for the other team. This is not cricket!" You should a seen that scrawny ass hole organiser wit' he squeaky voice. "Listen, I will not stand for this. I cannot bring more food. The original umpire is busy on the main field! I can not bring the television crews to film this match. They are already set up over there. For your information, I'm not in charge of the drinking laws of the province either!" He repeated several times that there was to be "no drinking in the park." I had no patience for this little man wit' his beady eyes and his stupid rules. A little brandy ever hurt anyone? Half of the team grab up our gears and walk off the field. I don't know if they continued without us. I don't care. Like I said, you can play for who you want. Me? I done wit' dose people. I stop playin' wit' dem.

Afro-Caribbean-Canadians resist racism from whites whose homes line the cricket fields on which they play. But this is not the full extent of race relations in Toronto cricket. There are other transnational histories and crucibles of diasporic trajectories "where Europe is not at 'the center' – which retain a critical bearing on understanding contemporary diasporic formations and their inter-relationships." Thus, it is necessary to deploy "diaspora space," which is a concept introduced by Avtar Brah (1996) to explore the lateral connections between diasporas – the ways "in which different historical and contemporary elements are understood, not in tandem, but in their dia-synchronic relationality" (p. 190). Diasporas can be understood based on their unities, disjunctures and their relationships to other groups. We must take a range of diasporas into account to understand the Afro-Caribbean diaspora.

The narrative "This Is Not Cricket," shared above, captures the bellicose and racist ways the Afro-Caribbean Mavericks referred to and interacted with Indians, Bangladeshis, Pakistanis and Sri Lankans (hereafter, South Asians) in Toronto's cricket spaces. It is the result of observations made at a local tournament combined with stories told to me by one elderly black Barbadian-Canadian club member, Warlie, who sometimes played alongside his 47-year-old son in friendly Master's games. I have no interest in either endorsing or excusing the Mavericks racist comments. Rather, I present their discriminatory words and capture their disempowered feelings to set them against a context of historical and contemporary Indo-Afro relations in the Caribbean and its diaspora. Their description of what is "not cricket" (not fair) at the cricket grounds highlights not only challenges to the socially constructed rules of the game, but also challenges to the socially constructed boundaries around their communities. Analysis of racialised and ethnic difference, Peake and Trotz (1999, p. 5) write of Guyana, "is not simply about different people with disconnected ways of doing things but rather about unequal access to power, about the relations through which differences are produced and reified." A range of fusions and new categories are created when people from different cultures meet. However, there may also be resistance to a mestizo identity, refusal to integrate and rejection of creolised cultures, based on historical antagonisms between groups. Hannerz (1997, p. 8) reminds us there "may be a preoccupation with cultural autonomy and the defense of a cultural heritage for its own sake, yet frequently this rhetoric of culture is closely linked to power and material resources as well." This chapter outlines the ways in which language, food, music, alcohol and cricket rules are used to create boundaries around the Afro-Caribbean community that excludes not only South Asians, but also Indo-Caribbeans.

Historical Indo-Afro Caribbean relations

Brackette Williams (1991) alerts us to how individuals continue to interact with people of other ethnic groups based on meanings of earlier periods. Today's hierarchies are

> constructed along paths well-trod by Europeans centuries earlier as they fashioned themselves into different races, nationalities, and nations ... if we are to provide informative accounts of [people's] struggles ... we must take into consideration the complexities of historically constituted interpretations of the nature of social and cultural interchanges. (1991, p. 15)

The history of Indo-Afro relations in the Caribbean is not incidental to the story of the Mavericks and sport in the Black Atlantic. Interactions with people of Indian heritage is foundational to the creation of boundaries around black Caribbean identity.

This history begins in a context where East Indians arrived in the Caribbean, in significant numbers especially in Guyana and Trinidad, as indentured labourers to replace enslaved African labourers after the abolition of slavery in the 1830s. The social subordination of both these groups in relation to European colonisers, their subsequent battles for power within postcolonial nation building projects, Indo-Caribbean subordination at the hands of Afro-Caribbean nationalists in nearly every territory, alongside creolisation of unequal social and cultural elements in the Caribbean and the diaspora politic must be included in any examination of Afro-Caribbean people and diaspora cultures.[1] In Trinidad, for example, where the descendants of enslaved Africans and indentured Indians comprise 34.2 and 35.4 per cent of the population respectively (Central Statistical Office, 2011, p. 94), calls for cultural unity belie intense economic, cultural and political competition between the two groups. Munasinghe (2001) shows a political movement to break free from neo-colonial political practices – in which government decisions were dictated by the economic interests of white and black middle-class elites – initially attempted to include lower-class Africans and Indians in solidarity; however, conflicts among ethnic groups at all class levels eventually divided the country. The black "majority" retained ownership and control of the government and economy, thereby subjugating the Indo-Trinidadian population.

In Jamaica, Africans are reported to have resented Indian competition for work and wages, and feared that Hinduism and Islam would have adverse cultural influences (Shepherd cited by Mohammed, 2009: 62). In Barbados, Indians are reported to have perceived Africans as lazy, materialistic and prone to criminal activity (Beckles, 2004). Across the Caribbean, what were once black lower class cultures such as calypso, were promoted to the stature of regional symbols, thereby making the ruling group ethnically 'invisible' as a consequence of its claims to represent mainstream national culture.

In a cricket context in particular, Afro-Indo conflicts were at a peak as the predominantly black Windies team ruled the world in the 1970s and 1980s. It is well known that Indo-Trinidadians and Indo-Guyanese fans commonly supported the team playing against the Windies if there were no Indo-Caribbean players on the Windies, as was generally the case during this period. Indo-Caribbeans were significantly marginalised from elite playing opportunities and the Indian national team, depicted by the black dominant group as weak and feminised in contrast to strong, fast, masculine black players, constitutes an important way the Mavericks understand their own embodied black sporting masculinities. Important for this study is also the increasing migration of South Asians to Toronto including areas such as Peel Region, with more wealth and political power than black groups who have been there for decades. The more recent decline of the Windies and improvement of South Asian teams in international cricket also shape the ways in which these older black men resist encroachment on what they believe are "their" cricket.

As Carrington (2007, p. 52, emphasis in original) has noted about identity, drawing on the work of James Clifford and Howard Winant, "identity needs to be understood as a strategic intervention by marginalised communities for cultural, political, and economic *recognition.*" That recognition may be sought from other black groups, dominant white groups, or the South Asian diasporas. Therefore, any study of contemporary Afro-Caribbean culture and politics must account for the historical ways in which Afro-Indo relations are loaded with the previous politics of slavery, indentured service and postcolonial nation-building projects in the Caribbean as well as contemporary issues of Windies decline and increasing South Asian migration to Toronto. This analysis extends the concept of the Black Atlantic beyond an inward-facing focus on shared transnational cultures and racial terror to an outward facing focus on relational boundary making and the real and symbolic violence enacted by blacks.

Space invaders

The Mavericks have vituperative interactions with South Asians who are portrayed as invaders because they use cricket spaces to perpetuate their own cultural heritage and gender performances. We know that ethnic groups generate boundaries around themselves based on shared criteria for evaluation. Their contrast to groups with other criteria for judging values, heritage, gender and ethics allows boundaries to be delineated. Importantly, contact with other groups is necessary to clarify where the boundaries are and to structure "interaction which allows the persistence of cultural differences" (Barth, 1998, p. 16). In the diaspora context, then, conflicts among the predominantly black Mavericks and other South Asian teams and tournament organisers, as well as disagreements among differently identified MCSC members over music, language, food and alcohol consumption at the cricket ground challenge our understanding of the Afro-Caribbean-Canadian diaspora as an independent group. And, while we may be eager to explore relations with African-Americans and black British men, we must acknowledge that diasporas are complex, multi-generational, ethnically heterogeneous, constructed in relation to other diasporas and embedded in historical and local contexts.

The Mayor's Cup (which originated in 1998, sponsored by the cities of Mississauga and Toronto) was spurred by a number of South Asian municipal councillors and members of the Federal and Provincial Parliament from the suburban cities of Toronto: Brampton and Mississauga. These cities in Peel Region are affectionately (and by some, pejoratively) referred to as "Bramladesh" and "Mississaugistan" for their rapidly increasing South Asian populations. The organiser, Akash, claimed the "aim of the tournament is to recognise and encourage the sporting contributions of ethnic minorities in the city." Although Caribbean boys and men had been playing cricket in Toronto for nearly two decades prior to the inaugural Mayor's Cup, it was not until South Asian politicians were willing and able to organise the event, find sponsors and gain media coverage that cricket came to be recognised as an important sport for the region's ethnic minority groups. The Mayor's Cup occurs at a multi-field venue with four simultaneous games. The event opens each year with a speech by the organisers and local politicians and then Toronto Mayor David Miller, an avid cricket fan, participated in a symbolic over in 2008. The Mavericks were invited to play in the Mayor's Cup via the Toronto police team, which always has a berth in the tournament among seven other predominantly South Asian teams.

The police team has always played friendly games and was once comprised predominantly of Caribbeans, but is now run by South Asians. "I captained the police team for 10 years" Vilroy, a 68-year-old black Barbadian-Canadian, claimed:

> It used to be 95% West Indian ... But as guys retired, not too many West Indians came up to replace them. They rely on immigration from cricketing nations to fill the spots. That's why you see so many Asians on the team now. In the 1970s and 1980s there was more immigration [from the Caribbean] and more black players. (Vilroy)

Many of the Caribbean police officers who started working for the police force in the 1970s, including Vilroy, have retired from it and/or from cricket. Nevertheless, a number of MCSC members still come to watch the police games and socialise with their friends and some are recruited to play when the police team's numbers are low. In 2008, four South Asian police officers joined ranks with eight Afro-Caribbeans (current and former officers and their friends) for the Mayor's Cup.

At every public park in Toronto, public drinking is prohibited. The Mayor's Cup featured no obvious sharing or selling of alcohol or food from cars in the parking lot. There was no loud music playing during the game and the atmosphere was serious and competitive, rather than the joking, festival atmosphere of typical Maverick matches. The cultural influence of the organisers was seen and heard at the tea break: aloo gobi (potatoes and cauliflower) and naan (flat bread) were served along with tandoori chicken and rice, and the classical music of Pandit Hariprasad Chaurasia was played over the loud speakers. Some of the Mavericks managed to drink in a clandestine fashion out of water bottles, coloured plastic cups and coffee mugs. Their surreptitious actions were noticed and they ended up in conflict with the tournament organisers and some of their own South Asian police officer teammates.

"You cannot drink beer here!" Akash, one of the organisers, passed by the Maverick's bench to remind them. "You see dis?" Otis, a black 47-year-old Barbadian-Canadian, indicated the clear blue skies and warm weather, as well as his frustrations with the organisers. "All dis an' me cyaan't even have one beer?! Raaaas!" Erol echoed his sentiments "Raaaas! What is the point of the weekend?" Akin to Caribbean women's kissing of their teeth, the expletive "Raaaas!" indicated frustration among many of the Caribbean men in the club.

Akash explained, "I don't make the laws, but we have to follow them" Otis promptly replied, "I ain't following no Indian nowhere," which resulted in a momentary stand-off before the Indian-Canadian police team captain, Prasham, interrupted the palpable tension and the tournament organiser walked away. As Akash left, he called out, "You are here to score runs, leave the celebrating for after!" That led to an explosion of expletives among the Mavericks: "Listen to this jackass!" "You gotta be kiddin' me!" "Fuck him an' all dese coolies" "Try an' stop me!" The Mavericks grumbled in disbelief that their fun was being curtailed. Though none of the current police officers was drinking, it was clear that outsiders were policing the "police team."

This argument must be situated within a context of Caribbean culture, which members of the Afro-Caribbean diaspora strive fervently to replicate; historical and local politics and entrepreneurial power, from which black Canadians have been effectively marginalised; and international cricket politics, in which the Mavericks are embedded as fans. Their imperative to relax on the weekends and celebrate cricket with "one beer" during, rather than after, the game, exposes the degree to which they are assimilated into the typical Canadian working week from Monday to Friday. The "point of the weekend" is to relax and turn that world upside down. The world of carnival, as many writers on the theme have stressed, is a negation or subversion of the structures, hierarchies and values that obtain in society during the rest of the year. Carnival is 'the world turned upside down'" (Burton, 1995, p. 95). For these Caribbean men and women, cricket spaces are carnival spaces that allow for a make-believe counter-society. If they spend their weekdays in paid and unpaid employment, ruled by the clock, stress and a (in many cases white) supervisor, MCSC members negate those norms on the weekends at cricket matches. They aim to enjoy themselves, abandon oppressive rules and be with people like them. They use the cricket grounds as a venue in which to relax. For them, drinking is an essential component of relaxing and performing black masculinity.

Warlie, exasperated, walked away from the field as fighting erupted among his black and Indian team members. I followed him and asked his opinion about the disagreement. At 50 years of age, he had been frustrated that the South Asians were "too aggressive and too cliquey," prompting him to leave league cricket:

> Just about 20 years ago I switched to friendly games … The reason for that is in my late stages they had (pause) there were lots of (pause) I don't want to say (pause) Indians and Pakistanis and Sri Lankan people coming … They're very aggressive. They're a very aggressive people and they want to fight. They come to the games and change the rules. When the decisions don't go their way they want to fight the players, they want to fight the umpires, and that's when I realised that's not for me and I left and I joined the older group, my age group and I play friendly cricket.

Warlie had vowed to play cricket only with his age group and only with other Caribbean players and is comfortable in that environment at the age of 70:

> I used to play for Police, but their style of cricket don't suit me because the police team has black people, white people, Indian people, and I find dat I used to play with them. When the black guy's runnin' the show, you get a game. But then the Indian guy he takes over, and then the next thing he does he bring all his Indian friends to play …Then you know there will be some fight like this … I say "no thank you." I came today because [Arnold] ask me, but mark my words, today … I stop playin' wit' dem.

Arnold, a 63-year-old black Barbadian-Canadian who continues to work for the police services, remains one of the few links between the Mavericks and the Police Club. His overt attempts to keep the peace between his two communities are increasingly futile. Warlie's frustrations demonstrate that unlike the "fights" MCSC members have among each other, where they act miserable, yell, swear and ridicule each other, but always walk away as friends, the loud exchanges with South Asians are laden with an animosity that is not resolved. MCSC members criticise South Asians for being too cliquey, competitive and argumentative. While these acts are seen as uncivilised and "not cricket," MCSC members remain comfortable with their own yelling, drinking, swearing and cliquey behaviours. In fact, these behaviours are how they define their black masculinities, which is relational to South Asian masculinities. As Brah (1996, p. 183) states: "The manner in which a group comes to be 'situated' in and through a wide variety of discourses, economic processes, state policies and institutional practices is critical to its future. This 'situatedness' is central to how different groups come to be relationally positioned in a given context."

From a historical point of view, Afro-Caribbeans were situated as antagonists to Indo-Caribbeans. As Caribbean planters faced the prospect of the end of indenture, any hint of solidarity between black and Indian labourers "was speedily crushed ... [and] images of the shiftless, lazy African and the industrious coolie [Indian] circulated with increasing frequency" in Trinidad (Niranjana, 2001, p. 262). Throughout the Caribbean, Indo-Caribbeans stereotype Afro-Caribbean men as having an overly strong emphasis on *liming*, socialising and conspicuous consumption. People with Indian heritage, in contrast, are seen as obsessed with work, highly organised and financially stingy. It is in relation to these differing stereotypes and self-descriptors of ethnic groups within a Caribbean setting that we must read interactions between the primarily black Mavericks and their South Asian teammates and tournament organisers in a diasporic setting.

In just a few decades, many South Asians have transformed their transnational migration experiences into successful businesses that sponsor the Mayor's Cup, successful careers in mainstream Canadian politics, and successful media outlets such as the Asian Television Network, which covers the tournament. Their entrée into business and politics in Toronto stands in contrast to Caribbean-Canadians, who have historically been excluded from these fields owing to economic constraints and racism (Henry, 1994). Caribbean migrants who have been playing cricket in Toronto for twice as long have significantly fewer resources at their disposal. Now that they are (nearing) retirement age, they are even less likely to mobilise resources to secure their own grounds, build clubhouses, or organise large-scale, televised tournaments. Nevertheless, retrieving and claiming space for cultural autonomy remains one means of survival within Canadian society for both of these marginalised ethic groups.

If the everyday stories we tell ourselves, individually and collectively, come to stand for who we are, it is clear that the Mavericks tell themselves they are not like South Asians. The groups' alternate definitions of sport – as a space of leisure or competition, as a place to use business contacts and political resources to build up the local profile or to relax and enjoy oneself – demonstrate that sport is always a dynamic object of struggles, with various groups vying for the capacity to impose the legitimate function of sporting activity. For the Mavericks, who choose only to play "friendly cricket," that legitimate function includes celebrating black culture through music, food and drink, whenever possible.

The most skilled of the Mavericks play friendly games with the MCSC and continue to compete on league teams. When I inquired, "What is the biggest difference between friendly and league teams?" Riddick, a black 54-year-old Barbadian-Canadian, immediately responded, "Bus trips! A lot of Indian guys don't travel. That's their culture. The bus trips are black trips." But, I interjected, "What about [Michael]?" Michael is a 56-year-old Indo-Guyanese-Canadian who is always present on the bus trips Riddick described. In fact, Michael is one of the informal team social coordinators and often recruits people for dances, parties and bus trips. Riddick clarified: "[Michael] goes everywhere. He is the blackest black man on the team!" Riddick tried to clarify, "He likes to dance and party. Indians don't drink. They wouldn't fit in so we don't invite them." He points out two important aspects of Mavericks cricket: travelling and drinking, and labels these activities "black."

The majority of club members self-identified as black, though the full range of phenotypes and ethnicities found in the Caribbean were represented. More important than any biological or essential definition of blackness is the hegemony of black culture in the majority of the Caribbean territories (Segal, 1993), in Windies cricket (Devonish, 1995), and in the Caribbean diaspora (Joseph, 2014).[2] Black is used not to refer to African heritage, or dark skin, but as a marker of Caribbeanness. Or, as Niranjana (2001, p. 261) put it: "[i]n spite of the ambiguous nature of the relationship between nation and nationalism in the West Indies, what is evident is the Afrocentric basis of the claim to being West Indian." The Caribbean diaspora is reproduced through the same hegemonic processes that promote and privilege black culture (e.g., carnival, steel pan and calypso) and identity as "authentic" across the Caribbean region, and suppress the cultural expressions of other groups (Brereton, 1979; Hintzen, 2002; Mohammed, 2009; Munasinghe, 2001). While there are of course, many "Indians," (both Indo-Caribbeans and people from the subcontinent) who drink alcohol, Riddick uses the biased idea that drinking is "black" to justify his club's exclusionary practices. Only those who embrace Afro-Caribbean culture, such as Michael, were welcomed "while the Mavericks ignore, subordinate and exclude expressions of Indo-Caribbean identity such as abstaining from alcohol, or listening to chutney-soca, Bhojpuri, or bhangra music, because they don't "fit in" on the bus trips" (Joseph, 2014, p. 680).

Cricket is an area in which the signifier "Caribbean" is internally contested in Canada. Rather than flying to Trinidad or Guyana to experience racial antagonisms, one merely needs to drive to the suburbs of Toronto. There, it is likely that a man like Michael will cite the Black Stalin calypso song "Tonight the black man feelin' to party/ tonight the black man feelin' to jam" in reference to himself, despite his Indian heritage. Similarly, Lawrence, who has Spanish and Portuguese ancestry and light skin once exclaimed, "All o' we black, you know. In Canada dey tek a look at me and dey don't know I black till I start talkin' ... That Negro culture *is* Trini. I go die black, you know."[3] These claims seem to expound racial solidarity between Afro-Caribbeans and other ethnic groups when, at the same time, they conceal racial antagonisms. If Lawrence entered the Mavericks spaces and tried to assert a white Caribbean identity, or advocate for creole (as opposed to "negro") culture, his membership might be short-lived.

One man who has been an MCSC member and cricket player for nearly 30 years was born in Pakistan. He describes himself as an "adopted West Indian" and over the past three decades has learned to perform Afro-Caribbean masculinity alongside MCSC members. Another member, a 68-year-old white man, learned to play cricket in his native England and has occasionally played with the Mavericks since the early 1980s. He stated, "If you join a black club, that's what you expect," with reference to the Mavericks dancing to soca for hours after their games. He was careful to avoid asserting English ways of playing and celebrating, or vying for a leadership role in the "black club," despite his 25-year tenure, because of his racially subordinate position.

Each of the Mavericks is "black" in relation to the white dominant group in both Canadian society and the South Asian dominant group in cricket. White- and Indo-Caribbeans, Pakistanis and English players are included in MCSC activities only insofar as they are willing to perform and adopt "black" Caribbean culture, defined as dancing, partying and drinking. One exception to this is Indo-Caribbean music with an emphasis on *liming*; for example, chutney-soca, a carnivalised expression of Indo-Caribbean culture, from artists such as Ravi B. and Hunter.[4] Puwar's (2004) advice to pay attention to which bodies are missing or "out of place" helps to hone my focus on the ethnic groups absent from the bus, the cricket pitch, or the Mavericks social events. Because older South Asians and Indo- and Afro-Caribbeans are equally fervently passionate about cricket, we might expect more ethnic mixing within teams or between opponents. Especially as the Mavericks age and are desperate at times for local opponents of their age and calibre, it might be helpful to have an Indian or Sri Lankan team against which to play. However, language, food, age, religion, drinking and other cultural differences lead to conflicts among the groups.

Barriers of language, food and drink

Verbal misunderstandings between Afro-Caribbean and South Asian cricketers were one of the most common reasons given to justify why the Mavericks' segregate themselves from local South Asian teams. Riddick, a black 54-year-old Barbadian-Canadian claimed that at the cricket ground "Indians speak in their own language. You know, this makes me really, really upset. I don't know why they do this. It creates a barrier. Are they saying things they don't want us to know?" He was vehement that "we are in Canada" and he communicates in English "so that should be the language on the field!" Hussein, a 66-year-old Indo-Trinidadian-Canadian, reported feeling excluded by South Asians when he attempted to join a league team in Mississauga: "The Indians tend to speak their language all the time, although they can all speak English. Don't know if that was a power thing, to 'don't let other people know what I'm talking about' you know? … They just shut you out. And they just keep you out." Hussein's position as an Indo-Caribbean man made him acutely aware of the differences between Indians and Indo-Caribbeans and the linguistic barriers he experienced fuelled his attachment to the MCSC and a Caribbean identity: "So I just come here [to Mavericks' games] and stick with the West Indians."[5]

Wesley's experience was similar. The black 57-year-old Jamaican-Canadian was eager to continue playing competitive league games, but saw the influx of South Asians as a problem. He considered moving to another team because of the shifting demographics in Brampton: "There are only five West Indians left and all of the other 195 club members are Pakis. There are too many and I can't understand what they're saying half the time." My discussions with Wesley and others about their use of the term "Indian" to refer to all South Asians and the derogatory name "Paki" revealed (1) an assumption on their part that I, as a racial insider, would not be offended, and (2) their feelings of anger and disempowerment in what were once "their" spaces. South Asian players increasingly use local grounds as their population in Toronto continues to grow rapidly. Between 1996 and 2001, for example, the number of people in Canada who reported a South Asian origin rose by 33 per cent (Lindsay, 2007b, p. 9), whereas over the same time frame the Caribbean population grew only 11 per cent (Lindsay, 2007a, p. 9), with the majority moving to Toronto. With this increase in population came an increase in the use of a variety of South Asian languages in cricket spaces.

The Mavericks resented the ways in which South Asians turned "their" cricket grounds into Bengali, Hindi, Tamil, or Urdu spaces when there are fewer and fewer places in which Caribbean people can comfortably speak in their native languages in Canada. Despite the Mavericks' admonishments that South Asians should speak "proper English," the Mavericks chose to speak in a combination of Canadian English and their native languages, fusions of the English or French of the colonisers of their respective islands and territories and the West African languages of their ancestors. When I sought him out after a game in order to conduct a formal interview, George, a 47-year-old Barbadian-Canadian, replied "me noh wan' fall dung you know! Leh we go fin' some food an' t'ing" (I don't want to faint. Let's go find something to eat). He put on a thick accent when he discussed food, which foreshadowed the delicious traditional Bajan meal he was about to eat. His predominant use of patois or speaking English with a Caribbean accent at the grounds with his peers directly contrasts with the Canadian English that he chose to speak in his daily work as a Registered Nurse and while I formally interviewed him: "Janelle, I've been here since 1986 and this is a multicultural society, I get that, but my free time is spent predominantly with black people. That's my preference and I make no apologies for that. This is my club." His ability to speak both languages fluently evinces a duality that can be framed as bi-national belonging, acculturation and double consciousness. His disdain for hearing languages other than those of his community evinces his use of cricket grounds for much more than sport.

Nakamura (2009, p. 100) explains that although shifting accents can be endearing or friendly, done to "tease" an outsider, it can also be used to exclude. While I could understand most of what they were saying, when the Mavericks were keen to say something (often private, sexist, lewd, or racist) they did not want me to hear, understand, or record in my field notes, they would pour their accents on thickly, or use terms I was unfamiliar with, to mark me as "Other" and exclude me from conversations. The Mavericks' own resistance to using "proper English" may keep South Asians away. At the same time, South Asians use their own languages to create a boundary around their communities and exclude black people from conversations. In Western societies, Caribbean languages and accents are banished to the domestic realm or "black space" (Carrington, 1998), in which Caribbean people are separated from non-speakers and feel comfortable to use their native tongue without being judged. Language is yet another way the boundaries around Afro-Caribbean-Canadians are drawn. When the linguistic boundary is challenged, an opportunity arises to reflect on what makes these black Canadians unique and what makes them feel safe in a black Caribbean homespace.

In addition to barriers of language and accents, the ways club members use language is incomprehensible for, or unappreciated by, outsiders. Afro-Caribbean men experience an inextricable link between talking and drinking, playing cricket and eating at the same time. Their talking also involves aggressive and derisive joking and making lewd or racist commentary. For them, the content of the words with which they communicate is less important than the style of their delivery (Abrahams, 1983) and cricket is a space in which talking is used to develop and express their gendered "reputation" values (Wilson, 1973). The amount of time the Mavericks spend making fun of the ways South Asian men talk indicates that particular communication modes are valued. The Mavericks perceive performances of South Asian masculinity through speech codes as incongruent with Afro-Caribbean values.

Especially as they get older, Mavericks are concerned less about sport and more about camaraderie, meaning that talking around the boundary, in a manner they feel comfortable, is increasingly important. Learie, a black 56-year-old Guyanese-Canadian, laments that times have changed and it is not only differences in language, food and jokes that keeps the Mavericks away from South Asian cricketers.

> Before I left [a competitive cricket team] there was a big influx of Sri Lankans and the problem was that when they came, the whole atmosphere changed ... In the pas', we hang out as one, a whole group after each game. We either went to a pub or a bar or went to somebody's house and they'd cook up curry ... But the Sri Lankan guys started coming in and there was quite a number of them. Then they started hanging out by themselves, you know pretty much and then you know, having their own little cliques kind of t'ing, didn't want to eat wit' us and t'ing.

It is interesting to note that curried foods might have been a point of convergence for the two ethnic groups, given the predominance of the spice in their regional dishes, but Learie blames Sri Lankans for excluding the Caribbeans and their cooking. These types of conflicts over food are characteristic of the meeting, clashing and grappling Pratt (1991, p. 33) describes when different ethnic groups find themselves sharing the same space; these "contact zones" can become contentious if conflicts are not resolved.

In addition to eating their favourite, home-cooked foods as they play, or after their games, the MCSC members prioritise drinking alcohol, mainly in the form of rum, brandy, beer and wine which puts them into conflict with some of their South Asian, in particular, Muslim, counterparts, who prioritise the sanctity of sport, leaving the celebrations until afterwards, and abstaining from alcohol. During a home game scheduled for fifty overs, some club members began to complain that the game was too long. "This should be a 20–20 game!" Marshall exclaimed. Riddick responded "Yeah, it's a lot of overs. [I want] bang bang (he emulates the sound of the ball hitting the bat) and let's drink." He made the true intention of the gathering known: "At least the water break is a beer break." Under the auspices of cricket, drinking and its attendant socialising are the foci for many of Afro-Caribbean men (Joseph, 2011a). I arrived to many games early enough to watch the Mavericks' pre-game routines and noted that players were constantly complaining about joint and muscle soreness, but few did any warm-up routines or stretches. My attempts to suggest a fitness regimen elicited a lot of laughs: Winston, a black 59-year-old Antiguan-Canadian joked, "The only fitness these guys do before the game is the bottle! Well, you see it in the morning. That's the only fitness (motions drinking a beer). They got very strong elbows and biceps (laughs)."

At every game, before the captains tossed the coin to determine who would bat or field first, sideline drinking had already begun. "Jamaica Rum" is not a real brand name. Nevertheless one spectator, announced, "Jamaica Rum is the official sponsor of the match!" as he offered cheers to other spectators. He continued, "My sport start!" By lifting a bottle of beer to his mouth, he indicated that he is involved in a pre-game drinking competition with only one objective: keep drinking. Spectators were not the only ones involved in that "sport." Many of the cricketers enjoyed a few brandies before taking the field. Layton, a black 48-year-old Barbadian-Canadian, explained why he did not need to stretch or exercise before his matches: "You will see a lot of cars and you will see the trunks open and once the trunks are open we are having our little ritual, which is our pre-game spirits. We call it "blood thinners" which keeps the body loose." A few players performed two or three stretches and gentle throwing and catching drills before some of the games, but this did not preclude them from imbibing also. Although drinking in public is technically a breach of local laws, if it is done from a cup or plastic bottle, or a glass bottle covered with a paper bag, the Mavericks do not seem concerned. This type of behaviour is in direct conflict with the values of some South Asian and in particular Muslim cricketers, who eschewed the breaking of local laws, were more concerned with sport success than socialising and disliked being surrounded by intoxicated teammates and opponents.

Fighting for power

On the rare occasions that they played on integrated teams, the Mavericks engaged in regular arguments with their South Asian teammates over adherence to the rules of cricket. As the Mavericks became more intoxicated over the course of the afternoons their arguments became louder and some players' tirades attacked individual South Asian men. Their rants must be read as a combination of a stylised performance of anger congruent with Caribbean masculinity and expressions of a kernel of fury owing to feelings of dispossession and decline in physical and social power.

One afternoon late in the summer of 2009, in a game between the Mavericks and the police team (which also featured some Maverick players), a fight broke out over whether players should be called off the field once they make fifty runs so that others can bat. Prasham, the police team captain wanted to give everyone a chance to play. The Mavericks were adamant that the rules of cricket should never be changed regardless of the circumstances: "If he is out there to make 100 runs then let him have the spotlight!" "What he doing out there? Making runs! You gonna call him in, send another man out dere do the same thing? Dat make sense?!" "Every cricketer takes a chance when he comes out to the grounds that he will not bat, especially if he is late in the order. Every cricketer knows that!" "If the lead batsmen stay out dere all day I consider it like myself staying out dere. Some people here ain't see a ball! Dat don't matter! Dere are rules! You don't make it up as you go along." The Mavericks' vehemence about adherence to the rules of cricket is reflective of the era in which they grew up, their commitment to cricket traditions, and perhaps most importantly, the passion with which they protect their spaces from the intrusions of other diasporic groups. Prasham shouted to the Mavericks to "Stop that! Stop that! It's just a game so we should all have fun and get a bat." On his side were other South Asian Canadian police officers, one of whom was next in the batting order, "I don't leave my house 10 hours to go field! ... We all want a knock!" He yelled back.

Cricket has always been a space in which black Caribbean men could assert their physical and intellectual prowess, generate a welcoming community and reinforce their heritage; however, MCSC members are decreasingly able to use cricket for this purpose due to club members' moribund physical potency, declining number of active players and miniscule representation in politics and media, relative to South Asians. The strong links that MCSC members are able to generate with Caribbean communities within Toronto and other diasporic nodes, provides an "option for escape or exit, which coincidentally may dampen the immigrant's interest in political participation in general, or radical political action or systemic reform more seriously" (Rogers, 2001, p. 184). Thus, a cycle occurs where Caribbean-Canadians feel marginalised by the host, turn to the homeland or other sites for a sense of comfort and security, fail to invest in improving their status and degree of assimilation in the host land, and continue to feel marginalised.

Ironically, the Mavericks admonish South Asian players for not speaking English, eating a restricted diet, fighting at the grounds and behaving in an uncivilised manner, criticisms that are often levelled against their own communities. They do not consider how their own behaviour is exclusive and raucous, or how they might be simultaneously alienating or subjugating Indo-Caribbean or South Asian members of their own teams who do not share their values. As Carrington (1998, p. 291) argued about cricket in the Caribbean diaspora, we must carefully qualify claims that this sport is fully emancipatory and unifies the Caribbean community. He used as an example the lack of women's teams in the club he studied, but the conflicts that arise among cricketers of Indian and African descent in a diaspora space provide another example of the disjunctures of black communities.

Afro-Caribbean-Canadian cricketers feel increasingly marginalised within Toronto's official cricketing communities, in part owing to the small numbers of second-generation or new immigrant Afro-Caribbean cricketers. Recreational and youth cricket are brimming with South Asian players, and as a result, the Mavericks efforts to protect the cultural exclusivity of "friendly" cricket are intensified. They resent the intrusion on what they consider to be their spaces by South Asian cricketers and use terms such as "invasion" and "interference." This language is reminiscent of popular Afro-Caribbean discourse of the 1970s, of an East Indian "takeover." In particular, in Trinidad and Tobago strides made by East Indian business and professional classes into sectors that were long considered Afro-Trinidadian preserves were alarming to Afro-Trinidadians (Munasinghe, 2001). The Mavericks goal is to generate a sense of home at cricket grounds. The more firmly they hold on to their nostalgic reflections on the way things were before they encountered so many South Asian cricketers, the more conflicts they end up in with South Asian teammates, opposition and tournament organisers. To avoid these conflicts, they try to limit their play to black-only teams.

Analysis of the Afro-Caribbean-Canadian Mavericks interactions with South Asian-Canadians helps to expand Paul Gilroy's narrow analysis of the Black Atlantic cultural forms as created through the racial terror of modernity (1993, p. 73). While those terrors were inaugurated by slavery, the resulting identities cannot be understood outside of the process of indentureship as well. The project of racial emancipation in the Caribbean did not occur in a world merely "split into white and black halves, and where the darker half was held back by race prejudice and legal bonds, as well as by deep ignorance and dire poverty" (DuBois, cited by Gilroy, 1993, p. 116). In fact, in the postcolonial era, black people dominated the majority of the Caribbean territories (Guyana and Trinidad are exceptions). The desire for a black homespace among cricketers and their supporters perpetuates a black Caribbean dominance that excludes, marginalises and denigrates Indo-Caribbean cultures as "inauthentic" representations of Caribbeanness and masculinity.

Although the Mavericks generally do not enjoy playing alongside South Asians, there are teams in Toronto that feature many positive interactions between Caribbeans and South Asians (see Razack, 2009). The main difference between these teams and the Mavericks is the age of players and the value of competition. The Mavericks are older men who have enjoyed primarily Caribbean-only cricket since the 1970s. In Canada, young Indo-Caribbean migrants and female cricketers in particular have been exposed to mixed-ethnicity cricket throughout their competitive careers. Also, these groups are more often engaged in league play in their schools and communities where the competitive nature lends itself to recruiting the best players regardless of ethnic background (Walter et al., 1991). Because the Mavericks' objectives include (re)generation of their Afro-Caribbean cultures, communities and consciousness, they are unable and unwilling to share cricket sites with South Asian-Canadians who may be good players, but interrupt the (re)making of Afro-Caribbean homespaces.

Demanding that ethnic "Others" speak proper English and using derogatory names are racist tropes used by ethnic groups that feel their hegemony is being threatened. Drawing from John Clarke's "magical recovery of community," Fletcher (2011, para. 3.2) similarly argues that, "when one's community identity is under threat, community members may attempt to recreate, through symbolic manifestations, a sense of their traditional cultural identities as a substitution for its 'real' decline." In the case of the Yorkshire County Cricket Club, exclusionary practices, racist language and normative whiteness are couched as "tradition" but efforts "to protect their heritage by denying many ethnic minorities access to the imagined community" reveal the club's institutionalised racism (Fletcher, 2011, para 6.12), and practices of exclusion. Inter-diasporic group conflicts reflect the shifting social hierarchies and identity-making processes of migrants. Any analysis of racialised diasporas cannot be read only in relation to the dominant white group because sources of conflict and identity marking often stand in relation to other minority ethnic and diaspora groups. As examination of diaspora space, that is, lateral and horizontal interrelationships within diasporas is necessary to move beyond "racism" in our historical and ethnographic theorisations of diaspora among black and Caribbean diasporas. As Thomas and Clarke (2006, p. 14) note: "[O]ther circulations [are] equally critical in the unveiling of counter histories and the constitution of community"; for example, examining overlapping networks that connect transnational communities such as Caribbeans and South Asians demonstrate the importance of other axes of power such as language, religion, age and political and economic power in the making of culture and marking of identity.

Afro-Caribbean Canadians rely on *liming*, which involves socialising, consuming an abundance of traditional Caribbean foods, drinking alcohol, playing domino games, sharing nostalgic memories, recounting ribald jokes and playing cricket to claim not only a black Caribbean identity, but also a Canadian one. As Walcott (2003: 147) puts it, when "[w]atching cricket [in Toronto ...] bodies of colour actually and symbolically refigure Canadian space and make their presence felt beyond the confines and restrictions of immigration legislation, multicultural discourse and policies, and the local police." Making connections to other Afro-Caribbeans through sharing a sport known to be central to anti-colonial efforts is one way of assuaging the racialised exile that is life in Canada. The Mavericks' conflicts with South Asians draw attention to what Munasinghe (2001, p. 1) describes as, the "contestation over the power to define the cultural coordinates of the symbolic space of the nation." Although Munasinghe was referring to the nation of Trinidad, it is worth thinking through how *liming* is essential to (re-)making Canada as well.

The Mavericks' version of the sport is impeded by the presence of South Asians (and their foods and languages) within a diaspora space. At cricket matches, the home team is always responsible for providing the food. Increasingly, when the Mavericks play with or for the police team, the chicken offered is tandoori instead of jerk. Ladoos and samosas have supplanted plantains and dumplings, and drinking is prohibited. Curry and rice may be the only staples on which South Asian and Caribbean groups can agree; however, the ways in which these dishes are prepared seem to continually keep the groups apart. These conflicts are characteristic of "diaspora spaces," where different ethnic groups find themselves together, negotiating for material and discursive power (Brah, 1996). The Mavericks are at once part of a community that is "dispersed" and "at home." Their cricket games in the Greater Toronto Area require excluding South Asian bodies in favour of competing against Afro-Caribbeans. Theirs is "a practice of dwelling (differently) ... an ambivalent refusal or indefinite deferral of return" (Clifford, 1994, p. 321). They do not need to return to their homelands to recreate homespaces and their national affiliations proliferate with each year after emigration. The grounds offer a place for solidarity both to an elsewhere and to the Canadian nation-state. The next chapter explores the various ways in which nations are differentiated and reproduced in this itinerant cricket and social club.

Notes

1 Munasinghe (2001) remarks that during the 1980s and early 1990s, "Indo-Trinidadian cultural activists, religious and political leaders, moderates and radicals, were united in their efforts to challenge hegemonic Afro-Creole representations of the nation" (p. 7). In Trinidad as in Guyana and Surinam, Indians were relegated to a fourth tier in the social structure, behind Europeans, elite blacks and creoles, and lower-class blacks. Their social and spatial isolation during indentureship operated to situate them symbolically outside the core of society (p. 10).
2 My own positionality, as a dark-skinned black woman, and the knowledge of my research as a project on the "Black Atlantic" potentially influenced how MCSC members chose to identify themselves and others in conversations with me.
3 "Negro'" is a term used as a conscious sign of respect among older Caribbean persons (Peake and Trotz, 1999, p. 26).
4 It is notable that conservative Indo-Caribbeans fiercely resist the "cross-over" from chutney performed in Indian wedding tents "to the further hybridized chutney soca, the "Africanized" and carnivalised form of chutney performed during carnival" (Puri, 1999, p. 26), which potentially renders invisible its Indianness and publically stages the sexuality of the Indo-Caribbean woman. The point here is that by Afro- and Indo-Caribbeans alike, chutney-soca is seen as a blackened art form and it should be no surprise that this is the only form of Indo-Caribbean culture welcomed by this cricket and social club.
5 The cultural specifics of Indo-Caribbean cricket experience is worthy of attention; there is something similar yet different at stake for Indo-Guyanese or Indo-Trinidadians in this Caribbean community. Their reasons for distinguishing themselves from South Asians, desire or capacity to forge alliances with South Asian or Indo-Caribbean teams, or feelings of exclusion within the MCSC deserve to be explored, but are outside the scope of this study. Sport in the Black Atlantic does not capture all the makings of Caribbean identity through cricket in the Caribbean diaspora.

6

Nationalisms

Although diasporas remain interconnected across multiple national borders, each is founded upon movements from a "cultural hearth" to a "diasporic node" (Voigt-Graf, 2004, p. 38), a process that, since the early 1990s, has been linked to globalisation and the decreasing significance of national boundaries. Madan (2000, pp. 33–34) argues that describing an ethnic community as a diaspora is a "political act signaling the fact that large, globally connected, migrant communities are shifting away from ethnic and national subjectification into postmodern spaces that are beyond the Nation ideal, beyond assimilation." A focus on the everyday activities of diasporas demonstrates, however, that they are at once situated globally and nationally, especially through family and social networks that knit members across multiple nations (Bashi, 2007; Olwig, 2001; Sutton, 2004; 2008), or within racial formations that link them to compatriots with similar ancestry (Edwards, 2001; 2003; Thomas and Clarke, 2006). After all, in order to cross borders, as members of diasporas so often do, passports and other means of documenting national affiliations are compulsory.

As black masculinity formed in the Caribbean without clearly defined national communities, black male subjectivity has always been outward looking, linked to black men in other places. Michelle Stephens writes of the black diaspora that "[w]hile in contemporary discourse the terms nation and diaspora are often posed in opposition to each other, in certain forms of black discourse from the early decades of the twentieth century they constituted two equally determinative and linked notions of blackness" (2005, p. 36). Later in her text, she describes the Caribbean diaspora as also determined by national and transnational discourses: "to say we are all Caribbean without interrogating our own location in relationship to empire and the nation state" is not useful (Stephens, 2005, p. 271). In this chapter, I consider Clifford's (1994, p. 307) question, "But are diaspora cultures consistently antinationalist?" The answer is a resounding "no." This chapter builds on other work on the Afro-diaspora that notes the importance of distinguishing the nations from which migrants come, and equally important, cautions Schmidt (2008), avoiding blurring the nations in which migrants settle. Referring to the Caribbean diaspora in general is insufficient: "We must distinguish between Caribbean New York, Caribbean London or Caribbean Berlin" Schmidt (2008, p. 30) warns. The politics of the place of residence as it intersects with migrants' class status, gender, time since migration, sporting performance and other characteristics will have a profound influence on how they interact with the diaspora and the connections they are able to make (or interested in making) across the Black Atlantic. This chapter highlights the many ways in the early decades of the twenty-first century, in which black men continue to be positioned diasporically and nationally.

The final events at one tournament in St. Lucia, in March 2008, clearly elucidate the multiple affiliations of Afro-Caribbean men. Tournament organisers posited white and black teams against each other, naming them The West (England and Australia) and The Rest. The Mavericks, a group of Antiguan-, Barbadian-, Grenadian, Guyanese-, Jamaican- and Trinidadian-Canadians joined Trinidadian and Jamaican nationals to celebrate unity and pride in black masculine sporting prowess, exerting a unified black identity despite their varied Caribbean origins and current places of residence. The following is an excerpt from my field notes.

The West vs. The Rest

> They began the final game of the tournament with friendly heckling of their opponents and boasting about the aptitude of a unified black force. Unity was fleeting, however, as The Rest could not help but acknowledge their national differences, especially as tensions rose throughout the game. With just two overs left, there were eighteen runs needed to beat the English–Australian team. The batsmen had their sights on the boundary for each of the twelve balls left. If they could just hit a few fours or sixes, the game could be wrapped up in short order. Players and supporters yelled instructions from the stands: "Hit them!" "Tek dem out. Bap bap!" "Don' waste time. Run! Take three runs! Ok. Take two!" They quietened only when the umpire raised his index digit. Batsman out: leg before wicket. A moment of silence pervaded the usually noisy stands before The West began cheering. The players and supporters for The Rest then erupted with blame being placed not on individual umpires or batsmen, but on national groups: "Jamaicans always droppin' catches!" "De Trinis and dem cyan't hit four fe save dey life!" "Why we never put de Canadians in firs'?"

The easy slippage between racial and transnational unity in one moment and national discord in the other is striking. Despite their similar regional origins and racial affiliations, the Canadian Mavericks and the Jamaican and Trinidadian cricketers of The Rest continue to entrench boundaries around the nations in which they were born and where they now live, depending on the context.

Ongoing salience of nationalisms within diasporas

In the Canadian setting, a few studies have highlighted the unique experiences of Caribbean-Canadians, their relation to global geopolitics and racial discourses, and their specific nation-of-origin differences. For example, Jamaicans in Toronto are well known for their ongoing efforts to celebrate 1 August, the day on which their nation of origin transitioned from a colonial outpost to a sovereign nation, although they have seemingly left behind the area of nation building. Burman's (2002) interrogation of this celebration raises questions about Jamaican, Canadian, Caribbean and black belonging. These operate simultaneously and depend on ongoing desires to return home, a capacity for transnational travel, proliferating social networks, national policies, cultural exports, family celebrations and political conflicts. A double consciousness of being simultaneously Canadian and "not quite" fixes Jamaicans' and other MCSC members' connections to both here and there.

Similarly, this chapter points out the range of national groups to which Afro-Caribbean Canadians belong and the ongoing salience of nationalisms within diasporas. Rather than posit a false binary and fall into a trap of romantic, pure nationalisms, this chapter draws from empirical evidence to interrogate how Caribbean-Canadians embody multiple, hybridised national identities, and explores the ways in which they draw boundaries around their communities and use dominant discourses to demonstrate national identities that are distinct and pure. The use of national iconography and symbols such as the maple leaf (Canada), or curry goat (Jamaica), is central to the attempts to fix national identities in cricket spaces. The active handling of meanings of various local and foreign cultural streams "can allow them to work as commentaries on one another, through never-ending intermingling and counterpoint" (Hannerz, 1997, p. 323). In other words, the Mavericks come to know themselves as Canadian or Jamaican through their interactions and interminglings with players from the United Kingdom, Australia and Jamaica among others.

Certainly, the family and friendship ties of cricketers lead them to visit regularly their nations of origin in the Caribbean, or Caribbean spaces in the United

States and England, criss-crossing geopolitical borders to maintain their relationships, connections to their homelands and a deterritorialised community (see Chapter 3). Their interpersonal networks and movements within the diaspora show their "simultaneity" within plurilocal homelands (Levitt and Glick Schiller, 2004). However, their multi-placedness and desires for affiliation with a regional Caribbean elsewhere does not negate their understandings of themselves as national citizens. The purpose of this chapter is to highlight the relationships between deterritorialised communities, or diasporas and bordered geopolitical regimes, or nation-states; it demonstrates how nationalisms are reinforced, not dissolved, in transnational spaces. This chapter conceptualises two different types of nationalisms Afro-Caribbean Canadians passionately espouse through their cricket-related travel: Canadian and nation of origin.

It has been suggested that the experience of racism is what connects black people in Canada (Henry, 1994); however, racism is too broad a brush for painting ethnic, gender or national particularities, and it cannot "solely account for the constitutive differences among Afrodiasporic peoples in Canada" (Campbell, 2012, p. 50). Black populations are often made to appear itinerant, fleeting, new or unexpected as Canadian nationhood, belonging, geography and citizenship is coded as European and white (McKittrick, 2002). This coding may be responsible for pushing black people towards an elsewhere, but it does not tell the whole story.

Co-existing with the discourses emphasising Canada as a white, French and British nation (Indigenous peoples are also erased or at best marginalised in dominant national representations) is the view of Canada as a mosaic. The Canadian response to growing immigrant populations of colour has been a multiculturalism policy that encourages maintenance of "ethnic heritage" (Mackey, 2002; Thobani, 2007). In this mosaic model, ethnic minority groups celebrate their nation of origin cultures through "saris, samosas, and steel pans," noted by James Donald and Ali Rattansi (1992, p. 2) in reference to the English education system as cultural elements given the power to represent difference and pluralism, and to stifle conversations about racism and structural inequalities. Caribbean and black popular cultures are produced by people "crucially and simultaneously engaged in a politics of how to belong to the nation-state as not-quite-citizens and how to desire beyond the too rigid confines of nation-state governmentality" (Walcott, 2003, p. 134). Whether they understand Canada to be white or multicultural, Afro-Caribbean-Canadians continue to identify with their ancestral cultures and ethnic identities through connections to the Black Atlantic and Caribbean diaspora.

If popular culture is a political practice, as Walcott (2003) suggests, then Afro-Caribbean-Canadians can use cricket in combination with the Canadian discourse of heritage within multiculturalism to stake their claim to nationhood, negotiate tensions of home and elsewhere, reconcile their stasis and movement, and include in their communities their friends and family from the United States and England. Symbols, language, food, media, politics, travel and sports continue to connect them to their nations of origin, even as they are hailed into entirely new "imagined communities" (Anderson, 1983). The ability to celebrate their heritage at cricket games where they wear their white uniforms, eat traditional foods, speak in their native languages and dance to music from the homeland is commemorated by the Mavericks as a source of both Caribbean and Canadian pride.

Canadian nationalism

Most of the Mavericks were little fish in a big sea in the jobs they found when they arrived in Canada in the 1960s and 1970s, but through cricket some of the MCSC members were revered for their skill and enabled to represent the province and the nation, which gave them a sense of Canadian national pride. Their above average talent, opportunities to compete among experts, and the centrality of cricket to their social circles and senses of self, all led to the intensely competitive cricket they played upon arrival at their new homes in Canada. Warlie and Riddick, both black Barbadian-Canadians, moved to Montreal, Quebec as young men and began playing elite-level cricket immediately. Warlie explained: "I played inter-province games which Ontario play Quebec every year. And they go like one year they play in Quebec and one year they play in Toronto, here. So I represent Quebec at that time. I did well in those games too." Warlie expressed great pride in being a provincial representative. Similarly, Riddick explained, smiling, that "When I was 18-years-old I started playing for the Quebec provincial team. It was an all-black team. We went to tournaments in Calgary, BC and Ontario. The Quebec and Ontario teams were the strongest in Canada." The "all Black" provincial cricketers hailed from the Caribbean. Riddick points out the racial difference of the team from the white mainstream in British Columbia, Ontario and Quebec in the 1960s and from the current provincial and national teams dominated by South Asian-Canadians: "Now it's all Indian, but back then we dominated." Winston, a black 59-year-old Antiguan-Canadian, also proudly represented the province of Ontario. He "never played on a white team," neither in Antigua nor in Canada:

> With my performances it gave me an opportunity to be selected for the trials to play for Antigua ... many times I found myself in the final 16. I didn't quite make it to the final 11, you know, or 12 guys. I just missed out. But I represented Ontario in cricket. I remember one year we played, I topped the batting average in the competition, of all the provinces, I was top.

The Mavericks' pride in their ability and opportunity to represent their new nation is expressed in the memorabilia they retained from those days, including provincial uniforms, brochures or newspaper articles with their names on them and the ways in which they discuss their success. They do not merely recount that they played provincially, but also insist that they (blacks and Caribbeans) "did well," were "top," and "the strongest" in the intra-provincial leagues, and therefore among the best in Canada. There has been a tendency in Caribbean cultural studies to emphasise the anti-hegemonic cultural practices that take place during carnival and in dancehalls, whereas, this study shows that rather than being transgressive, Caribbean peoples (especially those of the middle-class) are often embedded in mainstream, bourgeois and assimilationist nationalist projects and sentiments.

In a touching moment, one player, Jared, a black 57-year-old Antiguan-Canadian laments not being selected for the Canadian national team as a defining moment of his life. He was in his late twenties and had been living in Canada for three years: "I really wanted to make the Canadian team so that we could come up against the West Indies team in a tournament. Then I could play against Viv. I used to dream of that. Me on the Canadian team, him playing for West Indies." Jared grew up with Vivian Richards, who was knighted in 1999 for his outstanding contributions to international cricket. Jared did not want to believe that his migration (which had been forced upon him as a result of his financial and emotional commitments to his family members who had already moved to Canada as well as those left behind in Antigua) meant an end to his elite cricket aspirations. Unfortunately, it was not migration but his lacking specific skills and "fit" on the team that kept him out of cricket's top ranks in Canada. Some of his contemporaries made it, however:

> Dey called me up. An' dey had dis team touring to Barbados an' I got a game playing for Canada. In Barbados! ... After leaving Barbados to come to Canada an' wear Canadian colours it was a great t'ing fe me. I really enjoyed de time I got to spend dere and got to show who I am ... [but] I very outspoken an' dat prevent me from progressing farther into it because, for me, I look at it like life is difficult an' [I] come from West Indies to play for Canada an' I recently married an' I had a kid on the way ... I figure if I gonna leave [work] to represent de

> Canadian team I should at least get something fe compensate me .... Dey call me at certain times for their uses an' I refuse ... Yeah at de time (pause), funding was critical in dem times dere. (Otis)

Otis, a black 47 year-old Barbadian-Canadian, was unable to continue playing for Canada because the amateur sport system relied (and arguably still relies) on the idea of self-funded, middle-class athletes who are willing to devote their lives to the sport without substantial remuneration. Playing for Canada also meant adopting dominant attitudes, which for Otis meant remaining silent about racial and economic oppression. Although he aspired to respectability through assimilation and the chance to "wear Canadian colours," he ultimately drew from a Caribbean reputation value system (Wilson, 1973) and became "outspoken," transgressing rules around decorum, which got him released from the team. He, too, was told that he would no longer "fit."

Riddick, originally from Barbados moved from Quebec to Ontario in his twenties and found that his cricket skills were the cultural capital he needed to network with some important people. Ironically, his cricket contacts got him a job with the Toronto police force, which ultimately stunted his cricket career:

> I came here and was an exceptional player by their [Canadian] standards. There were lots of guys at my level back home ... I played for the Ontario team and the Canadian national team versus the USA for three to four years, but at that time it was 80–90% West Indian. Even the selectors were West Indian ... I was selected to play for Canada in the World Cup in 1967, but cricket was not in the police peripheral so I couldn't get the time off. I was new and I had to choose between police as a career versus cricket as a career. (Riddick)

Unfortunately, many players echo the experience of having to choose to work over playing cricket in those years due to obligations to feed their families and a lack of national funding for the sport (which continues today). Many migrants come from the Caribbean with short-term educational and economic goals in mind. As James (1963) describes, regarding Learie Constantine's decision to play professional cricket in England in 1928, many of the Mavericks were talented cricketers and never would have settled abroad if they "had had not only honour but a little profit" in their own countries (p. 109). Their decision to migrate "was the result of personal choice arising from national neglect;" with white or even light skin, they "would have been able to choose a life at home" (p. 110). Instead, they moved to Canada, where they were not greeted by professional cricket opportunities that could pay the bills. Their pride in being able to represent their new nation was not enough to sustain their participation at elite levels.

Forty years later, the Mavericks continue to represent Ontario or Canada in international cricket competitions, though as 'friendly' masters cricket players.

When they do so, they battle the stigma of Canada being regarded as a weak cricketing nation. At one of the Mavericks' home games versus a team visiting from Boston, one Jamaican-American man commented that he was "surprised" that the Canadians could beat them. Erol chimed in: "See what happen when dey say Canadians cyan't play cricket? [Once] we were on a tour in Barbados. I go in wit' my partner an' he hit dat ball so far, I t'ink dat ball still flying down Bridgetown today!" In a pep talk on the bus before the first game of the 2008 tour in England, one of the players stood up, hoisted a uniform into the air and reminded everyone that they were playing for Canada: "The uniforms might say [Mavericks], but they also have that maple leaf, so we're representing Canada in a sense. Play good!"

The trip to England was significant for many of the Mavericks who had never been before, both because it was the birthplace of cricket, and because it was the colonial motherland. These men had lived over half a century with an embodied understanding of cricket as a game that exemplified civility, gentlemanly behaviour and fairness, which they equated with Englishness. They would agree with Malcolm's (2013, p. 13) observation "that 'Englishness and cricket' amounts to a pleonasm (the use of more words than is necessary to express an idea)." At the same time, cricket has come to represent a challenge to British hegemony; a black masculine identity associated with strength, speed and dominance; and a space for breaking colonial rules. These conflicting perceptions of English cricket as a benchmark for ideal masculine behaviour became a central issue for the Canadian team, even before they left for the trip.

At a meeting two months prior to departure, the Mavericks' newly elected manager, Marshall, a 58-year-old black Barbadian-Canadian, promptly enacted his first order of business, a rule that no member of the team would drink while in the maple leaf uniform at games in England. This rule meant that if the Mavericks batted first, cricketers could not drink until the end of the game (six to eight hours in most cases), and if they batted second, alcohol could only be consumed after they were caught, bowled, run out, or what the Mavericks call "t'ief" or "steal" out. "Get steal out means you got robbed – not bowled out, but the umpire stealin' for the other team," Erol explained to me. "It's the only good part about getting steal out," Vilroy said with a broad smile across his face as he exited the field after the first game and walked directly into the changing room to take off his uniform and the cap on his bottle of beer.

Controversy blossomed, however, when some players expressed alternative ideas about how to perform or demonstrate their gender, race and Canadian identities in a cricket environment. At the first game in England, one member of the opposing black British team joked to a late-arriving teammate of his, "Listen, there's no drinking today," making fun of the Mavericks' rule. The player stopped frozen in his tracks for a second before saying "No what?! Just hush you' mout' jackass!" The opposition and black British spectators taunted the Mavericks by pouring extra-strong drinks for themselves. Erol, a black 55-year-old Barbadian-Canadian, who had been chosen to bat eighth in the second innings, decided he could wait no longer before opening a cold bottle of beer. He was stealthily sipping from a plastic cup when the team manager noticed him, confiscated his drink and suspended him for one game. Erol was extremely upset and called the manager a "dictator" as well as other more crude names. The opposing team's captain remarked as he shook his head, "Man cyaan't drink?! What?! But I thought this a touring team. Man cyaan't drink, man cyaan't happy!" He was truly sorry for Erol, who walked away from the field ripping off his uniform.

Despite openly raising no concerns when the rule was proposed at the meeting, most players saw the restriction on alcohol during games as too severe once it was in effect. Layton explained to me the opposite rule typically in effect for their bus trips: "You *must* drink from the time you get off the bus, then bat your age at least! These are the rules of the road for every man." His suggestion that a 60-year-old man could score 60 runs every time at bat was an exaggeration, but conveys the idea that drinking, being intoxicated while playing and performing well are important ways in which these Afro-Caribbean men "do gender" (and race) when they travel outside of Canada. The Mavericks did not see drinking while playing as incompatible with representing the nation. Barth indicates that boundaries are drawn around ethnic groups through overt signals and signs that show identity, such as dress, language and general style of life, along with basic value orientations, the standards of morality and excellence by which performance is judged. "Since belonging to an ethnic category implies being a certain kind of person" (Barth, 1998, p. 14), the Mavericks' policy brought into question whether they were the same kind of men as their black British opponents.

This confrontation is a classic example of what Peter Wilson (1973) referred to as the conflict between exhibiting Caribbean "respectability" and "reputation." If respectability is gained through approximating a standard of dress, use of language and conduct of the middle- and upper-class British colonisers, and Canadian culture more broadly, the aspiring, respectable Afro-Caribbean must embrace a restrained and obedient demeanour. The primary institutions to inculcate respectability included the Christian Church, nuclear family and education. Within the latter, school cricket also played no small role in teaching young black boys how to be "civilised," in education institutions across the Caribbean (Sandiford, 1998). It was not only the sport itself, but the style of play that conferred a respectable habitus. However, as is the wont of (post)colonial subjects, a simultaneous alternative value system developed: "reputation." Within cricket, a "respectable" habitus was rejected in favour of a style of life that gave value to breaking the rules with impunity, dominating through athleticism; being loud, ready to fight and proficient with language; and demonstrating a capacity to drink. Without the opportunity to display these characteristics to their fullest extent, club members' authority, as blacks and as men, felt threatened.

When the rule was introduced, the manager explained that the Mavericks would be travelling as a representative team. He reminded his teammates that they represent Toronto and the entire nation of Canada and must show the Englishmen that they are serious about cricket. On the bus to the first game he announced: "They [English players] need to know that even though we're from Canada, we know 'bout cricket. We need to play like home." For him, "play like home" meant play to win, like the West Indies team used to, and like they do in Toronto. One player piped up "I drink when I play home!" and Marshall responded, "Ok, then, don't play like home!" Marshall's desire to show the English players what serious cricketers they were is a reflection of insecurity about his cricketing authenticity as a Canadian citizen, despite his Barbadian background. Yet, in England as in Canada, older Afro-Caribbeans are serious only about *liming*, their performances of Caribbean masculinity and its associated drinking culture. The expression "Man cyaan't drink, man cyaan't happy!", spoken with a Caribbean accent, directly links Caribbean masculinity and alcohol consumption. If pleasure, fun and happiness are motivating factors for men's participation, then alcohol is a necessity in Canada and England. "Dese guys cyaan't play 'less dey drunk!" Terrel exclaimed when the sober Mavericks' wickets started to fall. Marshall's desire to manage a team presenting as sophisticated and authentic cricketers ended up in a rule that elicited the opposite effect. Instead of being regarded as gentle*men*, the Mavericks were ridiculed for being "soft," "weak," "poofs" (homosexuals) and "too Canadian."

This episode highlights another of the disjunctures of diaspora. Within the black diaspora, Brent Hayes Edwards insists, there are moments of *décalage*: misunderstandings, lack of translation among members of a globally dispersed population. Though the conflicts that erupted were not a result of linguistic divergence in the Black Atlantic as Edwards had studied, the ideas associated with the authentic or "proper" cricketer and national identity were different between those Afro-Caribbean men who only imagined cricket in England and those who had lived it. The misreading of the diasporic culture, in this case as different, when it was actually the same, demonstrates the influence of geographic separation, and the necessity of travel in forming embodied understandings of culture within the Black Atlantic and to break down barriers between plurilocal Afro-Caribbean groups.

MCSC members and their opponents spent a lot of time around the boundary keeping noise about Marshall's rule, and when the resistance of his teammates became too strong to ignore – nearly one week into the two-week tour – Marshall renounced the no-drinking rule on the bus while returning home from a game. I suspect this was owing to his sense of impending mutiny and because he recognised that his original purpose, to show the English how serious they were and that they had not lost their talent after being in Canada for 30 or more years, was not validated. The Englishmen he wanted to impress were diasporic Caribbean men like himself, whose primary reason for playing cricket was to have fun and socialise; limiting the Mavericks' alcohol consumption limited their enjoyment of the tour as well as the pleasure of their opponents. He acceded that the rule would remain relaxed as long as the players did not embarrass themselves, their region, or Canada. The team was very happy about this news. They had already been drinking cognac clandestinely at the back of the bus, but Marshall's announcement was cause for overt celebration. Another round was poured openly and they toasted "To Canada!"

This overt Canadian pride was matched by the use of symbols and iconography of the nation. When touring, the Mavericks enact a significant ritual that is not present at their home games in Toronto. They typically travel with the national maple leaf flag and find a way to affix it close to their changing room, their side of the clubhouse, or the stands where their supporters sit. In Barbados, England, St. Lucia or the United States, playing against Caribbean men with other national affiliations opens up the contest to be more than a friendly game between Caribbean "brothers." Sport plays an important role in the construction and reproduction of a national identity. When the game is represented as an international competition, it becomes linked to national heritage and pride. It is interesting to note that the Mavericks' desire to shore up a Canadian identity, by placing the Canadian flag on one side of their opponents' clubhouse, occurs solely outside of Canada, in black spaces where it is necessary to mark their national difference from their opponents.

After every game when the Mavericks were on tour, the two teams made presentations to each other to "trash talk," show gratitude for the opportunity to play and exchange gifts. During his post-game speeches, the Mavericks' captain, Sam, a 61-year-old black Barbadian-Canadian, handed out Ontario flags and maple leaf pins, and invited his opponents to come to Canada so that the Mavericks could extend the same hospitality. At one game, he stated:

> I would like to bring greetings on behalf of the [Mavericks] of Ontario and Canada to England ... So as I said we have a part of Canada to share with you. As you know we are part of the Commonwealth, so part of us is still ruled by England and the Queen, so we have – well this is the Ontario flag and it has the Union Jack and the [crest] from Ontario – to share with you and we also have some pins ... we didn't know so many Jamaicans would be here [in England] so it's our pleasure to meet our West Indian brothers here and any time you come to Canada you are welcome. (Sam)

The symbols of the province and nation, Ontario flags and maple leaf pins were given to every player the Mavericks encountered on tours and at tournaments. Four players were charged with going to their local city hall and obtaining twenty-five pins or flags so the team would have enough to hand out to each opponent. In addition, the Mavericks travelled with statuettes of beavers, deciduous trees and loons (divers), which they handed out to honour the captain and man of the match of their opposing teams. These exchanges of Canadiana were important parts of every game, signified by the gathering of players to photograph the exchanges and speeches made about the symbols. Sam explained the significance of each gift: "The beaver is our national animal." "Everywhere in our province you can see this kind of tree." "The maple leaf is the symbol on our flag." He effectively articulated the Mavericks' connection with, and pride in, the nation. Some players also wore Canada hats and T-shirts when they were out of their cricket uniforms, proud to represent their home. Their immersion in an urban lifestyle – perpetually distinct from the woodland symbolism used to represent the nation – is obfuscated in favour of a celebration of Canadian flora and fauna. Their use of these symbols to represent themselves, when many admit they have infrequently accessed wooded camp grounds or cottages, or ever seen a real beaver, articulates the tensions between diasporic identities and powerful discourses, signs and symbols of nationalism. Taking from the land without acknowledging indigeneity (not to mention ongoing colonialism) is well rehearsed in dominant Canadian discourses. Club members are not immune to the charms of the language, imagery and ideology of Canadian nationalism, demonstrating that deterritorialisation has destabilised identity, but it has not created subjects who are free-floating nomads, despite what is sometimes implied by those eager to celebrate the freedom and playfulness of the postmodern condition (Gupta and Ferguson, 1992, p. 19).

Though the wildlife statuettes are inadequate for representing MCSC members' hyphenated identities, they are wholly embraced. What authorised symbols of nation could they share with their black British brothers to connote an urban, *Caribbean*-Canadian identity? This illuminates one of the many powerful paradoxes of Afro-Caribbean-Canadian identity. Club members self-consciously make themselves the spokesmen and guardians of Caribbean and Canadian cultures at different times and the criteria for judging national identity are flexible. Sam lauds the label of "Commonwealth partner," in conversation with other Barbadians living in England to demonstrate his passion for his "adopted nation," Canada, as well as the bonds of Empire. At other times, he was known to rail against the monarchy, colonial powers and state-sponsored racism that limited his freedom. MCSC members' privilege as mobile, middle-class citizens allows them to celebrate Canadianness and brotherhood with the English through the representation of the game as one between Canada and England, instead of a game between two groups of Caribbean or black men, similarly oppressed by, and continually challenging, their nation-states.

Loyalty to Canada is also fashioned in less obvious ways. Despite being embedded in a Caribbean cricket and social club, some players detach themselves from a working-class, Caribbean identity and are critical of the loud, raucous and what they refer to as "ignorant" behaviour of many of their Afro-Caribbean peers. On one occasion after a game in Barbados in one player's hotel room, a number of the Mavericks became embroiled in a loud argument over how *bakes* (a flour dumpling) are made. Some thought they were deep fried, others, pan fried and still others insisted they were baked, hence the name. For nearly 10 minutes, five club members all talked at the same time, yelled, slapped the table for emphasis and clinked glasses full of cognac with others who shared their opinions.

Sitting at the periphery, Hussein, a 66-year-old Indo-Trinidadian-Canadian distanced himself from the conversation "You see this?" he asked me, "This is why Caribbean people don't get anywhere. Sit around all night talkin' stupidness. You know what the other [English] team is probably talkin' something intellectual, politics ... Here we goin' on 'bout bakes for half an hour!" Hussein, who had retired after 30 years of teaching in Toronto, often noted his surprise that Caribbean immigrants did not change their ways "after so long in Canada." Abrahams (1983) notes that when Caribbean men talk it is not the content that is important; rather, the competition takes priority. A "man of words" communicates his power and personality and aims to "capture the attention, the allegiance and the admiration of the audience through his fluency, his strength of voice, and his social maneuverability and psychological resilience" (Abrahams, 1983, p. xxx). Hussein remained unimpressed by the performances of his teammates, taking their discussion topic and words seriously. He complained that he moved to Canada to "get an education and get away from rum shops and foolishness," but it seems he was unable to escape fully from his masculine, working-class, Trinidadian culture, especially when his peers were drinking and competing with words.

Hussein's Indo-Caribbean status also complicates his critique of his mainly Afro-Caribbean teammates; however, the emphasis of this scene as an example of Indo–Afro-Caribbean conflict is minimised when the words of Learie, a black 56-year-old Guyanese-Canadian are taken into account. Learie was equally critical of the Mavericks "simple-minded" arguments, which he attributed to a "backward," "underdeveloped" Caribbean mentality. He quietly removed himself from the group and read or slept when the conversation was "too base" for him: "You notice that in 50 years since most of these islands became independent we have produced little of international consequence. We came to the developed world and still we're not contributing anything." The dominant Canadian attitude that black Caribbean immigrants have not contributed to Canadian history, literature and scholarship is perpetuated by some of the Mavericks. It is interesting to note that neither man challenges the group, but both detach themselves silently from this mode of representing Caribbean-Canadian masculinity. Invested in working for a municipal education board and a provincial electric company, respectively, Hussein and Learie's lack of acceptance of this means of representing Caribbeanness may be related to their identities as intellectuals and choice of professions for the past 30 years. Their commitment to reproducing the Canadian nation and shifting to a middle-class status with "respectable" values may have influenced their perception of their peers who are more devoted to reproducing their homeland culture through the "reputation" value system.

While MCSC members see themselves as part of a borderless black nation, one defined in social rather than geographic terms, or a Caribbean community with a regional identity, they also endorse the symbols and ideologies of the Canadian nation-state. As Basch, Glick Schiller and Szanton Blanc (1994, p. 3) note, immigrants are bombarded with ideologies that promote their "ongoing incorporation … into the society and polity of the country in which they have settled." Yet, their identities can be manipulated and contested depending on the agendas of interlocutors and the particular situation. Although they performed a decidedly Canadian nationalism on the one hand, on the other hand the Mavericks disavowed Canadianness in favour of an identity linked to their nation of origin.

Nation-of-origin identity

Economic, military and political forms of power in the nations of origin continue to influence national loyalties and resistances despite the deterritorialised or diaspora settings in which they occur (Alexander, 2005; Glick Schiller, 2005; Glick Schiller and Fouron, 1999; Walcott, 2003). Members of the MCSC who emotionally long for the past and the homeland; regularly send remittances to the family members they left behind; or remain invested in their nation-of-origin news, weather, or politics from a distance, are intricately linked to a national identity that is neither diasporic, nor Canadian. For some of them, this (re-)claiming of the home nation may be an anti-assimilation move (Walcott, 2003); nevertheless, they remain committed to their pre-migration heritage.

Several events occurred on the MCSC two-week cricket tour in England that exemplify the ways in which many of the Mavericks were quick to reject their Canadian status in favour of their nations of origin. On one of the first days without any games, some club members took advantage of the opportunity to do some shopping and sightseeing. We spent hours in a variety of sport shops, looking for a warm-up suit that the entire team both could afford and would find aesthetically pleasing, only to leave empty handed. If ever there was any doubt that the Barbadian nation-state had its hold on some of these migrants, that doubt could be dispelled when they made a point of abandoning the team track-suit search in favour of visiting the Barbados High Commission in London, their national government representative office. Coincidentally, when we arrived at the commission a ceremony was about to begin. Four parish ambassadors (18–30 years of age) from Barbados were being recognised for their role in a development programme that aims to involve youth in the national independence celebrations via a "Spirit of the Nation" competition. The ambassadors each spoke about "just taking the opportunities available to all," "reaching out to the underprivileged," and "the honour of working in one's community." The final ambassador to speak was the youngest. At just 18 years old, she appeared to be the most confident and well spoken of the group:

> Without the parish ambassador programme, I wouldn't be stan'in' here in dis cold country ... please come back and support people in Barbados ... Help our people become strong, make a better representation for the island. Come to Barbados – that's what ex-pats can do to help. This trip to London is part of our community outreach. Thank you.

She received an overwhelming round of applause. The High Commissioner introduced the Mavericks as a "cricket team visiting from Canada, primarily Barbadian and wholly supportive of the diaspora efforts." He then proposed that there be two youth ambassadors from the Barbadian diaspora in each of London, New York and Toronto. The crowd seemed pleased with this suggestion that "will help to keep the broader Bajan community together." The team captain, Sam, a black 61-year-old Barbadian-Canadian, was presented with the opportunity to make an impromptu speech. He boasted about the fundraising projects he had already begun and the association the Mavericks have with the Poverty Alleviation Bureau in Barbados. As such, he marked himself as a good Bajan citizen who mobilises funds to give back to the homeland. This formal ceremony was followed by a traditional Bajan meal, for which the Mavericks were grateful after a long day of window shopping. They mingled with other diasporic and visiting Barbadians and other Caribbean people as they ate and learned about current development projects in which they could become involved, or how they could mobilise youth in Toronto upon their return to Canada.

It did not take long for their cemented Barbadian status to be challenged. Just a few days later, an argument broke out around the boundary during a game, and many of the Mavericks were quick to assert that they are not Canadian and identify as Bajan "through and through." A local passer-by, Dudley, who identified himself as "pure Bajan ... just off the rock" stopped by the grounds to watch the game on his way home from work. He boldly stated that "these Canadian ol' men don't know nothing 'bout no cricket." The Mavericks did not take this lightly and began to heckle him. He was significantly younger than them, believed his skills were superior and offered to "embarrass" them at the next game. "I'll make a call tonight an' I go be dere tomorrow. I go bowl dung half a you!" The Mavericks did not accept this prediction that he would get half of them out with his superior bowling skills.

Otis, a black 47-year-old Barbadian-Canadian tried to explain to Dudley that although they are old, they have the benefit of experience and that many of them were elite players in the 1970s. "We talking BCL (Barbados Cricket League)! Whose era was better? We had Joel Garner, Gordon Greenidge, Desmond Haynes! Legends! You understan'? I came up wit' dese players!" Sam chimed in "Dem t'ink we from Canada don't play no good cricket. Dey say we from snow white. Not one tour we go on where dem noh say looka dese ol' men. Dem nah know we!" Sam is passionate that living in Canada, the land of snow, for half their lives and being old, does not mean they cannot play cricket. "Dem nah know we" (They don't know who we are or what we are capable of) indicates that he does not like to be judged and his use of patois authenticates his Caribbean (and not Canadian) status. "It's the background that's important!" Vilroy, a black 68-year-old Barbadian-Canadian adds to the debate with Dudley. He attests that Caribbean-Canadians and "just off the rock" Barbadians are on equal footing because they were brought up in the same cricket systems.

Drawing on a stereotype of Canadians as white and reifying the idea of the impossibility of belonging to Canada for blacks/Caribbeans (Walcott, 2003), Winston, a black 59-year-old Antiguan-Canadian called out, "I look Canadian to you?!" Pabst (2006, p. 119) explains "black Canadians are cast out of authentic Canadianness … [and] similarly cast out of discourses of blackness." They constantly struggle to (dis)avow their Canadianness and blackness in the face of challenges from "more authentic" subjects. This binary suggests that they are unable to affirm the hybrid identities they actually experience on a daily basis. The discourses available to them place them in or out of national, ancestral, or phenotypical categorisations when their impure, hybrid, culturally intermingled lives situate them in multiple locations and identities at once. In fact, Canadian national discourses of multiculturalism, that encourage immigrants to protect their ancestral heritage are coeval with discourses that reject racial others, restrict their citizenship rights and position white nationals as masters of national space (see Thobani, 2007). This makes a hybrid Canadian identity difficult to name. At the same time, these men came of age during the 1960s and 1970s black power movement. Rather than black self-hatred, their commitment to counter-hegemonic expressions of black self-regard, such as "black pride" and "black is beautiful" campaigns, which were linked to assertions of racial purity (Cohen, 2007, p. 377), also prevent them from embracing the mixture so evident in their daily lives and ancestral heritage.

As a young, newly immigrated man, Dudley regarded himself as a "true Bajan," and a "mighty black" in contrast to older Caribbean-Canadian Mavericks whose temporal and spatial distance from home leaves them inevitably disconnected from Barbadian (cricket) culture, old age prevents them from enacting physical cricket superiority and masculinity, and embedment in a white culture leaves their blackness in question. Dudley's own lack of a sense of security in his new English home may be a precursor to his outer-national identification and attempt to mark his authenticity by lashing out against and denigrating other men of Barbadian origin. He probably maintained a plan to live abroad for only a few years to make money and then return home, just as many of the Mavericks once did. Some of them recounted: "the plan was to come here just five years" or "I came to be a cop but you know the kids start coming an' I just stay." Dudley assumed that these men, who had stayed in Canada for 30 or 40 years could not possibly be true to their Bajan roots, and owing to the image of Canada as a non-cricketing nation, they could not possibly have maintained their skills. These factors, combined with the arrogance of youth, were used to construct a boundary between himself and Barbadian-Canadian Mavericks.

In response, the Mavericks deployed aspects of their culture such as the patois language ("dem nah know we!") and the ancestral ties ("it's the background that's important") in order to show their authenticity as Barbadian subjects. They even posit their age as an asset, owing to the experience it affords. In an interview, Sam, a black 61-year-old Barbadian-Canadian explained that he is able to play more cricket now than he could as a youth at home in Barbados because there are multiple teams to play for in Toronto and he has the time and money to travel due to his early retirement at 60 years of age. Schmidt (2008, p. 31) argues that diasporic groups "sometimes struggle with each other about the dominant feature" of what she terms the "polyphonic bricolage" (Schmidt, 2008, p. 24) that creates culture. Composed of heterogenous voices and constantly changing cultural practices and identities, members of the diaspora, even from the same nation of origin, may experience conflicts.

The players create fluid forms of solidarity and identity that do not rely on singular spaces or identities. Their de- and re-territorialisation "forces us to reconceptualize fundamentally the politics of community, solidarity, identity, and cultural difference" (Gupta and Ferguson, 1992, p. 9), and to recognise that our social boundaries are created and expressed in conversation with people similar, but also different to us around such characteristics as age, time since migration and integration into the host community. If we consider diasporic cricket locations as yet another type of border zone that the MCSC members occupy, we see that they are sites of heightened consciousness where identities become defined, constructed and articulated. As Brubaker (2004, pp. 81–82) points out, race, ethnicity and nation are overlapping terms with multiple dimensions of differentiation including phenotype and other visible markers, distinctive language, customs, religion, degree and nature of territorialisation, fixedness versus fluidity of group membership, and claims to membership, criteria which are hotly debated. The boundaries we create, to divide "us" from "them" require classification and categorisation; these are cognitive process that create diasporic group (sub-)identities.

Their sojourner mentality, dreams of permanent return, frequent trips to the homeland, remittances to family and friends left behind, property holdings and other assets in the nation of origin, reading of Caribbean newspapers, tuning into back-home radio shows, following cricket scores on www.cricinfo.com, belonging to immigrant national associations and performing well on the cricket field all point to a transnational identity that allows the Mavericks to disavow their Canadianness in favour of a Caribbean nation of origin identity when it suits them. Barth (1998, p. 14) describes ethnic groups as ascriptive and exclusive, but the nature of continuity of ethnic units is clear:

> it depends on the maintenance of a boundary. The cultural features that signal the boundary may change, and the cultural characteristics of the members may likewise be transformed, indeed, even the organizational form of the group may change – yet the fact of continuing dichotomization between members and outsiders allows us to specify the nature of continuity, and investigate the changing cultural form and content.

The Mavericks constantly make boundaries around their national identities to distance themselves from "others" and delineate their communities. Because Warlie lived in Barbados until he was 30 years of age and travels back every year, he considers himself "a real Bajan" and enjoys getting into discussions with others about the prowess of Bajan cricketers. "My name is [Warlie Michaels], and I'm a real Bajan. All the others are counterfeit!"

In July 2008, referring to the election of Tillman Thomas in Grenada, Curtis, a black 41-year-old Grenadian-Canadian exclaimed "So I hear we have a new prime minister!" and engaged in discussion with his Grenadian teammate about the political future of the island. When his teammate asked, "How you hear dat already?" in reference to a controversy within the National Democratic Congress party, Curtis asked, incredulously "You don't read News Now online?!" His teammate adamantly replied, "No I go down twice a year ... I'm not glued to the [Inter]Net." The club members highlighted regular travel to Grenada versus regular mediated access to the nation as contrasting means of performing nationalism. The constant discussions of criteria for belonging to the nation allude to the insecurity of this category. Connell (1995) describes a compulsory heterosexual masculinity that is so fragile that it is in need of constant reaffirmation in homosocial spaces such as sports teams. Within first-generation Caribbean-Canadian men's sport, the complexity and vulnerability of masculinity also requires nationhood's continual reaffirmation.

It should come as no surprise that some of the Mavericks identify as Canadian sometimes, Caribbean at others, and "truly" Bajan, or Grenadian, or any other national identity when it suits them. Within the Caribbean diaspora members each:

> interpret their culture quite diversely and individually, depending on their circumstances ... Each member marks different fixed aspects of their culture,

sometimes language, history, political conflicts or sometimes popular religiosity, depending on the place they live, the aims they are fighting for, the situation [with which] they have to cope, and the borders they want to construct. (Schmidt, 2008, p. 31)

During the conversations described above, we might wonder where were the Trinis (Trinidadians), Yardies (Jamaicans) and Kittitians (people from St. Kitts)? At times, they remained quiet while the Barbadians and Grenadians "kept noise" over who was the more authentic national subject. At other times, they used West Indies cricketers as proof of the relative merits of their nation of origin. For example, the famous batting skills of Rohan Kanhai, Garfield Sobers, or Vivian Richards were heralded as examples of the ingenuity of all Guyanese, Barbadians and Antiguans respectively. And, it should go without saying that female MCSC members, unable to prove their nationalism through cricket prowess, were also excluded from competing for national authenticity on these terms.

Nation-of-origin nationalisms also appeared strongly during holidays, in particular the Mavericks' respective National Independence Days. Nearly every Caribbean territory celebrates its independence in Toronto. On these days, the Mavericks appear less as a unified team and segregate themselves into groups based on their nation of origin. Jamaica's Independence Day, celebrated annually at Keelesdale Park is an opportunity to participate in island national affairs from a new dwelling place. The organisers advertise in the *Share*, *Pride* and *Caribbean Camera* Caribbean-Canadian newspapers, which promote a picnic with reggae music, a fête for insiders – and therefore "forge a direct connection between the Jamaicanised city and postcolonial Jamaica" (Burman, 2002, p. 59). Some of the Mavericks turned down the opportunity to play cricket and went to the Jamaican festival on Saturday, 26 July 2008, a notable decision given their devotion to the sport in the "short" summer and the importance attributed to the game against a visiting team from Connecticut.

For their Independence Day, Guyanese club members did not have to choose between cricket and a festival because their celebrations involved a cricket match:

Reggie: When is Independence, Guyana Independence, the Guyanese national team always come up … they have a big function at L'Amoreaux Park … and if you wanna reach a lot of Guyanese just fin' where that park is.
Janelle: So who do they play against?
Reggie: They play against the Ontario 11 or the Canadian 11, so it's a very very [competitive game]. One year I played in that.
Janelle: On which side? (laughs)

Reggie: I played in, (pause) Oh! (surprised) I can't remember now. Ah, I think it was the – oh yes, the Guyanese, because me and him (indicates Learie, another Guyanese-Canadian) played – yeah, we played on the Guyanese side … Of course! We represent South America!

Reggie's inability to remember initially which country he represented exemplifies the fluidity of choice of members of the Caribbean diaspora and their always already placement within multiple national frameworks. His exclamation, "Of course!" comes late as he suddenly recalls his national (and continental) pride. Hussein explained to me, in a joking manner, that the Guyanese see themselves as superior to the rest of the Caribbean, "We are no little islanders! … We are big country people. We know better than anybody else, regards cricket." The extended laughter at this joke, from Hussein and others within earshot, signalled how preposterous an idea it was that Guyanese could be superior to men from other Caribbean nations owing to (a) their mainland, South American status or (b) their expertise at cricket. The differences and hierarchies among the islands are typically presented as a joke when players are keeping noise around the boundary, but every joke is based on a kernel of truth from someone's perspective, and may strike a chord or play on an insecurity of some members of the seemingly homogenous Afro-Caribbean diaspora.

Afro-Caribbean-Canadians constantly draw on their networks of migrants, living in dispersed diasporic nodes to create opportunities for travel and reunions. Return visits to play cricket games, like family reunions, allow them to maintain their kinship and friendship bonds across national borders and throughout the Black Atlantic. Diasporas are not inherently anti-nationalist, however. Nationalisms within diasporas are selectively presented and contingent upon circumstances and location. This study shows how nationalisms manifest as the result of ongoing dialogues between differently positioned people. Members of diasporas are multiply located and able to draw on many national and regional discourses and symbols for the purposes of making identity. Although all Afro-Caribbean-Canadians may appear to eat similar foods and understand each other when they speak, they may choose to obfuscate the connections to their regional ancestry in favour of a Canadian identity, revealed through their participation on elite teams in the past and the contemporary flags displayed, uniforms worn, pins exchanged and discourses shared by and among the Mavericks when they travel to the United States or England.

Afro-Caribbeans often walk tall as they espouse the "out of many, one people" attitude from the Jamaican national motto. Nevertheless, they also eschew their similarities in favour of identification with their nation of origin in particular circumstances. Caribbean regionalism and specific Caribbean nationalisms are negotiated depending on the context, spatial opportunities and the perceived authenticity of interlocutors. Their discursive creation of a hierarchy of Caribbean nations reveals some of the fissures within the Caribbean community. As Clifford (1994) reminds us, nationalisms do not disappear when we discuss global flows; in fact, interactions within the Black Atlantic may make the boundaries around the nation-state more, not less salient. The following chapter links together the many boundaries (national, gender, racial, and ethnic) members of the Afro-Caribbean diaspora make and cross.

Conclusion

In my search for tidy conclusions and a singular confirmation of the meaning of sport in the Black Atlantic, I came up empty handed, or "wit' me two long arms" as cricket club members might say. There are so many dimensions to the transnational flows of peoples and cultures of the Afro-Caribbean diaspora that have important bearing on how we think about black masculinities, culture and sport. This book concerns the notion of the Black Atlantic, which was introduced by Gilroy in 1993, as a geographic region and a theoretical framework that helps in understanding the experiences of a racialised community that spans national borders. The Black Atlantic continues to be a valuable concept to signal attention to the racial identities within, and importance of travel between Canada, England, the United States and the Caribbean. This book is also concerned with the cultural flows and mobility within the Afro-Caribbean diaspora. As emigrant populations outnumber those who remain at home in Caribbean territories and islands, and as ethnic and national conversations, creolisations and oppressions influence black consciousness, more attention must be paid to the ways in which race, ethnicity, gender and cultural boundaries are regenerated in the diaspora.

In conversations about the Black Atlantic, Canada is often overlooked, but black Caribbean migrants offer a unique lens through which to understand black relations to other diaspora "nodes" (Voigt-Graf, 2004) and how Canadian national discourses manifest race. Also virtually ignored in conversations about race and gender in diaspora settings is the use of recreational sport to connect migrants to the homeland and each other. The ethnographic research presented here shines a light on the complexities of sport in the Afro-Caribbean diaspora to develop understandings of the Black Atlantic.

This study expands on C. L. R. James' (1963) text, *Beyond a Boundary*, which uses cricket to explain Caribbean nationalism and race relations. James was adamant that sport was important beyond the runs, wickets, bowling and batting because it could be used to draw attention to wider social and political contexts. His account of professional cricket(ers) is useful insofar as it explains the central importance of cricket to constructions of Caribbean identity and as symbolic of the intertwined anti-colonial, class and race struggles of various Caribbean nations in the early twentieth century. Though James himself operated in the United States, England and Caribbean, he did not use the language of diaspora and did not describe the importance of cricket for connecting Caribbean peoples across the Atlantic Ocean. This book extends his analysis and moves beyond James' boundaries to examine a more contemporary period, and focus on what recreational cricket and contiguous cricket spaces offer in an analysis of the boundaries we create around racial identities, relational performances of hetero-masculinities and femininities, ethnic antagonisms and persistent nationalisms that constitute the Afro-Caribbean diaspora. As Gilroy (2005) writes, "The knot of ideas around sport demonstrates that we cannot sanction the luxury of believing that 'race,' nation, [gender] and ethnicity will be readily or easily disentangled from each other" (p. 111). I extend contemporary Caribbean studies by investigating sport in Canada to open up the complexities of how boundaries are produced around race, nation, gender and ethnicity. I examin various social spaces created by a group of older, first-generation Afro-Caribbean-Canadians that is referred to as the Mavericks Cricket and Social Club (MCSC).

This study also owes a debt to, but expands on other, more recent works on sport and the black diaspora by Carrington (2010) and Abdel-Shehid (2005). I move beyond their reference to the black diaspora as a moniker for a broadly dispersed racial group and their focus on professional, black American and Canadian athletes. Instead, I identify a particular black sub-population (Afro-Caribbeans in Canada), focus on recreational sport, and enumerate how sport and its associated plurilocal social spaces are used to make (and break) the diaspora. The MCSC were primarily Afro-Caribbean-Canadians, born throughout the Anglo-Caribbean. They were mainly between 50 and 70 years of age, and knew each other in Canada for nearly four decades. I attended their parties, fundraising dances, banquets and cricket games at grounds throughout the Greater Toronto Area on weekends from early May to late September in 2008 and 2009. I also travelled with approximately 30 MCSC members to observe and participate in cricket tourism in Barbados, England and St. Lucia. I draw from this empirical research to outline the ways in which sport is what Nassy Brown (1998) calls a "diasporic resource": a confluence of symbols, materials, images, people and places that help to create transnational social fields that interconnect migrants dispersed across Europe and North America as well as those who stay behind. To Nassy Brown's list, I add corporeal practices, spectator activities, and sport-related travel, music and food as resources deployed to maintain the Black Atlantic.

A close look at what goes on before and during cricket matches, at cricket after-parties and on cricket trips provides insights into the influence of transnational flows of people and cultures on racial consciousness, community-making and the contradictions and complexities of Afro-diasporic identity performances that never remain static; they keep changing and moving in response to governmental projects and discourses as well as individual roots and routes. Sport is an important cultural flow that provides opportunities for the simultaneous representation of sameness and difference among Afro-Caribbean, African-American, black British, Indo-Caribbean and South Asian groups. Diasporas operate neither in isolation from each other, nor in an historical vacuum. Racial identities are formed in relation to other groups.

Sport and social activities organised by the club are used as a diasporic resource in two important ways. They produce unity and reinforce differences. First, the club allows members to maintain connections to their region and nations of origin through an association with people, places, cultures and memories of the "homeland." The club members under study here might be characterised elsewhere as members of the African diaspora, or African-Canadians, but they are not restricted by attachment to Africa. Even connections to their nations of origin are profound for some and scant for others. Rather, owing to their privilege as multiple-passport-carrying diasporic subjects, they interact across multiple national boundaries and draw from many similar ancestral and contemporary ties. Gilroy (1993) opines that, "it is important, while bearing significant differences in mind, to attempt to specify some of the similarities to be found in diverse black experiences in the modern West." He focuses on the black sense of unity that derives from experiencing, to use W. E .B. DuBois' term, "double-consciousness," feeling both black and American (or of the modern West) at the same time. Beyond double consciousness, I suggest that club members also experience a shared sense of plurilocal homelands.

The emotional, social, financial and material investments they make in the varied black Atlantic locations they visit for sport mean Afro-Caribbean-Canadians maintain connections not only in or to their nations of origin, but also to Canada, the United States and England. The batting order for the team has a similar national distribution to the West Indies International cricket team; the dinners served are as likely to feature flying fish as curried goat; and the participants easily discuss their monarch, president or prime minister. They are officially included in multiple nationalisms, and yet they desire more: a diasporic community formed from specific collaborations and exchanges among Afro-Caribbeans from many islands and territories, now living across the Black

Atlantic. Club members know that on any weekend in the summer they can head to one of the local cricket grounds and unite with other Afro-Caribbean people. For certain special events they are guaranteed to encounter visitors from abroad, thus restoring a sense of neighbourliness they once had in their nations of origin in plurilocal homespaces.

Members of the MCSC celebrate the unity across nation-state boundaries they are able to generate, but certain club members draw on the same diasporic resource in different ways: some may be passionate about sport while others emphasise the social opportunities the club affords; the specific languages spoken and music, foods and alcohols consumed at every game are significant means of creating distinctly Afro-Caribbean spaces and generating a convivial, status-free, welcoming, friendly environment. Men of all classes, including plumbers, postal workers, police officers and principals interact in friendships that are spontaneous in some cases and pentagenarian in others. They create a space in which they can reinforce the "reputation" values (Wilson, 1973) of working-class, outdoor Caribbean spaces through talking, joking, *liming* and storytelling.

Some of the priorities for the MCSC are the imaginative, material and financial maintenance of various homelands. Older men's ritual of sharing memories at the cricket field and MCSC social events is a means to recreate home and restore a sense of history, community, nationalism, regionalism and diasporic belonging. These club members are deeply embedded in nostalgia for the past; in particular, their lack of cricket resources as children is framed as an element of their upbringing that made them stronger, more courageous, more creative and more talented sportsmen. They tell tales of the supremacy of the Windies team and their own prior on-field greatness as demonstrations of their understandings of themselves as part of not only a community of men, but particularly of powerful black men. Their racial pride is demonstrated through continuous recounting and re-enacting how a few dozen black men from a tiny region dominated the entire world in cricket. While the stories of Windies supremacy might be true, other stories they tell are certainly embellishments, half-truths or fully acknowledged fabrications. However, in expressing their longing for times past and their gender and racial pride, they create a sense of stability and community.

In addition to the "imaginative rediscoveries" (Hall, 2003) of their homeland cultures, club members are able to contribute materially and financially to the amelioration and restoration of Afro-Caribbean communities in their nations of origin, throughout the Caribbean, in Toronto and elsewhere. Caribbean diaspora literatures highlight the importance of economic flows from the diaspora back to the Caribbean, which contribute significantly to the gross national product of the homeland. Through their economic commitments, including making donations to Afro-Caribbean organisations and individuals, the members of the MCSC maintain a connection to home. Club members feel a sense of obligation to help those in need who were unable or unwilling to migrate. Fundraising to pay for charitable donations, "authentic" Afro-Caribbean food, well-kept grounds, professional umpires and trips to the Caribbean or Afro-Caribbean diasporic cricket spaces, is important to replicate the cricket they were able to play at home, and to display and improve their social status (in Canada and the Caribbean) as prosperous, morally upright, benevolent and generous members of the diaspora. Meanwhile, their donation of cricket equipment to underprivileged boys in the Caribbean is a real investment in the making of masculinities at a local scale and an imagined contribution to regional cricket prowess on the world stage. Their donations to immigrant organisations and local charities in Canada, the United States and England allow them to participate in community making across the Black Atlantic. Participation in the sport of cricket helps to maintain the homeland and broader communities of their memories and reality.

This ageing group of migrants also promotes unity through the use of their sporting spaces and communities to collectively assuage the melancholy of their failing bodies, ill and dying friends and relatives, lonely retirements, homesickness and inabilities to travel regularly or return to the homeland as they had once planned. Their sharing of nostalgic stories about their youth, about the heyday of the Windies international cricket champions and about their own previous cricket travels provide talk therapy. Their foods, music and dancing reveal that a carnival atmosphere can operate as a salve for life's pains, with what Gilroy (1993) describes as the "racial terror" of the Black Atlantic being only one part. Ageing terror is an equally unifying force in the Black Atlantic.

The second way in which sport and social activities are a diasporic resource is that they provide a venue for differences within unity, that is, for class, gender, ethnic and national hierarchies to be expressed and reinforced. The diaspora, like the nations from which migrants come, are consumed with boundary-making projects that exclude as much as, if not more than, they include. Cricket spaces represented freedom for some powerful members. They were seen as a constraint for less influential others. Edwards (2003) describes diasporas as rife with *décalages*, that is "differences within unity," and calls for specific interrogations of exchanges among black interlocutors within transnational networks to generate multiple understandings of black culture and experience. Examining the hierarchies and disjunctures within diasporas indicates more complicated ways of thinking about Afro-Caribbeanness and/or blackness in Canada. It is the interactions and intersections among groups that allows for boundaries to be made and/or crossed. Paying attention to the members of the diaspora who are absent, marginalised, denigrated, or excluded from cricket and social activities reveals some of the hierarchies and disjunctures in Afro-Caribbean-Canadian communities and the power struggles of the homeland that are ongoing within diasporas. For example, not every club member is eligible for travel as a result of citizenship restrictions or a lack of disposable income and the culture of alcohol consumption excludes or at least marginalises their non-drinking peers. Three major groups are worth exploring for what their absences reveal about hierarchies in the Black Atlantic. Women, men of Indo-Caribbean origin and second-generation Afro-Caribbeans are conspicuously under-represented among the "unified" members of the MCSC and their community-making practices.

Though women of a wide range of ethnic and national heritages are included among the members of the MCSC, their numbers are miniscule compared to men's, especially at cricket matches. My analysis of the few women who do attend cricket games and particularly those who travel with the Mavericks could shift the discussion of sport and race in the Black Atlantic to relationships between heterosexual masculinity and femininity in the reproduction of black diasporic spaces. In order to disavow homosexuality, it is imperative that there are some women – girlfriends, wives and mistresses – present who can bolster the men's heterosexual identities. Cricket and social spaces are places for the performance of dominant Afro-Caribbean masculinities, which depend upon homosociality laced with homophobic jokes and banter that denigrate gays and transsexuals, and exclude or marginalise women while relying on their labour.

Most female club members support their husbands' participation through cooking, laundry, domestic and childcare, but do not attend MCSC games. Due to women's roles as the keepers of the insular nuclear family in Western patriarchal structures and nation building, Afro-Caribbean-Canadian women are more assimilated into Canadian structures than their menfolk and are limited in their ability and desire to reproduce Afro-Caribbean homespaces. Many Afro-Caribbean-Canadian wives "lose" their husbands to cricket every weekend, but they live with that because of a lack of support resources and discursive tools available to them for assistance with child-minding and domestic duties, because they want to grant their husbands the freedom to create homosocial environments, and because their respectability would be compromised by entering men's *liming* spaces. The Caribbean homespace cricket offers is something many Afro-Caribbean women migrated away from without desire to return.

Much research remains to be done on female club members. What do they do on summer weekends when they are not at games and with whom? What are their experiences at club dances and fundraisers? What are the roles and experiences of white, or East-Asian-Canadian women who marry into the Afro-Caribbean culture celebrated by the Mavericks? What types of opportunities are available for women who would prefer to be players rather than supporters or absent "widows" (Razack, 2009 provides insights in this regard).

In Toronto today, there are more Indo-Caribbean than Afro-Caribbean cricketers; however, the MCSC games belie this reality. Many Indo-Caribbeans, particularly Guyanese, have formed their own teams, it could be argued, because overt expressions of anti-Indo-Caribbean or anti-South Asian racism including the denigration of certain foods, music and language sends a strong message that they are welcome to participate among the Mavericks only if they accept and adopt an Afro-Caribbean habitus (Joseph, 2014). Carrington explains that sports contests are racially signified, that is, they "act as a key signifier for wider questions about identity within racially demarcated societies" (1998, p. 280). The acceptance of Afro-Caribbean cultural forms as the only representation of authentic Caribbeanness at the cricket grounds excludes many Indo-Caribbeans who may remember or wish to celebrate their homelands differently. This may explain the ongoing presence of Toronto's Guyanese or Trinidadian cricket clubs when many of the other nationally specific Caribbean teams have amalgamated into clubs such as the MCSC.

Another "absent" group comprises the second and third generations, who are referred to by Walcott (2001) as the authentic arbiters of black popular culture in Canada. Many club members expressed disappointment that their Canadian-born (grand-)sons were not interested in the sport of cricket. As Gilroy (2005) astutely observes of this generation in Britain, "[tall] children want to play basketball rather than bowl, and the fundamental idea that a wholly satisfying contest can endure for five days and yet produce no result increasingly defies comprehension" (p. 111). The Mavericks lament that they were unable to pass on this important aspect of Afro-Caribbean masculinity in a social setting where cricket has little salience among Canadian sporting rites of passage such as basketball, football, baseball and, of course, ice hockey. However, with the influx of South Asian youth, and now that cricket has been incorporated into the varsity sports system of many Canadian public and Roman Catholic secondary school boards, particularly those in and around Vancouver and Toronto, there are more opportunities for second- and third-generation Afro-Caribbean children and adolescents to play. The nostalgic storytelling of migrants may receive a new audience as youth of many ethnic backgrounds can potentially learn of the connections between the sport and racial and ethnic heritage from their volunteer coaches. A few of the Afro-Caribbean Mavericks are increasingly involved with secondary school cricket teams as they retire from paid employment and look for ways to fill their days. Whether cricket will become a corporeal diasporic resource for Afro-Caribbean youth, fundamental to their transnational community making and sense of deterritorialised identity, or gets categorised alongside other seemingly local, neutral sports in the Canadian landscape remains to be seen. What is clear is that for the older generation, those who were in their prime when the Windies team dominated the world in the 1970s and 1980s, cricket will remain central to the performative, corporeal and narrative production of their identities and this passion is a barrier for their unification with younger Afro-Caribbeans.

Exclusions of gender, ethnicity and generation are just three ways this Afro-Caribbean community experiences disjunctures. It is worth highlighting that there are at least a dozen other ways that the community is divided at certain times. Conflicts arise among wives and mistresses, fundraisers and misers, working- and middle-classes, organisers and revellers, patriots from different nations, those who travel and those who stay in one place, and so on. The Afro-Caribbean diaspora is internally divided and it is through the different ways people access and express themselves in cricket and its associated spaces, that we see how hierarchies within the community are established and dominant cultures formed.

Beyond the boundary of diaspora as a unified or internally divided entity, the evidence of black cricket spaces reveals that this diasporic resource may also be a Canadian national resource. That is, there are many ways in which the members of the Afro-Caribbean diaspora are creolised or acculturated Canadians and contribute to Canadian multiculturalism that are worth highlighting for the insights they provide into the Black Atlantic. Barnor Hesse (2000) introduces the term "transruptions" to account for the ways in which diaspora groups, by both drawing from their homeland cultures and generating cultural entanglements in their new homes, create recurrent, political contestations, unsettling the meaning of multiculturalism. Transruptions are *"any series of contestatory cultural and theoretical interventions which, in their impact as cultural differences, unsettle social norms and threaten to dismantle hegemonic concepts and practices"* (Hesse, 2000, p. 17, emphasis in original). The cricketers and club supporters examined in this study continue to embrace and at times challenge dominant ideas of what it means to be Canadian. Many are involved in interracial marriages and relationships; have children and grandchildren who express little to no interest in or knowledge of cricket; are embedded in white Canadian structures such as education, police services, or finance for their employment; and few will return to their nation of origin to retire as they had once planned. They have also experienced interpersonal and systemic racism, unfortunate hallmarks of Canadian nationalism. They are fixed to the Canadian nation-state.

When they travel abroad they share symbols of pride in Canadian nationalism with their black "brothers," demonstrating the complexity of their national affiliations. Afro-Caribbean-Canadians simultaneously oscillate between black diasporic consciousness, pan-Caribbean identity and hegemonic nationalisms. They are what Cohen (2007, p. 381) describes as creoles: "interposed between two or more cultures, selectively appropriating some elements, rejecting others, and creating new possibilities that transgress and supersede parent cultures, which themselves are increasingly recognized as fluid." Yet, they belie their own realities and constantly draw on essentialist language, describing themselves as "pure" black men, or "truly" Jamaican as circumstances warrant. Their high mobility, a result of their middle-class status, disposable income and retirement or vacation time, allows this group of older Afro-Caribbean migrants to access many different homespaces. Their constant redrawing of boundaries is a direct result of the increasing volume of cultural interactions they encounter in their plurilocal homelands and the constant challenge to their identities these present. The maple leaf flag that they hang on their clubhouse when they travel suggests that the Black Atlantic is a space for demonstrating Canadian pride.

Rather than orienting solely towards a singular homeland on one hand or feeling dislocated on the other hand, as diasporas are often described, Afro-Caribbeans can use cricket and its associated *liming* to recreate a homespace in their place of residence, which is part of, not instead of, their integration into the dominant Canadian culture. As Werbner (2005, p. 751, emphasis in original) notes of Pakistani immigrants in Britain, "increasing prosperity and indeed integration ... has been associated, paradoxically, not with cultural assimilation, as might be expected, but with ethnic cultural *intensification*, as the ritual celebrations of the elite have increased in scale, expense, frequency and cultural elaboration." As such, MCSC members' creation of vibrant homespaces across the Black Atlantic is an example of their affluence and performance of a highly valued Canadian ideology: multiculturalism. These migrants are able to feel emplaced in Canada because their local cricket grounds are a symbolic stand-in for the Caribbean and its hybridity, transnationalism and heritage. Yet, I do not wish to perpetuate what J. Lorand Matory refers to as the "illusion of isolation" in reference to South Carolina's Gullah/Geechee peoples. Though the MCSC is a significant case study of Afro-Caribbean "survivals" in Canada, and at times the cricket ground "feels exactly" like cricket in any of the Anglo-Caribbean islands, the spaces they create demonstrate the "evolving product of interaction" (Matory, 2008, p. 950), the reality of the permeability of ethnic communities in everyday life in the Black Atlantic, and the impossibility of an exact recreation of a home culture in a new diaspora location. Matory explains Black Atlantic culture as exemplified by two cross-cultural facts of life:

> First, the units of collective action and meaning-making that we call "cultures" are unique intersections, interpretations, and adaptations of translocal flows. They are not "islands" of *sui generis* distinction and internal homogeneity awaiting subsequent discovery by outsiders. Second, the consciousness and endogamous enforcement of heredity difference – or ethnicity – becomes a named reality only when and where one population and a co-present population share a desire to distinguish themselves from each other." (Matory, 2008, 951)

In other words, the cultures of the MCSC are defined against other groups and at times, even certain club members set themselves apart from each other, revealing that black masculine identities are reproduced in conversation with other gendered and ethnic identities, and are therefore affected by the "routes" of others as much as they draw from their ancestral "roots." The presence of multiple diasporas (e.g., from India and Pakistan) in Toronto are integral to the making of the Black Atlantic through the boundaries that groups create around themselves. Boundary-making is a process and boundaries must be constantly maintained by continual expression and validation to become meaningful.

Walcott (2003) argues that the continual erasure of blackness from dominant Canadian identities forces Afro-Caribbeans to look elsewhere for a sense of national belonging, and a plurilocal sense of home emerges as a result. This work fleshes out that notion with examples of the multiple elsewheres to which Afro-Caribbean-Canadians "look." Some travel to their nations of origin or another diaspora location to play and watch cricket and feel "at home." Those club members who travel do so regularly, and they typically visit their nations of origin, or a more broadly defined homespace found in other Caribbean countries, England, the United States and elsewhere in Canada. The MCSC creates opportunities for cricketers and non-cricketers alike to travel throughout the Black Atlantic to (re-)generate Afro-Caribbean cross-border kinships, friendships and networks. Club members engage in "roots tourism," but instead of returning to slave ports in Ghana or plantations in the United States for a glimpse of the past and to appreciate "the way things were," Afro-Caribbean-Canadian cricketers and their supporters tour Caribbean and diasporic parishes, towns and cities, visit world-class stadiums, national museums and heritage sites, and see consulate offices, beaches and shopping centres They, thereby, expand their knowledge and understanding of Afro-Caribbeanness, global cultural flows and racial communities (Joseph, 2011b).

They can also stay home in Canada and the past and their culture can "come alive" at the local cricket grounds, banquet halls and community events they attend, often with visitors from across the Black Atlantic. As Walcott notes, "any useful discussion of Afro-Caribbean popular culture in Canada is fixed between the transmigration of cultural artefacts, practices and peoples throughout the United States, Britain and the Anglo-Caribbean region" (Walcott, 2001, p. 126). Their travels and home games fuel their sense of belonging and provide them with new stories to sustain them for years to come.

Investigations of the Black Atlantic must take into account actual transnational travels, the memorabilia and memories of travel, and the differences among them. The unity of community and the class, gender, national and ethnic hierarchies that manifest in diasporic spaces are equally important. Sport is an aspect of culture that is used as a source of racial and national pride, but also produces conflicts between and within different diasporic groups in multicultural settings. "How, then, to describe this play of 'difference' within identity?" is a question asked by Stuart Hall (2003, p. 238). He refers to the "play" of history, culture and power that results in an identity not based on an essentialised past, but in a continuously changing narrative of ourselves. We can "play" with diasporic identities because they are forever unstable, unsettled and lack any final resolution. He also uses the word "play" to remind readers of the specific origins of dispersal for many black people in the West: the Caribbean. Here the varieties of Caribbean music "playing" exceed a binary structure of past/present, or them/us; Caribbean music signifies the mixtures, constant borrowing and creativity of Caribbean cultures. To his analysis, I add the "playing" involved in *liming* and sport in diasporic settings.

Liming is a complex phenomenon that entails playing language games, a play or performance of stylised aggressive talk, playing dominoes and playful cross-gender flirting, all of which are key to constructing Afro-Caribbean masculinities in the diaspora. Playing the sport of cricket includes bowling, batting, wicket keeping, fielding, cheering, heckling and strategising, which are all means of regenerating gender and race. This investigation of various types of play reveals the ways communities are built across borders and within nations. Understanding the centrality of masculinity and blackness and the political cultural expressions, such as sport, with which they are intertwined creates an opportunity to re-evaluate the Black Atlantic, particularly from a Canadian and Caribbean perspective. Playing sport requires making and crossing boundaries of race, nation and gender. Cricket, played both here and there, reveals multifaceted, plurilocal Afro-Caribbean communities, cultures and consciousness.

The final narrative, presented below, is based on both my observations and those of Kundell, a black 52-year-old St. Lucian-Canadian at a club meeting in August 2008. After showing him my documentation of events, he highlighted the importance of the transnational networks the club creates and mobilises for future travel plans. He also explained that the promise of *liming*, food, drink and cross-border "family" connections, were critical for his decision to join the Mavericks' next big cricket trip, indicating the importance of sport and its associated activities in the making of black and Caribbean diasporas.

Brothers Down Under

The cricketers gathered in a meeting room at the Howard Johnson hotel. It wasn't spectacular: forty grey chairs, four brown folding banquet tables and four peach-coloured walls with chipped paint and crumbling wallpaper borders. One of team members worked there as the evening supervisor and managed to reserve the room for them on a slow night, but they had only one hour to wrap up their meeting.

The club president and vice-president were first to arrive. Together they unfolded a table and placed it at one end of the room. They opened three metal chairs, one for each of them and the club secretary, and sat, facing the empty room, waiting silently for others to arrive. Though the meeting was scheduled to start at 7, it was 7.15 before any cricketers trickled in. As they entered, each took a metal chair from the stacks that lined the far wall, and arranged them in a semi-circle facing the club executive. Fifteen minutes later there was a quorum and the president called the meeting to order.

The first item on the agenda was the next big trip. Now that they had returned from a two-week tour in England, they were ready to organise future travels. The president raised the issue of fundraising for three weeks in Australia as though it was a done deal. The dissension was audible.

"Why we gonna go all the way to Australia when for that money we could finance five trips to Atlanta, or Hartford, or anywhere else in the States?"

"Who has three fuckin' thousand dollars to spend on a flight?!"

"What is gonna be so great there that we couldn't get in Englan'? I don't have no people in Australia!"

The tension built as some men got out of their chairs, not to speak, but just to stand, wide-legged and cross-armed to make their presence felt. The president explained gently that the last time they played in an international tournament in Grenada, the captain of the Australian side had approached him and said that he could guarantee them a half dozen games against men of their age and calibre, the combination of which was not easy to find. Though the cost of the flight was only two grand (some members sighed relief), the trip would cost four (those same members gasped). Well, the president explained, the club had to pay for accommodations, buses to take them from the hotel to the games, entry fees for tourist activities and fees for cricket matches, which would cover food and drink. That is why he wanted to talk about fundraising now, two years in advance of the trip. Most of the players grumbled their reluctance owing to the expense and the distance. Though most were retired, it would be difficult for those who still worked to get three weeks off. Those who wanted to travel around Australia or the South Pacific before or after would need even more time. And those who wanted to bring their wives or children would need even more money. As one man pointed out, he "better get started winning the lottery" to pay for such a trip on a fixed retirement income.

It took the testimony of the vice-president, who was probably vying to usurp his leader's position at the helm of the club, to convince the group. He had been to Australia when he played on a touring Guyanese team 10 years previously, plus he had also spoken to the Australian captain in Grenada. "Listen. Trust me." He began, begging for their attention, "Listen fellas, listen. It will be good. Australians are island people. They play like us. Bar open 10.00, Game start 1.00. You can eat an' drink in the club house all day! When I was there in 1998 we would go to the grounds, have a real meal for breakfast, rice and peas, ribs. Seriously, our fees pay for a full three-course dinner for breakfast. Then they open the bar. Me think, 'Wah, We cyaan't start drinking dis early?!" But I was only the manager on that tour. Lawd. I drink like a fish! And besides, they promise me we are gonna have a chance to play against an Aboriginal side. Yeah, dey play cricket too. We can meet our black brothers from down unda!" With that information the mood in the room shifted. Some of the men who were standing sat down and some nodded. One used the calculator on his phone to figure out how he could afford the expense. The discussion then swung to what they could do as fundraisers to alleviate the cost of the trip. The vice-president successfully showed the club members that in Australia they could still fulfil their priorities. As long as they are *liming* and networking, they can reproduce black and Caribbean cultures and communities.

Appendix

Table 1 Research participant demographics

Name	Year/nation of birth	Year of Toronto migration (year/city of initial migration indicated)	Date/location of interview	Occupation (retirement indicated)	Club status
Arnold	1945 Barbados	1972	26 Jul. 2008, Toronto, Canada	Police officer	Player
Bishops	1939 Barbados	1989	4 Aug. 2008, Toronto, Canada	Electrician (retired)	Supporter – former umpire
Camila	1949 Barbados	1978	17 May 2008, Toronto, Canada	Homemaker	Supporter – girlfriend
Charles	1941 Jamaica	1970	22 Aug. 2009, Toronto, Canada	Engineer (retired)	Supporter – former player
Ciskel	1961 Guyana	1982	19 Jul. 2008, Toronto, Canada	Automotive technician	Player
Curtis	1967 Grenada	1985	14 Mar. 2008, Rodney Bay, St. Lucia	Plumber	Player
Erol	1953 Barbados	1979	19 Jun. 2008, London, England	Car manufacture quality control technician	Player
Eunice	1962 England	1968	22 Jun. 2008, London, England	Teacher	Supporter – wife

Name	Birth year	Birthplace	Date/place	Occupation	Role
George	1961	Barbados	25 Jun. 2008, London, England	Electrician, registered nurse	Player
Hussein	1942	Trinidad	3 Mar. 2008, Rodney Bay, St. Lucia	Teacher (retired)	Player
Jared	1951	Antigua	11 Jul. 2008, Toronto, Canada	Chartered management accountant	Supporter – former player
Jean	1964	Jamaica	24 Jun. 2008, London, England	Registered nurse practitioner	Supporter – wife
Kundell	1957	St. Lucia	5 Jun. 2008, Toronto, Canada	Manager, courier service	Player
Lawrence	1937	Trinidad	15 Nov. 2009, Rockley, Barbados	Self-employed storekeeper	Player
Layton	1960	Barbados	23 Jun. 2008, London, England	Senior technical financial analyst	Player
Learie	1952	Guyana	17 Nov. 2009, Rockley, Barbados	Electric company technician (retired)	Player
Marshall	1950	Barbados	12 Mar. 2008, Rodney Bay, St. Lucia	Telephone company field technician (retired)	Player
Mason	1936	Barbados	15 Nov. 2009, Hastings Barbados	Self-employed financial advisor (retired)	Player
Michael	1952	Guyana	7 Mar. 2008, Dennery, St. Lucia	Fitness club vice-president	Player

(continued)

Table 1 (*cont.*)

Name	Year/nation of birth	Year of Toronto migration (year/city of initial migration indicated)	Date/location of interview	Occupation (retirement indicated)	Club status
Otis	1961 Barbados	1988	24 Jun. 2008 Brighton, England	N/A (Disability)	Player
Percelle	1967 Grenada	1980 (1980 Montreal, Canada)	17 May 2008, Toronto, Canada	Freelance business analyst	Supporter – wife
Reggie	1956 Guyana	1980	24 Jun. 2008, London, England	Millwright	Player
Riddick	1954 Barbados	1988 (1970 Montreal, Canada)	3 Sep. 2008, Toronto, Canada	Police officer	Player
Robert	1945 Barbados	1977 (1975 Montreal, Canada)	16 Aug. 2008, Toronto, Canada	School principal (retired)	Supporter – former player
Roland	1957 Guyana	1996	18 Jun. 2008, London, England	Welder, painter, fork lift operator	Player
Sam	1947 Barbados	1964	26 Jul. 2008, Toronto, Canada	Steel company office clerk (retired)	Player
Sutara	1943 Trinidad	1970	18 Mar. 2008, Rodney Bay, St. Lucia	Homemaker	Supporter – wife
Sylvanie	1948 Antigua	1970	23 Aug. 2008, Toronto, Canada	Department store accountant	Supporter – wife

Name	Born	Date & Place of Interview	Occupation	Role
Tayana	1962 Guyana	17 May 2008, Toronto, Canada	Cleaning business operator	Supporter – wife
Teresah	1950 Jamaica	13 Mar. 2008, Rodney Bay, St. Lucia	Registered nurse	Supporter – wife
Terrel	1952 St. Lucia	23 Jun. 2008, London, England	Automotive quality control technician (retired)	Supporter – former player
Thomas	1964 Barbados	23 Jun. 2008, Brighton, England	Engineer	Player
Vilroy	1940 Barbados	22 Jun. 2008, London, England	Police officer (retired)	Player
Warlie	1938 Barbados	23 Jun. 2008, London, England	Airport vehicle compliance officer	Player
Wesley	1951 Jamaica	16 Feb. 2008, Toronto, Canada	Self-employed home renovator	Player
Winston	1949 Antigua	5 Mar. 2008, Rodney Bay, St. Lucia	National postal service letter carrier	Player

Source: author's own data

References

Abdel-Shehid, G. (2005). *Who da man? Black masculinities and sporting cultures*. Toronto, ON: Canadian Scholar's Press.

Abrahams, R. D. (1983). *The man-of-words in the West Indies: Performance and the emergence of creole culture*. Baltimore, MD, Johns Hopkins University Press.

Ahmed, S. (2004). *The cultural politics of emotion*. New York: Routledge.

Alexander, J. M. (2005). *Pedagogies of crossing: Meditations on feminism, sexual politics, memory, and the sacred*. Durham, NC: Duke University Press.

Anderson, B. (1983). *Imagined communities*. London: Verso.

Andersson, M. (2007). The relevance of the Black Atlantic in contemporary sport: Racial imaginaries in Norway. *International Review for the Sociology of Sport*, 42(1), 65–81.

Angrosino, M. B. (1986). Son and lover: The anthropologist as nonthreatening male. In T. L. Whitehead and M. E. Conaway (Eds), *Self, sex and gender in cross-cultural fieldwork* (pp. 64–83). Chicago, IL: University of Illinois Press.

Anthony, T. (2005). (Director/Writer) *Da kink in my hair*. [Play]. Princess of Wales Theatre. 29 Jan. 2005.

Barth, F. (1998). Introduction. In F. Barth (Ed.), *Ethnic groups and boundaries: The social organization of culture difference*. Long Grove, IL: Waveland.

Basch, L., Glick Schiller, N. and Szanton Blanc, C. (1994). *Nations unbound: Transnational projects, postcolonial predicaments, and deterritorialized nation-states*. Amsterdam, Netherlands: Gordon & Breach.

Bashi, V. F. (2007). *Survival of the knitted: Immigrant social networks in a stratified world*. Stanford, CA: Stanford University Press.

Beckford, S. M. (2012). Always a domestic?: The question of Canadian redemption and belonging in selected literature by Black Canadian writers. *Southern Journal of Canadian Studies*, 5(1), 122–147.

Beckles, H. (2004). *Chattle house blues: Making of a democratic society in Barbados, from Clement Payne to Owen Arthur*. Kingston, Jamaica: Ian Randle.

Bourdieu, P. (1984). *Distinction: A social critique of the judgement of taste*. London: Routledge.

Boym, S. (2001). *The future of nostalgia*. New York: Basic Books.

Brah, A. (1996). *Cartographies of diaspora: Contesting identities*. New York: Routledge.

Brereton, B. (1979). *Race relations in colonial Trinidad*. Cambridge, UK: Cambridge University Press.

Brooke, B. (n.d.) Preserving history key to Caribbean Tourism. Retrieved from www.bobbrooke.com/caribbeanpreservation.htm (accessed 28 February 2010).

Brubaker, E. (2004). *Ethnicity without groups*. Cambridge, MA: Harvard University Press.

Burdsey, D. (2006). 'If I ever play football, Dad, can I play for England or India?' British Asians, sport and diasporic national identities. *The Journal of the British Sociological Association*, 40(1), 11–28.

Burman, J. (2002). Remittance; Or, diasporic economies of yearning. *Small Axe: A Caribbean Journal of Criticism*, 6(2), 49–71.

Burman, J. (2010). *Transnational yearnings: Tourism, migration and the diasporic city*. Vancouver, BC: UBC Press.
Burton, R. D. E. (1995). Cricket, carnival and street culture in the Caribbean. In H. Beckles and B. Stoddart (Eds), *Liberation cricket: West Indies cricket culture* (pp. 89–106). New York: Manchester University Press.
Campbell, M. V. (2012). "Other/ed" kinds of blackness: An Afrodiasporic versioning of black Canada. *Southern Journal of Canadian Studies*, 5(1), 46–65.
Canadian Heritage (2013). Sport participation 2010 research paper. Catalogue no. CH24-1/2012E-PDF.
Carby, H. (1998). *Race men*. Cambridge, MA: Harvard University Press.
Carrington, B. (1998). Sport, masculinity, and black cultural resistance. *Journal of Sport and Social Issues*, 22(3), 275–298.
Carrington, B. (1999). Cricket, culture and identity: An ethnographic analysis of the significance of sport within black communities. In S. Roseneil and J. Seymour (Eds), *Practising identities: Power and resistance* (pp. 11–32). New York: St. Martin's Press.
Carrington, B. (2007). Merely identity: Cultural identity and the politics of sport. *Sociology of Sport Journal*, 24(1), 49–66.
Carrington, B. (2008). 'What's the footballer doing here?' Racialized performativity, reflexivity and identity. *Cultural Studies-Critical Methodologies*, 8(4), 423–452.
Carrington, B. (2010). *Race, Sport and Politics: The Sporting Black Diaspora*. Los Angeles, CA: SAGE Publications.
Central Statistical Office (2011). *Trinidad and Tobago 2011 population and housing census demographic report*. Ministry of Planning and Sustainable Development, Government of the Republic of Trinidad and Tobago.
Chancy, M. J. A. (1997). *Searching for safe spaces: Afro-Caribbean women writers in exile*. Philadelphia, PA: Temple University Press.
Clarke, K. M. (2006). Mapping transnationality. Roots tourism and the institutionalization of ethnic heritage. In K. M. Clarke and D. A. Thomas (Eds), *Globalization and race: Transformations in the cultural production of blackness* (pp. 133–153). Durham, NC: Duke University Press.
Clifford, J. (1986). Introduction: Partial truths. In J. Clifford and G. Marcus (Eds), *Writing culture: The poetics and politics of ethnography* (pp. 1–26). Berkeley, CA: University of California Press.
Clifford, J. (1994). Diasporas. *Cultural Anthropology*, 9(3), 302–338.
Cohen, R. (1995). Rethinking Babylon: Iconoclastic conceptions of the diasporic experience. *New Community*, 21(1), 153–165.
Cohen, R. (2007). Creolization and cultural globalization: The soft sounds of fugitive power. *Globalizations*, 4(3), 369–384.
Connell, R. W. (1995). *Masculinities*. Cambridge, UK: Polity.
Connelly, M. F. and Clandinin, D. J. (1990). Experience and narrative inquiry. *Educational Researcher*, 19(5), 2–14.
Cook, I. and Harrison, M. (2003). Cross over food: Re-materialising postcolonial geographies. *Transactions, Institute of British Geographers*, 28(3), 296–317.
Cook, I. and Harrison, M. (2007). Follow the thing: West Indian hot pepper sauce. *Space and Culture*, 19(1), 40–63.
Crawford, C. (2003). Sending love in a barrel: The making of transnational Caribbean families in Canada. *Canadian Woman Studies*, 22(3–4), 104–109.
Crichlow, W. (2004). *Buller men and batty bwoys: Hidden men in Toronto and Halifax black communities*. Toronto, ON: University of Toronto Press.

Darby, P. and Hassan, D. (2007). Introduction: Locating sport in the study of the Irish diaspora. *Sport in Society*, 10(3), 336–346.

Davis, F. (1979). *Yearning for yesterday: A sociology of nostalgia*. New York: Free Press.

Davis, C. and Upson, G. (2004). Spectatorship, fandom, and nationalism in the South Asian diaspora: The 2003 Cricket World Cup. *The International Journal of the History of Sport*, 21(3–4), 631–649.

Devonish, H. (1995). African and Indian consciousness at play: A study in West Indies cricket and nationalism. In H. Beckles and B. Stoddart (Eds), *Liberation cricket: West Indies cricket culture* (pp. 179–191). New York: Manchester University Press.

Diawara, M. (1990). Englishness and blackness: Cricket as discourse on colonialism. *Callaloo*, 13(4), 830–844.

Donald, J. and Rattansi, A. (Eds). (1992). *Race, culture and difference*. London: SAGE Publications.

Duval, D. T. (2004). Linking return visits and return migration among Commonwealth Eastern Caribbean migrants in Toronto, Canada. *Global Networks: A Journal of Transnational Affairs*, 4(1), 51–68.

Edmonson, B. (2003). Caribbean women and the politics of public performance. *Small Axe: A Caribbean Journal of Criticism*, 13(7), 1–16.

Edwards, B. H. (2001). The uses of diaspora. *Social Text*, 19(1), 45–73.

Edwards, B. H. (2003). *The practice of diaspora: Literature, translation and the rise of black internationalism*. Cambridge, MA: Harvard University Press.

Fairley, S. and Gammon, S. (2005). Something lived, something learned: Nostalgia's expanding role in sport tourism. *Sport in Society*, 8(2), 182–197.

Farred, G. (2003). *What's my name?: Black vernacular intellectuals*. Minneapolis, MN: University of Minnesota Press.

Featherstone, M. (1991). *Consumer culture and postmodernism*. London: SAGE Publications.

Fletcher, T. (2011). 'Aye but it were wasted on thee': Cricket, British Asians, ethnic identities and the 'magical recovery of community'. *Sociological Research Online*, 16(4), www.socresonline.org.uk/16/4/5.html (accessed 15 September 2012).

Fletcher, T. (2012). 'Who do "they" cheer for?' Cricket diaspora, hybridity and divided loyalties amongst British Asians. *International Review for the Sociology of Sport*, 47(5), 612–621.

Foner, N. (Ed.). (2001). *Islands in the city: West Indian migration to New York*. Berkeley, CA: University of California Press.

Gadsby, M. M. (2006). *Sucking salt: Caribbean women writers, migration, and survival*. Columbia, MO: University of Missouri Press.

Garraway, J. (12 September, 2006). Untapped potential in 'roots tourism.' Panama guide. Retrieved from www.panama-guide.com/article.php/20060912200451663 (accessed 28 February 2010).

Gilroy, P. (1987). *Ain't no black in the union jack*. Chicago, IL: University of Chicago Press.

Gilroy, P. (1993). *The Black Atlantic: Modernity and double consciousness*. Cambridge, MA: Harvard University Press.

Gilroy, P. (2000). *Against race: Imagining political culture beyond the colour line*. Cambridge, MA: Harvard University Press.

Gilroy, P. (2005). *Postcolonial melancholia*. New York: Columbia University Press.

Gilroy, P. (2010). *Darker than blue: On the moral economies of Black Atlantic culture*. Cambridge, MA: Belknap Press of Harvard University Press.

Glick Schiller, N. (2005). Transborder citizenship: An outcome of legal pluralism within transnational social fields. In F. von Benda-Beckmann, K. von Benda-Beckmann and A. Griffiths (Eds), *Mobile people, mobile law: expanding legal relations in a contracting world* (pp. 27–50). Berlington, VT: Ashgate.

Glick Schiller, N. and Fouron, G. E. (1999). Terrains of blood and nation: Haitian transnational social fields. *Ethnic and Racial Studies*, 22(2), 340–366.

Gmelch, G. (1992). *Double passage: The lives of Caribbean immigrants abroad and back home.* Ann Arbor, MI: University of Michigan Press.

Goldring, L. (1998). The power of status in transnational social fields. In M. P. Smith and L. E. Guarnizo (Eds), *Transnationalism from below* (pp. 165–195). New Brunswick, NJ: Transaction.

Grainger, A. (2006). From immigrant to overstayer: Samoan identity, rugby, and the cultural politics of race and nation in Aotearoa/New Zealand. *Journal of Sport and Social Issues*, 30(1), 45–61.

Griggs, G. (2006). Calypso to Collapso: the decline of the West Indies as a cricketing super power. *Journal of Sport and Social Issues*, 30(3), 306–314.

Guarnizo, L. E. (2003). The economics of transnational living. *International Migration Review*, 37(3), 666–699.

Guarnizo, L. E., Portes, A. and Haller, W. (2003). Assimilation and transnationalism: Determinants of transnational political action among contemporary migrants. *American Journal of Sociology*, 108(6), 1211–1248.

Gupta, A. and Ferguson, J. (1992). Beyond "culture": Space, identity, and the politics of difference. *Cultural Anthropology*, 7(1), 6–23.

Hall, S. (2003). Cultural identity and diaspora. In J. E. Braziel and A. Mannur (Eds), *Theorizing diaspora* (pp. 233–246). Oxford: Blackwell.

Hall, E. T. (1959). *The silent language.* New York: Doubleday.

Hannerz, U. (1997). *Flows, boundaries and hybrids: Keywords in transnational anthropology. Transnational Communities Working Paper Series,* WPTC-2K-02. Oxford, UK: University of Oxford.

Harney, S. (1996). *Nationalism and identity: Culture and the imagination in a Caribbean diaspora.* London: Zed Books.

Henry, F. (1994). *The Caribbean diaspora in Toronto: Learning to live with racism.* Toronto, ON: University of Toronto Press.

Henry, F. (1999). Caribbean peoples. In P. R. Magocsi (Ed.), *Encyclopedia of Canada's Peoples* (pp. 331–340). Toronto, ON: University of Toronto Press.

Hesse, B. (2000). Introduction: Un/Settled multiculturalisms. In B. Hesse (Ed.), *Un/Settled multiculturalisms: Diasporas, entanglements, transruptions* (pp. 1–30). London: Zed Press.

Hintzen, P. C. (2002). Race and creole ethnicity in the Caribbean. In V. A. Shepherd and G. L. Richards (Eds), *Questioning creole: Creolisation discourses in Caribbean culture.* (pp. 92–111). Kingston, Jamaica: Ian Randle.

Hooks, b. (1990). *Yearning: Race, gender and cultural politics.* Boston, MA: South End Press.

Hooks, b. (1992). *Black looks: Race and representation.* Boston, MA: South End Press.

Houston, L. M. (2005). *Food culture in the Caribbean.* Westport, CT: Greenwood Press.

Hua, A. (2006). Diaspora and cultural memory. In V. Agnew (Ed.), *Diaspora, memory and identity: A search for home* (pp. 191–208). Toronto, ON: University of Toronto Press.

Jackson, F. Z. and Naidoo, K. (2012). 'Lemeh check see if meh mask on straight': Examining how black women of Caribbean descent in Canada manage depression and construct womanhood through being strong. *Southern Journal of Canadian Studies*, 5(1–2), 223–240.

James, C. L. R. (1963). *Beyond a boundary*. London: Stanley Paul.

James, C. L. R. (1986). Introduction. In A. Grimshaw (Ed.), *Cricket*. London: Allison & Busby.

James, W. (1993). Migration, racism and identity formation: The Caribbean experience in Britain. In W. James and C. Harris (Eds), *Inside Babylon: The Caribbean diaspora in Britain* (pp. 231–287). London: Verso.

Johnson, V. M. S. (2006). *The Other black Bostonians: West Indians in Boston 1900–1950*. Bloomington, IN: Indiana University Press.

Joseph, J. (2008). Going to Brazil: Transnational and corporeal movements of a Canadian-Brazilian martial arts community. *Global Networks: A Journal of Transnational Affairs*, 8(2), 194–213.

Joseph, J. (2011a). Around the boundary: Alcohol and older Caribbean-Canadian men. *Leisure Studies*, 31(2), 147–163.

Joseph, J. (2011b). A diaspora approach to sport tourism. *Journal of Sport and Social Issues*, 35(2), 146–167.

Joseph, J. (2012). The practice of capoeira: Diasporic black culture in Canada. *Ethnic and Racial Studies*, 35(6), 1078–1095.

Joseph, J. (2013). What should I reveal?: Expanding researcher reflexivity in ethnographic Research. *Sport History Review*, 44(1), 6–24.

Joseph, J. (2014). Culture, community, consciousness: The Caribbean sporting diaspora. *International Review for the Sociology of Sport*, 49(6), 669–687.

Joseph, J. (2015). A narrative exploration of gender performances and gender relations in the Caribbean diaspora, *Identities: Global Studies in Culture and Power*, 22(2), 168–182.

Joseph, J. and Donnelly, M. K. (2012). Reflections on ethnography, ethics, and inebriation. *Leisure/Loisir*, 36(3–4), 357–372.

Kearney, M. (1996). *Reconceptualizing the peasantry*. Boulder, CO: Westview.

Lamming, G. (1953). *In the Castle of My Skin*. Ann Arbor, MI: University of Michigan Press.

Levitt, P. (1998). Social remittances: Migration driven local-level forms of cultural diffusion. *International Migration Review*, 32(4), 926–948.

Levitt, P. and Glick Schiller, N. (2004). Conceptualizing simultaneity: A transnational social field perspective on society. *International Migration Review*, 38(3), 1002–1039.

Lindsay, C. (2007a) The Caribbean community in Canada 2001. *Statistics Canada Catalogue* 89-621-XIE-No. 7.

Lindsay, C. (2007b). The South Asian community in Canada 2001. *Statistics Canada Catalogue* 89-621-XIE-No. 6.

Mackey, E. (2002). *The house of difference: Cultural politics and national belonging in Canada*. New York: Routledge.

McKittrick, K. (2002). 'Their blood is there and you can't throw it out': Honouring black Canadian geographies. *Topia*, 7, 27–37.

McLaren, J. (2009). African diaspora vernacular traditions and the dilemma of identity. *Research in African Literatures*, 40(1), 97–111.

Madan, M. (2000). 'It's just not cricket!': World series cricket: Race, nation, and diasporic Indian identity. *Journal of Sport and Social Issues*, 24(1), 24–35.

Majors, R. and Billson J. (1992). *Cool pose: The dilemmas of black manhood.* New York: Lexington Books.

Malcolm, D. (2013). *Globalizing cricket: Englishness, empire, and identity.* London: Bloomsbury.

Manning, F. (1990). Overseas Caribbean carnivals: The arts and politics of a transnational celebration. In J. Lent (Ed.), *Caribbean popular culture* (pp. 20–36). Bowling Green, OH: Bowling Green University Popular Press.

Marcus, G. E. (1998). *Ethnography through thick and thin.* Princeton, NJ: Princeton University Press.

Marshall, P. (1983). *Reena and other stories.* New York: Feminist Press.

Massey, D. (1994). *Space, place and gender.* Minneapolis, MN: University of Minnesota Press.

Matory, J. L. (2008). The illusion of isolation: The Gullah/Geechees and the political economy of African culture in the Americas, *Comparative Studies in Society and History,* 50(4), 949–980.

Mintz, S. W. (1996). Enduring substances, trying theories: The Caribbean region as oikoumenê. *The Journal of the Royal Anthropological Institute,* 2(2), 289–311.

Mintz, S. W. (1998). The localization of anthropological practice: From area studies to transnationalism. *Critique of Anthropology,* 18(2), 117–133.

Mohammed, P. (2009). The Asian other in the Caribbean. *Small Axe: A Caribbean Journal of Criticism,* 13(2), 57–71.

Munasinghe, V. (2001). Redefining the nation: The East Indian struggle for inclusion in Trinidad. *Journal of Asian American Studies,* 4(1), 1–34.

Mundaca, B. G. (2009). Remittances, financial market development, and economic growth: The case of Latin America and the Caribbean. *Review of development economics,* 13(2), 288–303.

Murray, D. (2012). *Flaming souls: Homosexuality, homophobia, and social change in Barbados.* Toronto, ON: University of Toronto Press.

Nakamura, Y. (2009). Boundaries of belonging: Overlapping loyalties and multiple attachments – a study of the North American Chinese Invitational Volleyball Tournament. Unpublished doctoral dissertation. University of Toronto, ON.

Nassy Brown, J. (1998). Black Liverpool, black America, and the gendering of diasporic space. *Cultural Anthropology,* 13(3), 291–325.

Nederveen Pieterse, J. (2009). *Globalization and culture: Global mélange.* Lanham, MD: Rowman and Littlefield.

Niranjana, T. (2001). Left to the imagination: Indian nationalisms and female sexuality in Trinidad. In D. Parameshwar (Ed.), *Alternative modernities* (pp. 248–271). Durham, NC: Duke University Press.

Noble, D. (2008). Postcolonial criticism, transnational identifications and the hegemonies of dancehall's academic and popular performativities. *Feminist Review,* 90, 106–127.

Nurse, K. (1999). Globalization and Trinidad carnival: Diaspora, hybridity, and identity in global culture. *Cultural Studies,* 13(4), 661–690.

Nurse, K. (2004). *Diaspora, migration and development in the Caribbean.* Policy Paper FPP-04-6. Ottawa, ON: The Canadian Foundation for the Americas.

Olwig, K. F. (2001). New York as a locality in a global family network. In N. Foner (Ed.), *Islands in the city: West Indian migration to New York* (pp. 142–160). Berkeley, CA: University of California Press.

Pabst, N. (2006). "Mama, I'm walking to Canada": Black geopolitics and invisible empires. In K. M. Clarke and D. A. Thomas (Eds), *Globalization and race: Transformations in the cultural production of blackness* (pp. 112–129). Durham, NC: Duke University Press.

Peake, L. and Trotz, D. A. (1999). *Gender, ethnicity and place: Women and identity in Guyana*. London: Routledge.

Pierre, J. (2009). Beyond heritage tourism: Race and the politics of African-diasporic interactions. *Social Text*, 27(1), 59–81.

Portes, A., Escobar, C. and Walton, A. R. (2007). Immigrant transnational organizations and development: A comparative study. *International Migration Review*, 41(1), 242–281.

Pratt, M. L. (1991). Arts of the contact zone. *Profession*, 91, 33–40.

Price-Mars, J. (1928). *Ainsi parla l'oncle: Essais d'ethnographie*. New York: Parapsychology Foundation.

Puri, S. (1999). Canonized hybridities, resistant hybridities: Chutney soca, carnival and the politics of nationalism. In B. Edmonson (Ed.), *Caribbean romances: The politics of regional representation* (pp. 12–38). Charlottesville, VA: University Press of Virginia.

Puwar, N. (2004). *Space invaders: Race, gender and bodies out of place*. New York: Berg.

Radley, A. (1990). Artifacts, memory and a sense of the past. In D. Middleton and D. Edwards (Eds), *Collective remembering* (pp. 46–59). London: SAGE Publications.

Razack, S. (2009). Women's cricket spaces: Examination of female players' experiences in Canada. Unpublished Master's thesis. University of Toronto, ON.

Richardson, C. C. (1992). *The Caribbean in the wider world 1492–1992*. Cambridge, UK: Cambridge University Press.

Richmond, A. H. (1989). *Current demographic analysis: Caribbean immigrants, a demo-economic analysis*. Ottawa, ON: Ministry of Supply and Services Canada.

Rickford, J. R. and Rickford, A. E. (1976). Cut-eye and suck-teeth: African words and gestures in New World guise. *The Journal of American Folklore*, 89(353), 294–309.

Ritivoi, A. D. (2002). *Yesterday's self: Nostalgia and the immigrant identity*. Lanham, MA: Rowman & Littlefield.

Roberts, M. (2004). Cricketing fervour and Islamic fervour: Marginalisation in the diaspora. *The International Journal of the History of Sport*, 21(3), 650–663.

Rogers, R. (2001). Black like who? Afro-Caribbean immigrants, African Americans, and the politics of group identity. In N. Foner (Ed.), *Islands in the city: West Indian migration to New York* (pp. 163–192). Los Angeles, CA: University of California Press.

Ropero, M. L. L. (2004). *The Anglo-Caribbean migration novel: Writing from the diaspora*. San Vicente, Spain: Publicaciones de la Universidade de Alicante.

Routon, K. (2006). Trance-nationalism: Religious imaginaries of belonging in the Black Atlantic. *Identities*, 13(3), 483–502.

Rushdie, S. (1991). *Imaginary homelands*. New York: Penguin Books.

Safran, W. (1991). Diasporas in modern societies: Myths of homeland and return. *Diasporas*, 1(1), 83–99.

Safran, W. (1999). Comparing diasporas: A review essay. *Diasporas*, 8(3), 255–291.

Sandiford, K. A. P. (1998). *Cricket nurseries of colonial Barbados: The elite schools, 1865–1966*. Kingston, Jamaica: University of the West Indies Press.

Schmidt, B. E. (2008). The many voices of Caribbean culture in New York city. In H. Henke, and K. Magister (Eds), *Constructing vernacular culture in the trans-Caribbean* (pp. 23–42). Lanham, MD: Lexington Books.

Segal, D. (1993). Race and 'color' in pre-independence Trinidad and Tobago. In K. A. Yelvington (Ed.), *Trinidad ethnicity* (pp. 81–115). Knoxville, TN: University of Tennessee Press.

Sparkes, A. (2002). *Telling tales in sport and physical activity: A qualitative journey*. Champaign, IL: Human Kinetics Press.
Sparkes, A. C., Nilges, L., Swan, P. & Dowling, F. (2003). Poetic representations in sport and physical education: Insider perspectives 1. *Sport, Education and Society*, 8(2), 153–177.
St. Pierre, M. (1995). West Indian cricket part 1: A socio-historical appraisal. In H. Beckles and B. Stoddart (Eds), *Liberation cricket: West Indies cricket culture* (pp. 107–124). New York: Manchester University Press.
Steckles, G. (2009, November 17). Calypso cricket fades away. *Toronto Star*, S6.
Stephens, M. A. (2005). *Black empire: The masculine global imaginary of Caribbean intellectuals in the United States, 1914–1962*. Durham, NC: Duke University Press.
Stoddart, B. (2006). Caribbean cricket: The role of sport in emerging small-nation politics. *Sport in Society*, 9(5), 790–808.
Sutton, C. (2004). Celebrating ourselves: The family reunion rituals of African-Caribbean transnational families. *Global Networks: A Journal of Transnational Affairs*, 4(3), 243–257.
Sutton, C. (2008). Reunion rituals of African-Caribbean transnational families: Instilling a historical and diasporic consciousness. In H. Henke and K. Magister (Eds), *Constructing vernacular culture in the trans-Caribbean* (pp. 43–60). Lanham, MD: Lexington Books.
Tettey, W. J. and Puplampu, K. P. (2005). Border crossings and home-diaspora linkages among African-Canadians: An analysis of translocational positionality, cultural remittance, and social capital. In W. J. Tettey, and K. P. Puplampu (Eds), *The African diaspora in Canada: Negotiating identity and belonging* (pp. 149–174). Calgary, AB: University of Calgary Press.
Theopano, J. and Curtis, K. (1991). Sisters, mothers, and daughters: Food exchange and reciprocity in an Italian-American community. In A. Sharman, J. Theopano, K. Curtis and E. Messer (Eds), *Diet and domestic life in society* (pp. 147–172). Philadelphia, PA: Temple Press.
Thobani, S. (2007). *Exalted subjects: Studies in the making of race and nation in Canada*. Toronto, ON: University of Toronto Press.
Thomas, D. A. (2007). Blackness across borders: Jamaican diasporas and new politics of citizenship. *Identities*, 14(1), 111–133.
Thomas, D. A. and Clarke, K. M. (2006). Introduction: Globalization and the transformations of race. In K. M. Clarke, and D. A. Thomas (Eds), *Globalization and race: Transformations in the cultural production of blackness* (pp. 1–34). Durham, NC: Duke University Press.
Thomas-Hope. E. (n.d.) Trends and patterns of migration to and from Caribbean countries. Unpublished paper. Retrieved from www.virtualtradeportal.org/cms/index.php?option=com_docman&task=cat_view&gid=197&Itemid=11 (accessed 30 December 2014).
Thompson, R. F. (1984). *Flash of the spirit: African and Afro-American art and philosophy*. New York: Vintage Books.
Thompson, S. (1999). *Mother's taxi: Sport and women's labor*. Albany, NY: SUNY Press.
Trotz, D. A. (2006). Rethinking Caribbean transnational connections: Conceptual itineraries. *Global Networks: A Journal of Transnational Affairs*, 6(1), 41–59.
Trotz, D. A. (2011). Bustling across the Canada-US border: Gender and the remapping of the Caribbean across place. *Small Axe: A Caribbean Journal of Criticism*, 35(2), 59–77.
Voigt-Graf, C. (2004). Towards a geography of transnational spaces: Indian transnational communities in Australia. *Global Networks: A Journal of Transnational Affairs*, 4(1), 25–49.

Walby, K. (2010). Interviews as encounters: Issues of sexuality and reflexivity when men interview men about commercial same sex relations. *Qualitative Research*, 10, 639–657.

Walcott, R. (2001). Caribbean pop culture in Canada: Or, the impossibility of belonging to the nation. *Small Axe: A Caribbean Journal of Criticism*, 5(1), 123–139.

Walcott, R. (2003). *Black like who? Writing Black Canada* (2nd ed.). London, ON: Insomniac Press.

Walter, T. O., Brown, B. and Grabb, E. (1991). Ethnic identity and sports participation: A comparative analysis of West Indian and Italian soccer clubs in metropolitan Toronto. *Canadian Ethnic Studies*, 23(1), 85–96.

Ward, B. (1998). *Just my soul responding: Rhythm and blues, black consciousness and race relations*. London: University College of London Press.

Werbner, P. (2005). The translocation of culture: Community cohesion and the force of multiculturalism in history. *The Sociological Review*, 53(4), 745–768.

Whannel, G. (2002). *Media sport stars: Masculinities and moralities*. London: Routledge.

Wilde, S. (1994). *Letting rip: The fast bowling threat from Lillee to Waqar*. London: H. F. & G. Witherby.

Williams, B. (1991). *Stains on my name, war in my veins: Guyana and the politics of cultural struggle*. Durham, NC: Duke University Press.

Williams, J. (2001). *Cricket and race*. Oxford: Berg.

Wilson, J. L. (2005). *Nostalgia: Sanctuary of meaning*. Cranbury, NJ: Rosemont.

Wilson, P. J. (1973). *Crab antics: The social anthropology of English-speaking negro societies in the Caribbean*. New Haven, CT: Yale University Press.

Index

Abdel-Shehid, G. 6, 12, 23–24, 60, 178
Abrahams, R. 17, 37, 51, 86–87, 148, 167–168
African-Americans 23, 57, 77–78, 122, 139
ageing 6, 14, 16, 31, 44, 48, 52, 78,
    105–106, 124, 127, 129, 181
alcohol 43, 47, 53, 57, 119, 133n.2, 135, 137,
    139–140, 148–149, 165, 180
antiphony 17, 37, 50–51, 60
assimilation 57, 61, 80, 147, 150, 155,
    160–161, 169, 185

Barth, F. 5, 9, 139, 163, 173
Black Atlantic 7, 10–11, 21–23, 30, 63–64,
    154n.2, 177
  critiques of 11–13, 16, 24, 108, 129,
    151, 177
  diasporic resources 11–12, 19, 48, 61, 99,
    114, 132, 178–181, 184
  racial terror 6, 16, 37, 139, 151, 181
black power 41, 87, 95–99, 106, 107n.2, 171,
    180, 187
boundary crossing 6–9, 19, 23, 30, 32,
    49–50, 76, 80, 113, 124, 155,
    157–158, 179, 182, 188
boundary making 4–6, 31–32, 35–36, 83,
    121–122, 127, 132–133, 134n.2,
    137–139, 142–147, 152, 157, 163,
    172–173, 177–178, 181–182,
    185–186, 188

calypso 21, 41, 42, 58, 75, 94, 102, 119, 123,
    125, 138, 144–145
Canadian
  icons 56, 157, 162, 165–167, 185
    see also nostalgia artefacts
  identity 3, 21–22, 165–166, 171, 175,
    184–185
  national discourses 18, 155, 166,
    171, 177
  provincial and national cricket 159–162

racism 2, 4, 16, 21, 38, 43, 45, 77, 98,
    136, 143, 158, 167, 183, 185
white belonging 13, 16, 66, 141, 145, 152,
    158, 159, 171
carnival 6, 24, 41, 49, 68, 76, 78, 80, 84n.2,
    123–124, 141, 144–145, 154n.4,
    160, 181
Carrington, B. 21, 23–24, 27–28, 37, 40,
    45, 52, 109, 114, 139, 147, 151,
    178, 183
class 14–15, 17–19, 26–28, 33n.5, 39,
    43–44, 53–54, 57–58, 64,
    73–75, 80, 83, 89–92,
    95–96, 105, 117–118,
    120–127, 132–133, 138,
    154n.1, 160–161, 163–164,
    167–168, 180, 184–185
  see also reputation
cuisine 10, 40–41, 50, 55–58, 66, 68–69,
    80–81, 84, 101, 109, 112–113,
    129, 131–133, 135, 140, 147–148,
    153, 175, 180–181, 183, 188–189

dance 8, 25–27, 41–42, 47, 55, 58, 66, 69,
    77–79, 100, 102, 111–113, 120,
    123–124, 126, 128–131, 144, 159,
    178, 183
diaspora identity *see* transnational: identity
diaspora space 30–31, 34n.10, 135–137,
    151–153
diaspora studies
  black 8–10
    see also Black Atlantic
  Canada and 14–15, 18–19
  migration and 13–14
  sport and 20–24
disjunctures 30–31, 34n.10, 35, 106, 109,
    118–124, 132–133, 136, 151, 164,
    176, 181–184
donation *see* remittance

Index

drinking 2, 3, 5, 17, 19, 25, 30, 37, 40, 41, 44, 46, 48, 51–55, 101, 103–104, 113, 119, 128–130, 134n.2, 136, 140–142, 144–145, 148–149, 153, 162–165, 182, 188–189
   see also alcohol

Edwards, B. H. 8, 11, 34n.10, 35, 118, 132, 155, 164, 181

family and friends *see* kin
food *see* cuisine
fundraising 19, 31, 79–80, 109, 129–131, 170, 178, 180–181, 188–189

gender
  performances 12, 17, 31, 37, 42, 51–54, 57–58, 83, 86, 91, 95, 109, 112–113, 125–129, 142, 148, 162–164, 167–168, 170–171, 173, 182, 187–188
  women's absence 25, 31, 111–114, 116–119, 126, 132, 134n.3, 182–183
Gilroy, P. 6–7, 10–12, 16, 19, 21–23, 30, 34, 41–42, 53, 60, 63–64, 97, 100, 108, 117, 118, 123, 131–132, 151, 177, 178–179, 181, 183

homespaces 4–5, 30, 37–40, 63–65, 68–69, 71, 78, 80, 112, 117, 131, 133–134n.2, 147, 151–153, 180, 182, 185
homophobia 52, 60, 100, 120, 164, 182

Indo-Caribbean 6, 9, 26, 31–32, 46, 133, 137–138, 143–146, 151–152, 154n.1, 154n.4, 154n.5, 168, 179, 182–183

James, C. L. R. 2, 5, 33n.3, 52, 58–59, 93, 97–98, 108, 161, 177–178

kin 5, 13, 19, 30, 48, 59, 63, 68, 70, 72–73, 87, 155, 157, 175, 186, 188
  see also transnational: social networks

language 3–5, 8, 21, 29, 37–38, 41, 51, 65, 86, 88, 103, 120, 132, 146–148, 152–153, 159, 163–166, 172–174, 183, 185, 187

liming 30, 36–61, 88, 117–118, 127, 142–143, 145, 153, 164, 180, 182, 185, 187–189
love
  intimacy and 59–60, 129
  mock anger and 50–54, 57, 98, 136, 140–142, 148, 150, 156, 167
  see also gender performance
  see also dance; drink

narrative inquiry *see* stories
Nassy Brown, J. 11–12, 64, 108, 117, 123, 178
national
  borders 19, 23, 49, 124, 155, 175, 177–180
    see also boundary crossing
  cricket 24–25, 33n.7, 138, 159–161
    see also Canadian: provincial and national cricket
  culture 99, 103–104, 122–124, 127, 133, 138, 155, 157–158, 160, 165–166, 169–175, 180–182, 186
  identity 4, 20, 22, 27, 31–32, 50, 82–83, 100, 106, 121, 124, 155–159, 164–173, 175–176, 178–179
  independence 95–96, 157, 169, 174
nostalgia 30, 54, 56, 78, 81–83, 87–89, 92, 97–100, 103–106
  artefacts 85–86, 91–92, 100–102, 166

racial identity 5, 7, 21–23, 28, 30, 33n.6, 38, 40, 53, 56, 63, 85, 87, 89, 122, 133, 137, 139, 144–146, 152–153, 154n.5, 156, 162–163, 167, 172, 178–179, 183
reflexivity 27–28, 30, 125, 128–129, 133–134n.2, 134n.4
reggae 24, 41–42, 47, 58, 63, 102, 119, 123–124, 174
remittance 36, 65, 71–75, 80, 169, 172
repatriation 62, 65, 81–83
reputation 17, 37, 82–83, 86, 113, 118–121, 125–126, 134n.2, 148, 161–164, 168, 180
  see also gender performance; Abrahams, R.
reunions 18, 30, 62–63, 65–68, 71, 84, 175
roots *see* homespaces
routes *see* boundary crossing; transnational: mobility

second-generation Afro-Caribbean-
    Canadians 32, 42–44, 67, 99,
    151, 182–183
South Asians 31, 44, 112, 133, 136–154
stories 2–4, 8, 18, 28–31, 33–34n.9, 53, 82,
    109, 111, 121, 123, 136, 143, 180,
    181, 187
    see also nostalgia

transnational
    cultural circuits 16, 56, 139, 177, 179
    identity 4, 11, 16, 22, 28, 31, 35, 37, 40,
        42–44, 62, 65, 78, 101, 106–107,
        168, 173, 184–185
    mobility 25–26, 30, 40, 54, 59, 63–64, 80,
        109, 143, 157, 173, 175, 177, 179
    see also boundary crossing; tourism

social networks 7, 12–13, 16, 18–19, 21, 24,
    30, 45, 65, 70, 73, 76, 78, 152, 175,
    178, 181, 188
tourism 66–67, 70, 103–104, 130, 144,
    169–170, 178, 186–187

Underground Railroad 5, 76–77

West Indies 20, 32n.1, 39, 42–43, 46, 48,
    56, 78, 93–94, 109, 121, 135, 140,
    144–146, 161, 166
West Indian cricket team 20–21,
    24, 31, 59, 75, 84n.1, 87,
    91–100, 106, 107n.1, 107n.2,
    131, 138–139, 144, 179–181
Richards, V. 12, 93–94, 160, 174
Sobers, G. 1, 21, 68–69, 93–94, 174